Looking for Trouble

Leslie Cockburn

Looking for Trouble

ANCHOR BOOKS
DOUBLEDAY
New York
London
Toronto
Sydney
Auckland

AN ANCHOR BOOK
PUBLISHED BY DOUBLEDAY
a division of Bantam Doubleday Dell Publishing Group, Inc.
1540 Broadway, New York, New York 10036

ANCHOR BOOKS, DOUBLEDAY, and the portrayal of an anchor
are trademarks of Doubleday, a division of Bantam Doubleday Dell
Publishing Group, Inc.

Grateful acknowledgment is made for permission to reprint copyrighted material:
Excerpt from Canto XXIX from *The Inferno of Dante: A New Verse Translation* by Robert
Pinsky. Reprinted by permission of Farrar, Straus, and Giroux, Inc.

Library of Congress Cataloging-in-Publication Data

Cockburn, Leslie.
  Looking for trouble / by Leslie Cockburn.
     p.   cm.
  1. Cockburn, Leslie.   2. Women journalists—United States—Biography.
3. Investigative journalism—United States.   I. Title.
PN4874.C599A3   1998
070′.92—dc21   97-21479
[B]
CIP

ISBN: 0-385-48319-8
Copyright © 1998 by Leslie Cockburn
All Rights Reserved
Printed in the United States of America
First Anchor Books Edition: March 1998

10 9 8 7 6 5 4 3 2 1

For Chloe, Olivia, and Charlie

Acknowledgments

This book would not have been possible without Sarah Chalfant at the Wylie Agency, whose encouragement was crucial to the enterprise. Arabella Meyer at Anchor ushered it through to completion with patience and a ruthless eye for detail.

I owe a debt to family and friends who urged me to write about my perilous travels to the back-of-beyond. Ana Carrigan, Gloria Emerson, Flip Caldwell, Jeanne Redlich, Melissa North, Jennifer Phillips, Connie Bruce, Lindy von Eichel, Emma Gilbey, Gail Percy, Wade Davis, Joel McCleary, Alexander Chancellor, and Bill Broyles gave me indispensable support. John Hatt gave me champagne at the Oriental.

Contents

Speak civilly to blondes and they will speak civilly to you.
    —P. G. WODEHOUSE

Looking for Trouble

TV Mountain

W E BOARD the sleek white United Nations jet in Islamabad, the capital of Pakistan. U.N. is painted in huge letters on the wings. There is an illustrated land mine warning card in every seat pocket. Our destination, Afghanistan, is one of the most heavily mined countries in the world. Mine sweepers complain of vertical minefields in the ruins of Kabul, fifteen layers of mines planted in the sediment of homes rocketed into troughs of dust. Families are living in the ruins. Most Afghan women give birth to eight or nine children. Then the mines and rockets pick them off, one by one.

It is October 1996. This trip is a whirlwind assignment for ABC News. It begins with a call on a Wednesday morning from Phyllis McGrady, executive producer of *Primetime Live*.

"Diane wants to go to Afghanistan." Diane Sawyer is the *Primetime Live* anchor at ABC in New York. "I told her you were the only person who could produce this piece. Do you want to do it?"

"I can't think of anything I'd rather do." This is, in fact, true. The occupation of Kabul in September by the Taliban, an army of shadowy fundamentalist Muslims from Kandahar, has been catastrophic for Afghan women. Surgeons, engineers, and civil servants who have kept the capital functioning throughout eighteen years of war, during the Soviet occupation and its bloody aftermath, have been fired from their jobs. They can no longer appear in public without wearing a shroud. If there is a hint of an ankle, the Taliban enforcers beat them with sticks. The heavy silk burka has a three-inch embroidered screen to allow partial vision without the eyes being displayed. Their daughters have been expelled from school. Thirty-five thousand war widows, whose paltry income from menial work feeds some 300,000 children, have been forced by the bearded mullahs to quit work. The children are starving.

ABC's McGrady gives me carte blanche to assemble a team. I call Fabrice Moussus, a seasoned cameraman in Paris, and Carlos Mavroleon, a London-based fixer and troubleshooter who speaks Dari and Pashto, the languages of Afghanistan. He has ties to guerrilla factions dating back to his days fighting with the mujahedin against the Russians. A soundman and an assistant to coordinate logistics fill out the crew. We agree to meet on Saturday in Islamabad, the jumping-off point for U.N. aid flights. The Red Cross has suspended flights to Afghanistan due to bombing. No one flies commercially. The only other aircraft in Afghan airspace are MIGs, Russian-made fighter-bombers, in the hands of the Taliban and their opponents in the northern city of Mazar-i-Sharif. Carlos brings the steel-plated flak jackets.

I have now covered six wars and a revolution, as a producer for CBS and ABC News, correspondent for *PBS Frontline*, and writer for *Vanity Fair*. I have covered this war twice. For Diane Sawyer, this is unfamiliar turf. Foreign travel usually means a chauffeur-driven Volga to the Kremlin for an interview with Boris Yeltsin. Still, she weathered a Russian coup and seems game for anything.

Our last meeting before this expedition was at a transvestite magic show in Dublin. Diane's husband, Mike Nichols, was conducting research at a popular Irish club called Mr. Pussy's for his upcoming film *The Birdcage*. I was in town with my husband, Andrew, to write a *Vanity Fair* story on the American involvement in the impending cease-fire in Northern Ireland. The four of us sat primly in a booth while a drag queen placed his sequined accomplice in a box and proceeded to saw slowly through her. Diane and I discussed the state of television news.

We lamented the lack of foreign stories in the increasingly frothy tabloid mix of the network newsmagazines. Now, ABC News has been swallowed up by the Walt Disney Company. One of Disney's first acts was to install a Mickey Mouse souvenir shop in the lobby of the news headquarters on West 66th Street in New York. I call ABC News "Disney's Reality Division." The lead story on Diane's newsmagazine the week of our departure is a hard look at garage door openers.

Flying in the U.N.'s nineteen-seater jet over the Khyber Pass, we are a long way from the ABC archipelago on the Upper West Side. Below, the landscape looks as though the earth has just been formed. It is empty, dry, a buckling Precambrian crust. I can see the town of Jalalabad, surrounded by training camps for militant fundamentalists from Saudi Arabia, Egypt, and Algeria. To our left are the White Mountains, with a light snow cover like a white lace antimacassar. To our right is the Kabul River and ahead the Hindu Kush.

Before landing in Kabul, we must suit up in appropriate veils. I wear a voluminous white eyelet Pakistani veil that transforms me into the Virgin Mary. Diane wears my black Armani *hejab*, the Islamic dress favored by Shia women in North Tehran. Our wrists, ankles, and necks are covered. On the strip we see a battered but serviceable MIG fighter. Military junk is heaped everywhere from waves of military occupation. Since the Soviet withdrawal in 1989, several mujahedin factions, once on the payroll of the Reagan administration as "freedom fighters," have tried to annihilate each other. They have fought vicious battles with state-of-the-art weaponry left behind by the Americans and the Russians. I survey the detritus of the most expensive covert operation in CIA history.

Our pilot shouts at us to hurry off the plane. He leaves the engine running and takes off less than a minute after we have hit the tarmac. It turns out the opposing army beyond the front line ten miles north of town has just bombed the landing strip. Fortunately, they missed. Their leader is General Abdul Rashid Dostum, who supports a women's university in Mazar and is now harboring thousands of Kabul women who have fled the city. The disgusted Taliban call him the whiskey-swilling general. I wish for a moment that we are with Dostum in Mazar.

Taliban fighters in turbans, with rocket-propelled grenades and AK-47s slung over their shoulders, are milling around the airport, watching us intently. They have skin like saddle leather and eyes the color of amber and aquamarine. Carlos talks us through the crowd of armed men that passes for customs. The U.N. has sent jeeps to collect us. We barrel through the streets to their staff compound in what was once a leafy colonial neighborhood dating back to the British Raj. The landscape of the city is postnuclear, like Hiroshima after the blast. Even this does not fully describe the devastation wrought here after the Russians climbed into their Hind helicopters and left.

The latest wave of invaders, the Taliban mullahs, have been rocketing the city for a year. Now the largely illiterate horde, many reared in refugee camps from the Russian war, has taken the city. U.S. officials have been selling the Taliban as a stabilizing force. Their brutal treatment of women has made full American recognition awkward. U.S. Ambassador to the United Nations Madeleine Albright (and soon to be Secretary of State) has told the State Department to cool its enthusiasm. Her actual words were "You are out of your minds to recognize these people."

The U.N. staff house is next to a park with a large crater from a bomb dropped after dinner the night before. Inside the U.N. gates, a dozen men are furiously digging a trench. A retired Australian Army officer who is the U.N. security briefer grabs us for a presentation.

"The bombs dropped last night and this morning," he says in a heavy outback drawl, "were five-hundred-pound bombs. The shelter that is under construction outside the front door"—he points to the trench—"won't be much good to you. The nearest shelter is two blocks away. I recommend that you wear your clothes to bed. Oh, and lights out during the bombing raids. So they don't have a nice target to aim for." The security officer has the bravado of a soldier who has washed up in too many outposts like this. Most of Kabul has been without electricity or running water for years.

Diane and I check into room 2 on the ground floor. The room is clean and severe with two narrow beds and a wall of sandbags outside the windows to prevent bomb blast from shattering the glass. We are down the hall from the U.N. Club, where journalists, demining specialists, and aid workers come for forbidden gin and tonics. Carlos sets up the satellite phone inside another wall of sandbags, and aged U.N. retainers bring us pizza and chips.

Since the Taliban Army entered the city unopposed on September 27, they have instituted a Draconian vision of Islam. The mullahs have outlawed videos and cigarettes. They have banned music and forbidden the children to fly kites. Their soldiers obediently slash paintings and draw the magnetic tape out of audiocassettes.

Terry Pitzner, who runs U.N. relief operations, has a pleasant house stacked with VCRs and birdcages. Terry's Afghani staff have brought all electronic equipment here so the Taliban will not smash it. The cages are full of parakeets, refugees from the Taliban. Even birds are not allowed to make music. The Taliban are killing songbirds.

I am anxious to see the effects in Kabul of women being hounded out of their jobs. We head out in search of a large orphanage that had been staffed by women. We nearly break the axles of our ancient taxis driving down rutted dirt tracks to find it. The building is an ugly cement barracks. The windows are blown out from four and a half years of ceaseless rocketing. The children are perched in the open windows. They are ragged and barefoot. Winter is coming. In winter, the wind is very cruel, whipping off the peaks of the Hindu Kush. When the Persian shahs ruled from Kabul, they retreated to the warmth of Peshawar and built splendid gardens to amuse themselves while Kabul froze.

The children swarm around us. Diane asks how many live in the orphanage. The older children answer cheerfully that there are eight hundred orphans here. Inside is a warren of dark corridors. As we search for staff, an anxious man appears who tells me seventy women were employed there. Only four remain. They are risking a beating and prison. We wander through a bleak interior courtyard and up some stairs to the girls' section. Men are shouting at us to come back. We have no authorization from the Taliban. I tell Fabrice, the cameraman, to just keep rolling.

We enter a room with forty beds in it. The beds are tiny cots for children under five, stacked on top of each other with two feet of space between. Sixty-six of the women whose job it is to feed children who have lost parents to rockets and bombs, women staff who wash their clothes, change the bedding and diapers, scrub floors, sing and play, and give direction to their wretched lives are gone. The stench in the dank hallways of unpainted cement is foul. Urine sits in puddles on the floor. There are no toys.

When the tiny, filthy girls see us coming, they line up and burst into song:

> "We have one doll,
>   She's very beautiful,
>   She sings nicely and laughs.
>   My father is not cross with me.
>   We have a doll,
>   She sings and laughs.
>   My mother is happy."

Babies nine months old are in the arms of three-year-olds. We ask what they are eating. The skeleton staff of the Taaimiskan orphanage is providing its sad little inmates with breakfast of flat bread and weak tea. Lunch is plain rice. Dinner is watery broth with rice. Their lives are miserable beyond comprehension. I imagine my three-year-old son, Charlie, in this place.

In the crowded open markets with the ruined city as a backdrop like some macabre opera set, we see women gliding like ghosts under their shrouds. The silk is dyed the color of lapis lazuli and saffron. To make the film effective, we must convince women to unveil and talk about the Taliban occupation on camera. They will risk harassment, torture, ransacked homes, prison, or exile. We have to believe that their appearing on American television is worth the risk. The program will pressure Washington to censure the Taliban. The mullahs want aid, bank loans, multiple rocket launchers, a seat at the U.N. Our program will get in their way. These days, sadistic treatment of women is not a great calling card. If we do not believe this, it is unconscionable to ask others to make themselves a target for the mullahs' wrath just so we have some nice footage.

Back at the U.N. compound Terry is waiting for us. His long white hair is combed back neatly and he wears a dashing scarf. He is agitated. His face is full of fatigue and despair. Six of his female Afghani staffers, now out of work, want to talk with us. Terry has arranged a clandestine meeting behind the high walls of his house for the following morning.

I fall asleep before dinner at 8:30. At 11 P.M., there are explosions in the distance, the deep base rumble of aerial bombing. Then the sharp crack of antiaircraft fire. There is a MIG overhead.

"What's that?" Diane is awake.

I identify the sounds for her. Every weapon has a signature sound as distinct as a mosquito or cicada. Once you know them, you can assess what is happening in an otherwise ink-black city. The MIG itself is silent, flying high. I can track its course because of the positions of the antiaircraft guns. There is a full burst from one gun right outside our window. The bomber is overhead. The experience of being under bombs or rockets is always the same for me. I feel naked. My bedcovers, the locked door, the thick walls, the roof, are no longer of any use. I think, God, why am I here? Who are the soldiers manning the guns? What do they know about artillery? I'm being defended by the Taliban? What a joke. There is nowhere to run. There are no telephones. There is no one to call, no 911, no light. We take our chances. The firing stops. I lie rigid in bed waiting for the next MIG.

There are fresh explosions on the edge of the city. This is a second run. Both of us lie still. The antiaircraft fire echoes against the mountains that enclose Kabul like a teacup. The deep booms that shake the ground and the brittle rat-a-tat-tat come closer, roar around us, then fade. Tracer fire streaks across the sky like bullets of light. Then, dead silence.

In the morning, the gates at Terry's compound open and shut fast to conceal our cameras from Taliban spies. I decide to film the women in Terry's dining room where they can have coffee and feel relaxed. Veiled head to toe, they appear and take their seats. Diane explains that they will have far more impact if we can show their faces on camera. All of the women hesitate, then unveil together. They are strikingly beautiful, with high cheekbones and pale skin.

Fatima is a doctor, trained at the Kabul University Medical School. Mashe is an engineer. Five of the women around the table are the family breadwinners. One of them has five children to feed. Soon they will be destitute.

They describe the nightmare of Taliban occupation. Women are beaten in the mosque. They are forced to live in unsanitary conditions. With no running water in the city, they have relied on public bathhouses, but the Taliban have now closed them. Women doctors have been told to stay at home. Male doctors are forbidden from examining women patients, and therefore, women are going untreated. Women are giving birth without doctors.

Frustration wells up in their voices over being forced to stay home. "We are educated women. We cannot accept this." They are like the caged birds they have handed over to Terry. They hide photo albums so they won't be ripped to shreds by the Taliban on house raids. Books are stashed away in cupboards. Favorite dresses are hidden deep in the recesses of the bedroom closet. The Taliban have decreed that women no longer have any say in whom they marry. When they do marry, their wedding parties must be silent.

I need permission to film at one of the Red Cross hospitals. We stop by Red Cross headquarters to see the press officer. We get no further. The press officer is Dr. Zikria, actually a fine obstetrician. With the wave of militant fundamentalism that filled the vacuum left by the Russians, he was fired. "They were very tough on male doctors working on women. And the pay was eight dollars a month." His wife was a surgeon on the faculty of the Kabul University Medical School. The Taliban have now terminated her job. "She's very depressed," says Dr. Zikria. "She's asking to leave Afghanistan. If I leave, I will lose my job at the Red Cross. I have two kids, a mother, a brother. I have no money. All I have is my house and my car."

The Red Cross press officer begins to cry. He is crying quietly, tears streaming down his face. He confides that the Taliban banged on his door last night and accused him of being a former secret policeman. "Can you imagine me as secret police? They will come back. I am scared. I must decide tonight whether to leave. How can I leave my mother?" He believes he will be tortured and jailed or worse. Many people have disappeared from their homes at night. Kabul is being ethnically cleansed. Anyone not Pashtun like the mullahs is suspect. He agrees to do an interview in the garden of the German Club with his face in shadow. We shoot it against the sun. He says the Taliban have closed his daughter's kindergarten. He must make a decision. That night, he sleeps at his father-in-law's house. The next day, Dr. Zikria and his family flee to Pakistan.

The director of Kabul's military hospital is a general and the world's most experienced trauma surgeon. General Souhaila Sidiq has operated on over four thousand soldiers, some with their insides cut to ribbons. Sidiq successfully mended what was left of an English reporter who took a mortar round in the stomach. The general has been a surgeon for thirty-seven years, including eighteen years of war. The Taliban have forced this remarkable woman to go home.

She is reluctant to see us. I go twice down the dusty lane near the Chinese Embassy and knock on the garden gate. I am told she is out. I leave messages. Finally, we are admitted, face-to-face with this general, surgeon, and niece of the former king of Afghanistan. Her father ran the Afghan Red Cross and served as governor of Nangarhar Province, which has now spawned the monstrous Taliban.

The general is tall and exceptionally beautiful with a deeply lined face. She is inhaling Marlboros as though each cigarette is an oxygen machine. Her eyes are ringed with kohl, her hair swept up in a regal French twist. She wears a black velvet vest over a thin blue cotton traditional Afghan dress and a thin black scarf with scalloped embroidery. She sits on the sofa in this comfortable compound with a rose garden. "You know, my father was imprisoned by the Soviets. I've been a doctor here for thirty-seven years. I have given my blood for my people. I'm Pashtun. I don't want to leave. I'm an Afghan girl. I'm not afraid of anything."

General Souhaila is insulted by the Taliban leaders' claim that this new repression is simply the "rules and regulations," as one mullah put it, of Islam. "In Islam," General Souhaila says firmly, "men and women have equal rights. The first person to accept Islam was a woman. The first martyr was a woman. Mohammed discussed everything with his wife. She was the leader of a fighting faction. The doctor in the battle of Uhud, the first Muslim battle, was a woman."

Souhaila is trying to disguise her deep depression over recent events. "I'm a doctor. A doctor doesn't interfere in policy. When a patient comes to me, it doesn't matter if he is a friend, relative, or stranger." She pauses to smoke. "I'm very distressed at being kept from my job. Most women here have lost their husbands." She deliberately did not marry so she could devote herself to trauma surgery.

The general is staging one-woman protests. She walks out into the street unveiled. She wears traditional Afghan dress, a lovely long piece of embroidered scarf thrown loosely over the hair, the ends tucked back over the shoulders. It is the Grace Kelly look. "I don't wear a burka. I wear our national dress. If the Taliban stop me," she laughs, "I say I wear it for religious reasons."

Her sister Professor Sidiqa Sidiq has been forced to quit her post teaching architecture and engineering at the Kabul Polytechnic Institute. She was the first woman professor there. She is sitting on the sofa, another tall, striking member of the Afghan royal family. Fifty percent of her students, she says, are women. If the university reopens, they will not be allowed back. Even at Zarghoona High School for Girls the gates are padlocked.

Before we leave, the sisters hand me a precious letter for a third sister, Zafia, in San Diego. "Please give it to her," says the general with a fierce hug. "She thinks I've been killed." Later, at the gate, she says she is ready to die for the women of Afghanistan. I say I would like to pretend I could be as brave.

"You are a brave woman"—she smiles broadly—"coming here and risking your life."

Kabul is called the city of widows. Some of them live in the ruins that stretch for block after city block, heaps of blackened concrete and baked mud bricks, eerie shells of shops, businesses, restaurants, hairdressers, tailors, grocers, movie theaters—all exploded, sometimes hit by a dozen rockets over time. In those ruins with the widows and the broods are the unexploded rockets and the mines, layered in the ruins, a sandwich of death. Deminers work patiently with Russian-made probes and mine-sniffing dogs. They are losing limbs regularly. The problem, as the munitions experts gathered around the U.N. Club bar explain, is that under one mine there is another, and another. "There is nothing like it anywhere in the world," says one mine clearer from the Halo Trust. "Hundreds of thousands of mines in the middle of the city fifteen layers deep." Naturally, the widows and children step on the mines. Four hundred thousand children have been killed here since the wars began eighteen years ago. Most have been killed in the past four years, many from mines. Now the widows who squat in the ruins and work at odd jobs to buy food are forbidden from earning money. Aid agencies like CARE and the Red Cross are trying to feed them. They are feeding ten to fifteen thousand, but there are many thousands more. The widows we visit with a small 8-mm camera, hoping to be unobtrusive, are shattered. One stands with her nine children crying. "What will I do?" Everyone in Kabul cries. The resilience of making it through so many years of war, rockets, mortars, grenades, cluster bombs, mines, is unwinding like a peeled golf ball.

The blackened Intercontinental Hotel is now filled with Taliban fighters on the top floor. They survey the city, savor their victory. The fighters gaze across the ruins to the sharp ascent of TV Mountain. None of them know where TV Mountain got its name. It dates from the time years ago when people had electricity. They owned televisions. The television station needed a transmitter, and the rugged ridge across from the Intercontinental was just the place.

Over at the Foreign Ministry, a brand-new black Mercedes with smoke-glass windows purrs into the compound. There are no car factories in Afghanistan. This has come from Pakistan across the border, like so many advisers, rocket launchers, and rounds of ammunition. The Pakistani Ministry of Interior led by Nasiri Babar is sponsoring the Taliban. Perhaps they even gave them their name, the Seekers of Wisdom. Two years ago, no one here had even heard of them.

Inside the ministry building, the mullahs are in residence. They have agreed to receive us, even though Diane and I are women. They seem genuinely surprised that the world has recoiled from them because of the women's issue. Shir Mohammed Stanekzai, with milky skin and a straggly beard to Taliban code, sails briskly into the conference room. The camera is ready. The microphone is pinned to his flowing robes. All of the leaders are young. Stanekzai's boss, Mullah Mohammed Omar, who refuses to leave Kandahar, is in his mid-thirties. Stanekzai's title is deputy foreign minister, but he is a key member of the mullahs' team because he speaks English fluently. He can converse with the U.N. Special Mission, the U.S. State Department, and the CIA station chief in Islamabad, who meet regularly with the Taliban.

The deputy foreign minister is perfect for television. Regardless of what he says, his face tells the truth. The camera loves his face. It records the venom, arrogance, and disgust. The Taliban spokesman is saying that the mullahs have brought peace and security to Afghanistan. They are not against women's rights. They are not against "girls' education in schools or universities. But," says Stanekzai, "we want them to be educated in a proper manner, according to our religious rules and regulations." This is a major theme. "We have set up a commission in order to solve all these problems, to introduce our rules and regulations, and announce it through radios, so that everybody knows. They should be strict. We have closed the schools for girls."

Diane asks where in the Koran it says that women cannot work. The Taliban minister is irritated. He cannot answer the question directly because there is no such prohibition in the Koran. "No. It's not that women cannot work. Women can work. We know the importance of a woman in society. Obviously, we realize that. And further, I can tell you that in every society, women play 50 percent of the role in a society for men. But there are certain rules and regulations." He responds to the facts on the ground by saying everything is temporary, only "for a short time." How short? "That's up to the committee." Diane takes off the black Armani veil and the minister turns away.

Rules and regulations dictate that videocassettes must be screened and stamped by the Taliban censors before they leave the country. On top of this, the U.N. rules forbid taking videocassettes on U.N. planes. I intend to break all of the rules. If we abide by them, our tapes will be damaged, stolen, or lost. After the interview with the minister, we tear over to the airport. There is a U.N. flight due in minutes. Carlos has stuffed all of our belongings in the taxi. At the loading dock, Diane and I disappear into a dark passage with our veils and the box of cassettes. We divide them equally and begin stuffing them into our clothes. We emerge buxom and veiled. The Taliban are unlikely to body-search us. The difficulty is getting through the airport without a cassette slipping to the floor. We smile a lot and move slowly. Fabrice, Carlos, and the others will drive out of the country to get "pickups," footage we must have of Taliban soldiers, rocket launchers, and antiaircraft guns, and scenic shots. They can be stopped and searched anywhere en route. We board the jet awkwardly. I am worried now about the effect of sweat on the cassettes. Once the plane is in the air, I remove the tapes one by one.

The U.N. jet acts as a taxi, stopping at several Afghan cities. We land in Jalalabad to collect Colonel Bill Egar, the Senior Military Advisor to the U.N. Special Mission to Afghanistan. He is an Irish colonel from Cork, with sharp blue eyes, gray hair, and a trim physique. He has met with the Taliban many times. Since his tour began in April, seven months before this meeting, the colonel has traveled all around the country observing military equipment, training, strategy, and tactics. I ask about Pakistan's role in supplying military hardware and support. The Pakistan role, he says, is "major." He adds with a winning smile that "Pakistan cannot afford what they are sending."

"Where is the money coming from?" I ask.

"The U.S.," Colonel Egar says matter-of-factly. The Senior Military Advisor to the U.N. Special Mission smiles again. This is confirmation of what I have heard repeatedly from Afghani and diplomatic sources.

I press the point. "Why is the U.S. so keen on the Taliban?"

"Anyone who is against Iran is okay in Washington," the colonel explains. Iran shares a common border with Afghanistan. "Iran is Shia Muslim. The Taliban are Sunni Muslim. Sunni fundamentalists are okay. Shia are not." The Irish colonel shrugs. "Then there is the terrorism problem. The Taliban promised to close the training camps. I know firsthand that at least one camp outside Jalalabad was shut down. It's empty now with a Taliban guard. And the Taliban claim they will stop opium poppy production. They won't allow the planting of next year's crop. This is very appealing for the Americans."

There is also the matter of the gas pipeline. An American oil company called Unocal wants to lay pipeline across Afghanistan, pumping gas from Turkmenistan, one of the former Soviet republics. Unocal has befriended the Taliban. The Taliban's peace and security will ensure profits from the pipeline. Unocal also has a good working relationship with the SLORC government in Burma, the military dictatorship that kept Nobel Peace Prize winner Aung San Suu Kyi locked up for five years.

I wonder about the CIA's judgment. In territory controlled by the Taliban for the past year and a half, drug traffickers have profited handsomely from the heroin trade. Some of the world's most famous terrorists are sheltering around Jalalabad, including Osama Bin Ladin. The CIA's own analysts say Bin Ladin is financing Saudi bombers in Riyadh and Dhahran. So it would seem the Taliban have not kept their bargain.

We say good-bye to the U.N. in Islamabad. From there, we fly halfway around the world to New York. I have a week to cut the piece, so I shuttle down to Washington to go trick-or-treating with Charlie on Halloween. The following morning, I am back in New York in the edit room to screen the tapes. I get an urgent message from Phyllis McGrady, the executive producer. I have to cut a piece for *World News*. It is Friday. The piece will air tonight. I race downstairs and start constructing a short news piece in my mind. Just when I have worked it out, McGrady walks in. There will be no short news piece. Instead, the entire story will air tonight on *20/20*. That way we beat *60 Minutes*, which plans to air Christiane Amanpour's debut story, her piece on women in Afghanistan, on Sunday. Christiane left Kabul the day we arrived. *60 Minutes* will have had seven days to cut a piece. I have, checking the clock, seven hours.

Phyllis sends me legions of helpers. I am constructing sequences in my head and reading off time code numbers to identify where shots can be found on the tapes. Producers are lining up to take sections of the piece, the orphanage, the high 8 footage of the widows, the central interview with the unveiled women. I give them the rundown, the outline for building the sequences, and all the best shots. I have marked the "sound bites," the sections of interviews we will use. I am concentrating on the interview with the Taliban minister, which is the key confrontation. Working this way is chaotic. There are transcript pages in four edit rooms. All of the "mods," modules or sections, must be "married" in a final edit. This is done minutes before air.

The piece looks coherent, even moving. It is a strong story. Diane and Barbara Walters introduce and close the piece in the studio. Barbara is wonderful. She is outraged. The fact that these two titans of television news have agreed to share a set gives the story added luster. I am relieved. The women did not show their faces in vain.

With any luck, the White House is watching.

TWO

The Oasis

PEOPLE become journalists because they cannot decide what to be when they grow up. We are like troublesome children, asking too many questions. When someone probes to get to the bottom of why we do this, the answer is often a shrug and "Well, it beats working for a living."

I started down this road as a traveler with a taste for danger. At the age of eighteen I landed on a strange continent in pitch-darkness. It was like diving off a waterfall. I was alone in Africa, with no idea that I was entering journalism boot camp.

Taking time off after my freshman year at Yale to live in an African village would prepare me, I thought, to be an anthropologist. I had already made a pilgrimage to the Collège de France in Paris, home of the great Claude Lévi-Strauss. I would study the women's role among the Akamba tribe in Kenya. Because their home terrain was shrinking to make way for game parks, their culture was under terrible pressure. They had withdrawn into the isolated hill country of central Kenya, high above the herds that once sustained them. Hunters with poisoned arrows got in the way of photo safaris.

I arrived in Nairobi armed with names and addresses and one small suitcase. In 1971, Nairobi was a low-built and sleepy town, with markets crowded with Indian traders and Kikuyu women in hot-colored Manchester cottons. Burned maize was hawked from street corner barbecues under the burning-red canopies of flame trees and the purple shade of flowering jacaranda. Jomo Kenyatta, father of Kenyan independence, drove the streets in a long motorcade with outriders, sirens blaring. The Ngong Hills smelled of bog myrtle, as they did when Isak Dinesen first passed that way.

I pitched up on the doorstep of the African Medical and Research Foundation, the ground team of the Flying Doctors, whose principal work was rescuing the sick and the wounded from the remote bush. The ground team penetrated the most inaccessible areas in the country to gauge the severity of health problems. The team leader, a large affable man called Toluungua, was from the tribe I was hoping might adopt me. He had little use for an untrained student but gave in to my pleading and settled me under the foundation's wing in a village in the Mbooni Hills of Ukambani.

I was in fact learning one of the most basic tenets of journalism: barge through the door even though you have no business being there.

I squeezed into the back of a battered Peugeot taxi, already loaded with villagers returning home from Nairobi down the Mombasa road. It was too hot to breathe. Once the windows were opened as we sped east, we were all coated with dust. This was the main eastern artery to the coastal towns and the Indian Ocean. My destination was the Kombu district, in the hills above Machakos, on a direct axis between Mount Kenya to the north and Kilimanjaro to the south. We crossed the baked plains, dotted with thorn trees shading giraffe, and occasionally stopped in an utterly desolate spot to deposit a passenger, who headed purposefully toward the horizon. There was nothing in his path for a hundred miles.

It was rare for a Mzungu, the Swahili term for "European" or "foreigner," to travel in these overloaded taxis, and my presence raised eyebrows. The mood improved when a baboon crossed our path. This was a good omen. Under a cloudless sky, we arrived at the teeming Machakos bus depot, where I attracted a crowd who directed me in unison to the Nzaikoni bus. The bus was a shambles, full of chickens and heaped with baskets and bundles tied on the roof with sisal. I felt nervous and exhilarated. As we climbed through thick pine forest to the summit, the earth turned rust red and fields of bananas and sugarcane fell away sharply to the plains. To the south, the horizon was filled by the magnificent volcanic cone of Mount Kilimanjaro, rising nineteen thousand feet. Any second thoughts I had about the expedition vanished.

Nzaikoni was a hilltop marketplace. A dozen brick hovels that passed for shops sat on the prow of the ridge, surrounded on market days by women with cicatrized skin (covered with decorative welts) and teeth filed into points. They wore indigo-blue scarves and smoked clay pipes stuffed with homegrown tobacco. Freshly picked bananas, loquats, and guavas were displayed on the ground. I was offered loam black snuff wrapped in dried banana leaves and herbal remedies for typhoid, rheumatism, and V.D.

The ancient bus deposited me at the "counselor's" shop, a tiny shop selling general provisions, where the chief and subchief of the district took charge of my welfare. My mission, as defined by the indulgent Toluungua, was to gather information that might help explain why this area had the highest infant mortality rate in the country. My ability to communicate was rudimentary. I had spent two months in the reading room of the British Museum studying every known text on their language, but their selection was so meager that I was forced to start from scratch in the shop, asking the name of everything in Swahili for translation into Kikamba. Would-be teachers swarmed in and I was nearly crushed as they tore down bars of soap, cooking oil, and lamp wicks to declaim their proper Kikamba names.

The chief, who managed to look distinguished in his threadbare fedora and sandals made from old tires, came to my rescue. He cleared a path through the crowd with his polished cane and spirited me into a smoky café, which boasted one table with an open pit fire. In this sort of place the chicken was dispatched and plucked after the order was placed. All of the district elders had gathered to meet me, drink Tusker beer, and discuss politics.

When everyone had polished off their share of seared meat, I was called upon to describe the American political structure in my basic Swahili. Not one of my inquisitors knew what or where America was. "Across the ocean" drew a blank. I scored points with the revolt against the British and drew approving nods with the separation of powers, which I couched as chief versus the elders. Their one association with the word "America" was maize falling from the sky. John Kennedy, while president, had ordered an airlift of famine relief to the Mbooni Hills and earned their everlasting gratitude. Slang for their finger millet was "Kennedy." My hosts fell over themselves to buy me Fanta soda to repay the debt. I was then escorted by the most distinguished locals and a very long train of children on a ten-mile hike to my hut.

Most of the villagers had never seen a white woman before. They believed that white women could not walk. We needed bearers, litters, Land-Rovers with chauffeurs. What I assumed was an innocent trek down the red dirt gullies, along switchbacks through the banana and sugarcane plantations, was in fact a traveling circus for everyone along our route. I found some privacy in the bathhouse, a mud structure containing one bowl of water, one sponge, and a hole in the wall at eye level so one could admire the view while bathing.

I remained the big draw of the region for the next several months. My waist-length hair had to be piled on top of my head to stop gossip that I was a witch. It terrified the children. The more benign explanation for my hair was kinship with the bush baby, a common tree monkey with a voluminous tail. My Kamba name was Bush Baby.

Being watched night and day, whispered about, followed, touched, made it easy to later work as a journalist in the teeming refugee camps that spring up like weeds around every war.

The young woman who offered to share her thatched and wattled hut was a "primary school" teacher (a generous description of the primitive school) who was suspected to be barren and thus unsuitable for marriage. In Ukambani, Kamba women became engaged and did their best to become pregnant before marriage to ensure fertility. Thamba Museo's fiancé of two years was growing impatient. She had been unable to conceive ever since a first child was stillborn. She consulted every *mundu mue*, a witch doctor, herbalist, and psychologist combined, for forty miles around. She followed every bizarre instruction to the letter. She dragged me on expeditions to collect white stones from the river, where she swam and drank with her lover, soil from the hilltop where they slept, a golden hen from his family compound, a branch from a tree at her mother's shamba. These were the ingredients for a cure.

The witch doctor sat in the gloom of her round hut, warming the skin stretched over an enormous drum. She offered Thamba and me *baki*, homemade snuff, and we sneezed as tears poured down our cheeks from the acrid smoke of the fire. The interior walls of the hut were soot black, with dried maize hanging from the rafters. Once the drum, a hollow tree trunk with cowhide fastened with hobnails, was supple enough, she played to summon ancestral spirits. She accompanied the hypnotic rhythm with a high-pitched ethereal chant. I watched her exquisitely lined face through a veil of smoke, geometric patterns cut into her skin. The spirits she sought lived in the branches of sacred *muumo* fig trees and baobabs. They were roused by the drum and another queer instrument, a bow strung tight and plucked with a smooth baton. The witch doctor, in a trance, listened to the vibrating bow and dispensed instructions for a cure. Everything failed.

Any malady was connected with ill will, a slighted relative, a jealous neighbor. A child dying of kwashiorkor with a belly like a balloon was not the victim of hunger but of someone's evil intentions or a mother's failure to follow ritual procedures. It was not possible to mix an egg with a child's morning porridge, ground at dawn from bemba wheat, because the child who eats an egg will grow up to be a chicken thief.

There were dozens of such prohibitions, all contributing to the poor health of anyone under three. Recording them was important because in the remote hill country, taboos changed in the space of twenty miles. I was learning to doggedly pursue reasons—in this case, for 50 percent malnutrition. These beliefs, mixed with malaria, chronic chiggers, parasites that nested in open sores, eyes, and ears, and the famine that came regularly with dry weather and erosion, left children weak, vulnerable. When the rains finally came, the air was thick with flying termites, which everyone greedily devoured, cooked lightly in oil. Even I developed a taste for crispy termites.

My bedroom consisted of a bare floor. There was no electricity, no telephone, no water, no windows, no mirror. Much of my small suitcase was taken up with books. No one in these hills, with the exception of my hutmate and a fellow teacher who read selections from the Bible, had ever read a book. There was no conversation about books, no references or allusions. It was a rare villager who had seen a film. Once during my stay, a mobile projector arrived on the back of a truck in the nearest market town. A spaghetti western was shown to a good crowd sitting comfortably in the brush. The villains wore black and galloped around furiously on their stallions. There was rustling in the audience, confusion over the size of images on the screen. If a horse appeared tiny because it was a mile down the road, the suggestion that it was a horse was preposterous. It was surely a beetle.

People amused themselves with conversation. They sat, as night fell, around the fire dug into a pit in each hut, where the maize and beans were cooked in a tall *nungu*, a handsome black pot. Everyone told a story. Because Kikamba was as yet an unwritten language in these hills, their memories were superb, matched only by their appetite for gossip. The worst sins that could ignite gossip were laziness and sloth. There was perennial jealousy among first, second, and third wives over who was next in line for a conjugal visit.

In exchange for their hospitality, the village women made demands. They would stop me along the road, and peering at me from beneath huge bundles strapped to their heads, test my progress speaking their language. They invited me to join them chopping down eucalyptus trees and handed me an ax. This was women's work. I chopped until my palms were a mass of bleeding blisters and was led into the nearest hut where my hands were rubbed with strange herbs and cauterized with hot coals. This was a kind of rite of passage. The blisters disappeared the next day.

I walked ten to twenty miles each day, hauling water by gourd from the river, and survived an attack of bilharzia—an invasion of tiny river parasites through the skin—which can ravage, among other things, the central nervous system. Nairobi doctors informed me I was living in the bilharzia capital of East Africa. The creatures were in my drinking water and bathing water. No one had warned me. I was treated with a massive dose of Ambilhar. I was also spared the effects of infectious hepatitis, which doctors were amazed that I failed to contract. I learned how to recognize the signs of parasites and to dig chiggers out from between my toes. It was difficult to remain squeamish in such conditions. Weakness was squeezed out of me like the sugarcane juice that Kamba women collected from long green stalks crushed in a mangle.

Tropical diseases are a great hazard to journalists. After living in Ukambani, I took care to avoid them, paying close attention when a new strain of malaria appeared that defied all of the pills or when the cholera shot that was required for so many years turned out to be completely useless. Nets and bottled water became essential. By the 1990s, the East African coast was afflicted with cerebral malaria, a cruel variation that inflamed the brain, leading to mental retardation or death.

During my months in the village, the outside world beyond the Yatta Plateau became an increasingly vague concept. I was honored with an invitation from the oldest man in the village. He was over a hundred and wanted to describe his memory of the British expedition in 1896 from the coast to what is now Nairobi to chart the course for the Mombasa–Victoria Nyanza railway. The building of the Uganda railway was a momentous event, opening the country to white settlers. The railway men saw that the conditions on the high plateaus were just right for British colonization, which exploded in 1903. The old man remembered seeing the first expedition cross the plain below, where Kamba men traditionally hunted big game with their bows and arrows. He described the strangers vividly as "transparent people with fire in their pockets." The transparent people were white. The fire was their guns. This conversation, a firsthand account of the British force crossing the frontier seventy-five years before, was my first memorable interview.

Most of the old hunting grounds, like Tsavo below us, were now game parks, reserved for men in bush jackets laden with Nikons. But Kamba men still made deadly poison arrows. One day I was invited for a lesson in making poison and a set of arrows, packed in a dried rhino skin quiver. This was a gift for me. I watched the tips dipped in black sticky sap, for which, I was told, there was no antidote. One prick of the skin was fatal. We wrapped the tips carefully in cloth to avoid killing someone by accident. The hunters, when not poaching on their old territory, got drunk on sugarcane beer, to forget they had become obsolete.

I became acquainted with families for miles around and interviewed the women regularly about everything from birth control to what they served for breakfast. Polygamous families lived in well-defined communities, a round hut in the center for the eldest wife, square huts extending outward for the lesser wives and their children. My visits began with a single wooden chair being produced for me along with a calabash full of warm sour milk. The women then fired a barrage of questions. What was my clan? I explained that I had already been initiated into the Lion clan. My inability to eat liver was a sign. Lions, I was told, shared my aversion. Clan members treated me like a relative. What were our rituals? Why were eggs painted and hidden at Easter? Why was a tree chopped down for Christmas? Did we sacrifice turkeys? What was our bride price? I was sometimes faced with two or three gourds of sour milk in a day.

The top price for a wife was forty-four goats, one bull, one cow, and one bushel each of maize and beans. This was a fortune, the equivalent of a Manhattan apartment and a trust fund. It often took years to pay the debt. Divorce in these circumstances was a financial disaster. The offer of marriage was made with great ceremony. A boy's mother wove an elegant *thonge* basket with leather straps to secure it on the forehead, and beaten copper bangles. Girls were then invited to the potential in-laws' for goat stew.

One morning, an emissary arrived with the basket. It seemed I had passed muster with the village women. They had decided I was a suitable wife and should remain in Ukambani. I was summoned to the compound of Kombu district's most eligible bachelor, the eldest son of the eldest wife of the most revered village elder. My presence was required. My fiancé-to-be popped the question as he took me on a tour of his estates. A banana plantation on the steep hillside, an arrowroot patch at the river's edge, it would all be mine, not to own, but to harvest.

"All this will be yours to work in," he announced proudly.

My bride price was an unprecedented eighty-eight goats, two bulls, and two cows. That was double the going rate. I could not simply say, "No thanks." The decision to accept or decline the herd was not mine, but my father's. I was instructed to send word to him of the offer. My suitor's family wanted details of how to transport the goats to my house. I did not mention that my father, running a shipping corporation in San Francisco, would know exactly how to move eighty-eight goats ten thousand miles by sea.

On my next trip to Nairobi, a ten-mile hike at dawn to meet the dilapidated bus, a terrifying ride down winding dirt roads with sheer cliff, rough riders hanging from the bus (cracking raw eggs with one hand and sucking them down), a hunt for a crowded taxi in the confusion of the Machakos market, I sent a cable to San Francisco. I stressed that I did not see my future tilling the fields of the Mbooni Hills. My father played his part perfectly. He replied immediately that I was already committed. His answer was translated, considered, and accepted, man-to-man. My views were irrelevant.

Living with these people, in a place that seemed the end of the earth, I began examining everything from their point of view. By the third month, white skin looked sickly, the massive baobab trees seemed like a reasonable nesting place for ancestral spirits, and a column of safari ants marching over my bed was to be calmly tolerated. This is what a journalist is always trying to achieve, the ability to see the other side. I drew the line at female circumcision, which Kamba women assured me was de rigueur for the complete woman. In their eyes, I was somehow androgynous without it.

I discovered the folly of arrogance, the assumption that Third World villagers are simpleminded. One day, I was asked to the hut of a woman with a pressing question. As I entered through the low doorway cut in the mud wall, I saw that she had pinned up pages from an old *Life* magazine. They were faded glossy pictures of the moon landing. While I was trying to think where she might have found them, my hostess was already hurling questions. How, precisely, had men traveled to the moon? What was a rocket? How was it made, powered, guided? What did they find on the moon? What was gravity? I dredged up every scrap of physics, every memory of Walter Cronkite's script, the odd description of stages, modules, heat shields, telemetry, from the live coverage of the NASA control room, a conversation that I had as a child with astronaut Alan Shepard. I felt hopelessly out of my depth. She was polite but unsatisfied. This illiterate, "uncivilized" old woman needed a rocket scientist.

Whenever I walk into a village in Africa or the Amazon, in the triple-canopy jungle of Southeast Asia, I imagine her there among the old women in the market, waiting to ask if I have the answers yet.

This early plunge into "primitive" society was a revelation. Leaving the biosphere of the First World, the giant terrarium of Safeways, pools, auto junkyards, and raked sand traps, was like falling into what physicists call a wormhole, a passageway to a higher dimension. Concepts we regard as inviolate like telephone communications, vanilla ice cream, orthodontists, and the collective experience of *I Love Lucy* were suddenly fragments of memory belonging to some parallel universe. Absolute frames of reference became mere choices on a menu. Seeing the world as a villager without a mirror allowed me to observe my own society from the outside. It was a bit like the African anthropologist who came to England to do his fieldwork studying village ritual along the Thames.

This heightened ability to observe also made it easier to step into someone else's shoes. I could feel at ease with Colombian hit men, Khmer Rouge guerrillas, members of the Saddam family, or Afghan fundamentalists. Once I felt at home fashioning poison arrows and sampling termites, I was comfortable anywhere.

I stumbled into television news on a spring day in 1976. I remember sitting in the glass pilot house of my fishing boat *Orpheus*, moored on the Thames in London, watching a sunset over Battersea. One of my roommates from Yale suddenly appeared on deck, having climbed across several boats tied up at Cheyne Walk to find me. She began recounting her adventures in the Moroccan desert where she had, by royal invitation, carried the flag at the head of King Hassan's "Green March" to take over the Spanish Sahara. The newspapers were full of photos of the human wave that set out across the desert in a grand gesture to undermine the Polisario guerrillas who wanted that particular spot for themselves. Laurie Frank rarely stepped outside Manhattan, and the image of her as a royal emissary in spiked heels bravely tackling the Sahara was irresistible, like Dorothy Parker playing Lawrence of Arabia. In the sand encampment at the front, she had been adopted by a camera crew from the London bureau of NBC News. As *Orpheus* rocked violently on a rising tide, Laurie lit a cigarette and pronounced the NBC team "heaven," adventurous, good poker players, and generous with food and drink. She convinced me to apply for a job at the network.

We had graduated together as Yale "superwomen," in the first batch of undergraduate women to navigate the shoals of the all-male university. I remember the horror of attending a "mixer," a college dance, and having to pretend that I had been bused in from one of the women's colleges, Smith or Wellesley, which was standard practice at the time. Yale women were too threatening, too dangerous, too smart. The admission that I lived across the street inevitably left me without a dance partner.

After Yale, I had decamped to London for graduate school at the University of London's School of Oriental and African Studies. I was immersed in African colonial history and the oral epic poetry of the Gambian griots, bards who sang the tale of the thirteenth-century founding of Mali, the only living Homeric tradition left. Seeing Laurie fresh from the Sahara convinced me that I was completely unsuited to academia. I was bored. I wanted to go back to Africa where I could stand on the escarpment of the Rift Valley and see the green flash over the sun as it set.

I had just won the *Vogue* writing prize, which yielded lunch with Princess Margaret's husband, Tony Snowden, a genial photographer, and an invitation to work for *Vogue*'s glamorous features editor called Joan Buck. (Years later, Joan and I both landed at *Vanity Fair.*) But British *Vogue* could not compete with the budgets of network news. For someone who wanted to explore the ends of the earth, there was no other news organization that could afford the sort of expeditions I had in mind. With Laurie's prodding, I walked into the Economist Building in London's West End for an appointment with the bureau chief of NBC News.

The handsome building at number 25 was the only thing modern on St. James's Street, a warren of men's clubs that smelled of leather and port, and wine vaults, where good clarets were put away for newborns and picked up at twenty-one. Christie's auction house was tucked around the back along with the dusty London Library. It was a three-minute walk to tea at the Ritz.

The bureau chief ushered me into his commodious office. The room was bare. The tall lanky man, with the features of a sparrow hawk, motioned for me to sit on the floor. I studied the walls, covered in royal-purple felt. The bizarre interview proceeded with both of us sitting cross-legged on the carpet. I had my doubts about the news business. The chief seemed preoccupied with his new designer chairs out for upholstering in shades like plum. Irv Margolis and I had little in common. He had learned his trade at the Chicago affiliate of NBC. I had never been to Chicago. I was a San Franciscan, whose brush with the Midwest was driving through at the rate of a thousand miles a day until I hit the New Jersey Turnpike. I hated local news and Irv's polyester shirts. They were short-sleeved, exposing arms like chalk. He needed sun. He wore thick beat generation glasses. Irv was the man with absolute power to determine what foreign news was fit for the American viewer, at least the NBC slice of viewers, which was considerable at the time.

I had to sharply revise my first impression once I saw him in action. He picked up the phone on the floor to take a call from Lebanon, where a civil war was raging. "What do you mean you can't get the film out of Beirut? See any boats in the harbor? Charter!" He rifled the pages of a fat ABC Airline guide poised on his lap. "Yeah, there's a flight out of Cyprus to Rome or Paris. Even a Zagreb–Frankfurt connection. I really don't see the problem. Or sail to Israel. Walk if you have to." Irv was in command. The words "I can't" were greeted with derision. News gathering required unorthodox tactics, stamina, and for best results, a criminal mind. As he probed my past, he was most interested by the fact that I had mapped the Yale steam tunnels and learned the technique of hopping freight trains from New Haven to Maine. I also spoke Swahili.

"Well," I said decisively, "if a job opens up in six months or a year, please let me know."

I left him sitting in the empty room plotting routes, neglected connections through Dushanbe or Baku, rust-bucket prop planes plying the routes of Central Asia. The next morning, I had just stoked the coal stove on *Orpheus* when the phone rang. It was Irv. I could have a job if I started immediately. He said this knowing I was slogging through my master's thesis and cramming for exams.

"What would you like me to do first?" I asked tentatively.

"I'm giving a lecture in Turkey next week on censorship in television. I need you to write a paper on global censorship, cover every continent, and deliver it before I leave. Come over to the office and pick up your press card. You'll need it to get into the Fleet Street morgues."

The morgues, as I discovered, were the vast clippings libraries of the great English newspapers. I lived in them for the next several days and turned in a hefty fifty-page report. I slept for two days and reported for duty. Irv let me know I had passed his initiation rite by saying simply, "Keep your press card."

I went on the payroll at the princely sum of 100 pounds a week ($160) plus 50 pounds for each radio spot. Someone at NBC should have been jailed for exploitation. I, however, was thrilled. I was finally being paid for the same skills that two universities had charged me for the privilege of using. My job was to find stories, on any continent, and develop them for *Nightly News* in New York. Irv's empire stretched from London to Hong Kong, with the war in Lebanon in the middle. The landscape was defined by trouble.

I began monitoring the terrorist group Baader Meinhof, who were then kidnapping German industrialists, and the South Moluccan independence movement seizing trainloads of hostages. I befriended oil sheiks who parked their wives to watch TV in Rolls-Royces outside the Dorchester Hotel on Park Lane while the sheiks consorted with their mistresses upstairs. I watched events in the "covert" war in Angola, which embroiled the White House, the South Africans, and the Cubans.

Irv created a floating slot for me and dispatched me under the wing of various members of the bureau to learn the foreign news business. The peculiar thing about my presence in that bureau was that every one of my American colleagues, whether in radio or television, producer, editor, correspondent, camera operator, or engineer, was a man. There was the occasional comely English secretary and bureau assistant. But this was veneer. I had landed in a tight fraternity.

Producers guzzled beer, smoked Camels, and threw footballs to punctuate conversation. Fortunately, Yale had trained me for those awkward moments when you realize you are the only woman in the room. I was a curiosity. If Irv had broken with precedent to groom a woman from the Ivy League, it never occurred to him that I was destined to carve a career taking on the news business's most dangerous assignments.

In 1976, combat reporting and the rougher Third World stories, famines and revolutions, were regarded as hazardous duty, a beat reserved for men in Abercrombie bush jackets. Somehow lost to history was the fact that one of the first newsreel war correspondents was Jessica Borthwick, a woman reporter who, at the age of twenty-two, covered the Balkan War of 1913. Distinguished war correspondents like Lee Miller in World War II and Gloria Emerson in Vietnam had displayed exemplary courage and endurance. All of the questions about women that seemed to vex military commanders and bureau chiefs—"Where will they sleep, change clothes, pee? Can they stand the noise?"—should have been long since resolved. Great women explorers like Gertrude Bell, Isabella Bird, and Alexandra Neal had endured unimaginable hardships and risked their lives daily in the Middle East and Asia. Still, Beirut was for boys. I fought long and hard for the privilege of being shot at.

In the meantime, I had a great deal to learn. In my first days, Irv sent me to the radio room to write scripts and select quotes, "bites" or "nat sound" as they were known, for London feature stories. My tutor was a soft-spoken Canadian reporter, Clark Todd, who patiently drilled me in radio skills. Clark was later killed by a sniper in a Beirut street. Remarkably, my first radio interview was with Margaret Thatcher, then a minor feature story, whom I billed with some gripping phrase like "Unlikely Conservative Party matron climbs the ranks." I had no idea that three years later she would be prime minister, installed in Downing Street. I thought it was a pity my listeners could not see the stunning texture of her skin, like a smooth plastic developed for NASA. She had the firm but reassuring manner of an English nanny, which is precisely what, her handlers wagered correctly, the country wanted in its leader. I wrote more about the grooming of Mrs. Thatcher for *Vogue*. But overall, I found British politics had a soporific effect on me. Writing domestic feature stories for radio was like chewing lettuce leaves for laudanum. Far more intriguing was London as the backdrop for the riveting politics of oil.

This was a huge story. Words like "gas lines" and "energy shortage" had resonance. I became a keen student of the oil states, paying close attention to events in Riyadh and Baghdad. I produced a series of oil stories with Garrick Utley for *Nightly News*. I was amassing contacts in the Middle East, in the oil business, and in the City, London's financial center. When an oil tanker called the *Argo Merchant* cracked up off the French coast, I was given the task of investigating the checkered past of the Liberian registered ship. I started at Lloyd's of London and ended up on Broad Street, Monrovia.

Finally, I was on the road. I flew to Liberia, via Geneva and the Ivory Coast, in search of clues to the shipowner responsible for a massive oil spill fouling the Channel. I was free to board a plane and follow a lead to another continent without a second thought. This was the lure of network news. It was the sort of freedom that is addictive.

I arrived in Africa at night after a rainfall, the air smelling heavily of earth and paraffin from the smoky lanterns. There was Zaire rock playing on scratchy radios and hawkers selling palm wine and groundnuts. I checked into the Dukor Hotel. My file from Lloyd's led me to a brass-plate office of the Liberian flag of convenience, a service that had brought a steady income to the Liberian treasury for decades, a supplement to the rubber plantations. The device of Liberian registry shielded owners of rusty tankers from massive claims and prying questions from investigators like me.

I was greeted by a scene out of Somerset Maugham. The Monrovia address yielded an American expatriate in a white three-piece suit smoking a cigar under a ceiling fan. This was the end of the paper trail. Gerald Cooper, the commissioner of maritime affairs, like Liechtenstein lawyers and Swiss bankers, was steeped in secrets. Liberia, on paper, had the biggest fleet of ships in the world. I was candid with Cooper and other Liberian officials about my investigation into the appalling state of one of their tankers. This was a bold approach, as the last NBC crew in town to investigate diamond smuggling had been thrown in jail. They were rescued by a Russian exile known as "Papa" who claimed to be the illegitimate son of Rasputin.

In spite of the Liberian registry's discretion, I did manage, through well-placed leaks, to track down the *Argo Merchant*'s ownership and get out of town in time for an hour special on the disaster, "The Last Voyage of the Argo Merchant," broadcast in March 1977.

I was learning how to investigate, develop sources, and "cut and feed" stories and "bird" them to New York. The bird was the satellite link between New York and London. Satellite transmission at the time was controlled from the labyrinthine BBC headquarters at Shepherds Bush, the model of George Orwell's *1984*. On Saturday nights, I was often in the BBC's smoky control room, shouting down the phone to an identical room in Manhattan, "Can you see a picture? You should see a tank and a minaret," another image from the infamous Green Line that divided the armies in Beirut.

Under Irv's wing, I learned how to operate in the shadowy world of journalism behind the Iron Curtain. He allowed me to finance and run a sensitive smuggling operation, to get precious dissident footage out of Czechoslovakia. Irv did not ask who my contacts were in the Czech underground or how they operated. Anonymity was the condition laid down by the dissidents involved, who shuttled 16-mm cameras and film cans between Prague and London. The risk of detection by the Czech secret police promised severe penalties, at the very least a long and unpleasant jail term. The pictures that flowed out were powerful evidence of repression of the movement that became known as Charter 77. My smuggling ring earned me a reputation I had not anticipated in the bureau. A rumpled veteran correspondent wandered into my office one day and expressed the new office view. "So, you're CIA?"

Bureau inmates seemed to have difficulty accepting that a woman could be resourceful and discreet. There had to be some explanation. Irv was bemused. He gave me a raise. He invited me to Africa for more field experience in shooting a story. We set out to do two light features, one on the mania in Nigeria for boxer Archie Moore and the second following the first *Roots* tour up the Gambia River. Within a few days of landing in the Gambia, I was arrested as a spy.

At first, the trip seemed promising. Irv and I, along with cameraman, soundman, and assistant, were collected in Volvo limousines, deposited at Heathrow Airport, relieved by porters of twenty cases of camera gear, and ushered into first class on Air France bound for Paris. Irv, of course, had studied the routing and found that the Concorde, flying to Brazil from Paris, required a fueling stop in Senegal on the African coast. That was our destination. We piled on board the supersonic jet, then spanking new. After takeoff, the cramped cabin was so laden with lobster, caviar, and *mousse au chocolat*, it was impossible to move. The South American matrons who had flown to Europe to shop sat in agony. We gratefully disembarked at the Dakar airport and drove south over the border to Banjul, the capital of the sleepy enclave of the Gambia.

Roots was American writer Alex Haley's best-seller tracing African American family roots past the auction block and the slave ships to a village near the banks of the Gambia River. Haley's book opened this malarial backwater to a stream of affluent black Americans who wore the same expression as Boston Irish in Killarney. We boarded a riverboat steaming up the wide river into the African interior, escorted by dolphins. It was as cinematic a "return" as anyone could script. The shore was thick with mangrove. A dock appeared, missing most of its wooden slats. The ladies clattered ashore in their sling-back heels.

There were no vehicles, no shops, no telephones, no running water, no ice. The party was received by an aged wood-carver who hobbled over from the shade of his hut. He remembered Haley as "the rich American." The few inferior sculptures he displayed were received with rapture by the tour. One enthusiast inquired through the translator whether the carver took American Express. The local economy was only just shifting from barter to paper money.

A footpath led the way to the nearest village, and the lawyers and stockbrokers trudged inland through cassava, millet, and ground-nut fields, to the birthplace of Haley's hero, Kunta Kinte, for whom dozens of American children were now being named. It was an unspoiled village of sun-baked mud and thatch huts. The exhausted hikers settled down amidst the dogs and chickens to hear a languorous speech from the village oral historian. The dust and flies shifted the thoughts of the listeners to when they might head back to the capital for some shopping and a stiff drink.

After the long return voyage, all of us palsied from the vibrating engines and slipping in winch grease, I was arrested for espionage. The Gambian government did not believe an NBC News team would venture from London for such a trifling story. Roots was a cover. We were spies plotting a coup.

This surprising news was revealed in an interrogation room, where a slow-moving ceiling fan barely stirred the wet heat. The interrogator looked satisfied with his catch. He took pleasure in denying me water and cigarettes, in the hope of forcing a confession. He wanted full details of the plan. Moments like this, when you are inclined to laugh and make disparaging remarks, are the most dangerous for journalists. This is when the P. G. Wodehouse maxim "Speak civilly to blondes and they will speak civilly to you" comes into play. The only thing standing between a journalist and a year of rotting in a tropical jail cell, prey to dengue fever, yellow fever, cerebral malaria, is a fulsome display of good manners.

My jailer, from the local intelligence service, never paused to ask why anyone would have the slightest interest in toppling the government. The Gambia's only blue chip asset was its epic poetry, sung as the *Iliad* and *Odyssey* were once sung, accompanied by a haunting long-necked string instrument called the *kora*. I failed to impress the member of the governing party across the table with my profound appreciation of Gambian culture. I merely deepened his suspicions.

I watched the sweat slide down my tormentor's cheek. After a long round of questioning, Irv and I were permitted to return to the hotel. We would be summoned in the morning. To legally exit the country, we needed a government stamp, one of the elaborate stamps that control passage in the Third World. We would be detained at the airport without it. As planes were flying once or twice a week, the airport option looked bleak.

We decided to make a run for it. For the dollar equivalent of their annual wage, two drivers were willing to risk imprisonment to deliver us by night to the northern border with Senegal. We were fugitives, without proper papers. Making it through the border checkpoint was problematic. Failure left a hard trek on foot through the African bush as our only option short of Amnesty International.

Removing ourselves from Banjul at a relaxed pace to avoid attention, we reached the border post after midnight. We could dimly see half a dozen armed men. My stomach tightened as a soldier approached the car, fingered his automatic weapon, and demanded our passports. He took a long look at the driver and struck up an animated conversation in Mande, occasionally waving the gun barrel in our direction as we sat like crash-test dummies, hoping to be ignored. Our pile of documents was tossed back through the window, and with machine guns held high, the soldiers waved us out of the country.

"How did you do that?" I asked the driver with a gasp of admiration.

"He's my cousin." The driver lurched the car forward to freedom. I wondered whether each of us has a reserve account of impossible luck, without which we would be facing the ugly consequences of the border check, the mortar shell, the ice on the mountain pass. (The Nigeria leg of the trip was unmemorable except that Archie Moore got food poisoning from Lagos fish sticks.)

It was sheer *bad* luck, it seemed to me, that I was then dispatched to Libya. It was December 1977. I had just flown over the north pole to France from a family Thanksgiving in San Francisco. Things took an inexorably downward course when I made the mistake of calling Irv in London to check in.

"Where are you?" asked the connoisseur of airline guides.

"Paris."

"There's a charter that leaves Orly for Emperor Bokassa's coronation in the Central African Republic in an hour. There's a fuel stop in Tripoli. Get off, find the crew, and get an interview with Qaddafi."

Colonel Muammar Qaddafi was flush with oil profits. He harbored terrorist Abu Nidal, had befriended Idi Amin, and did business with Armand Hammer. The Libyan's literary taste ran to airport thrillers about nuclear weapons smuggled into New York.

"Irv, I have no visa."

"Leslie, you have to put the phone down right now to make it. By the way," he added with relish, "the charter is fully booked." Mission: Impossible.

I convinced the Paris taxi driver that it would be worth his while to break the speed record to the airport to catch the coronation charter. Frantically, I dredged my purse for the card of my one Libyan contact. We had met by chance at a Libyan Embassy reception in London a few months before where I had been introduced to Vanessa Redgrave, a fixture at pariah state cocktail parties. The gifted actress with a taste for radical politics towered over the gathering of Arab diplomats in their Savile Row suits. Redgrave was explaining the views of the Workers' Revolutionary Party, a leftwing splinter group she championed (with members drawn principally from the actors' guilds), which Colonel Qaddafi greatly admired. We were interrupted by a polished Libyan who gave his name as Said. He hoped we might adjourn to Tramps, his favorite nightclub, a haunt of IWT patrons ("international white trash"). Redgrave's interest rapidly flagged. I was left stranded with Said, who extended an invitation to visit him in Tripoli. He added in an offhand way that he was Qaddafi's cousin.

Tearing through the outskirts of Paris, I found the card and noted the address in the Libyan capital, the Oasis Oil building. A cheerful palm tree was embossed next to Said's name. The taxi screeched to a halt and I was catapulted into the airport terminal. There was one no-show on the charter. Bedraggled and jet-lagged, I joined a planeload of drunken Antwerp diamond dealers. They were already celebrating their African host's weekend plans to crown himself emperor, change his country's name to the Central African Empire, and throw the most extravagant party of the decade.

I was the only passenger defecting from the planeload of raucous guests. My seatmate was the scion of the Armenian diamond family who supplied the 128-carat stone in Bokassa's crown. He made a very persuasive case for dropping my itinerary and going as his date to Bangui for the coronation. A bucket full of champagne was consumed and I vaulted across the Libyan tarmac, having promised to call next time I was in Belgium.

Immigration was already clogged with journalists swarming in from Europe, Cairo, and Beirut. An NBC camera crew spotted me and escorted me to a run-down hotel, packed with well over a hundred journalists who were, with the exception of one matronly correspondent, all men.

This was the bulk of the Middle East press corps. They were here for the Rejectionist Conference, an assembly of angry leaders from across the Arab world, including Saddam Hussein, Yasser Arafat, Hafiz al Assad, and a diminutive, stony-faced delegation from South Yemen, who came to register their complaint that

Egypt's Anwar Sadat had chosen to make a separate peace with Israel. Over five days, they drank gallons of coffee with cardamom, smoked thousands of untipped cigarettes, and talked into the night with frequent pauses for photo opportunities. They agreed on very little, except that the Egyptian president had betrayed them, breaking ranks in order to regain control of the Sinai desert, lost to Israel in the 1967 war, and collar a few billion dollars from the U.S. treasury.

The press encampment in the Mediterranean bar was littered with overflowing ashtrays and the dregs of Turkish coffee, medium sweet. In Muslim Libya, the embassies had their private stash of alcohol. The throng concentrated most of their energies on wrangling invitations to sample the stock in diplomatic cellars. Every journalist in the room, including the dons of the Middle East press corps, had requested an interview with the Colonel. Eric Rouleau of *Le Monde*, the senior correspondent in the crowd, was waiting patiently. My orders were to get the first interview, even though NBC News had no particular clout. Local press officials were overwhelmed with unintelligible Japanese, imperious Germans, shouting Americans, and laconic Englishmen. The conventional route of pandering to minor bureaucrats, assuring them of massive coverage and penning self-important letters of introduction, was not promising. The NBC team was waiting. My only hope was the card with the palm tree.

I arrived by taxi at the Oasis building in the glare of late morning winter sun. The steel and glass corporate headquarters I imagined, with elevators full of oilmen just in from Houston, was nowhere to be seen. In its place was a concrete skeleton, a half-constructed high-rise with one outdoor staircase. The elevators had yet to be installed. I began to walk, dragging myself up floor by empty floor, thinking Said must have played a practical joke. My prospects looked grim. The card read PENTHOUSE.

When I reached the top, miserable and out of breath, the wind whipping down the empty corridors, I was facing a door with a stolen London CARNABY STREET sign tacked on. I knocked. An ebullient Said answered. Inside, he proudly displayed a sound system with all of the latest tapes from Tramps and a wet bar that ran the length of his apartment.

"Gin and tonic?" he asked brightly. "Or Scotch?" The punishment for alcohol in his cousin's domain was flogging. Said seemed delighted that a six-foot blonde was in his apartment. It began to sink in that we were very much alone. I kept the conversation fixed on world affairs and the urgent need to convince his cousin that I was the one journalist he wanted to see.

"What do you want to talk to him about?" Said shrugged, as though a conversation with cousin Muammar was a duty rather than a pleasure and not nearly as stimulating as his new tapes. I delivered an earnest explanation about the critical need to record the Colonel's views on the future of the Arab world and the consequences of Sadat's Jerusalem liaison. This explanation seemed to satisfy him. He reached lazily for the phone and direct-dialed the boss. They spoke. Said translated. "He says okay."

My host, who was well into his second gin and tonic by midafternoon, shared a number of my interests, such as the Saudi Arabian scheme to tow icebergs from Antarctica to the Arabian desert for irrigation. We discussed the Shah of Iran's latest weapons purchases, the best chefs at the Paris Air Show pavilions, and the new Mirage fighter. "Let's go to my office," he said, and led the way down. Racing along in his jeep, we came to a security fence with guard posts. Inside was a low compound. Said was waved in with quaking respect. As we swept into the building, everyone seemed to be saluting. I was deposited in a cavernous office in the Libyan equivalent of the Pentagon, a rare stop for foreigners unless you happen to be an arms dealer. Said excused himself. He returned in a general's uniform, every bit the chief of the Libyan Army.

Later, when the Reagan administration declared that the greatest threat of terrorism came from a Libyan "hit squad" roaming Europe and North America, Said was named as the terrible éminence grise behind it.

It was the next morning after spending the day with Dr. Death that I found myself in disgrace.

It was Sunday. Colonel Qaddafi stood on the steps of his presidential palace in Tripoli like a matinee idol facing an empty house. He surveyed his capital from behind a pair of Ray-Bans.

"Where is this woman?" he demanded. My interview with the Colonel had been granted for nine. It was now ten. His Excellency's bodyguards and courtiers examined their watches, shuffled their Italian shoes.

Unfortunately, I was sound asleep.

The envoy dispatched by the Libyan leader to the Mediterranean Hotel to track me down was incandescent with rage. No one had ever dared do this to His Excellency before. My behavior was insulting. His tortured face was a blur of virulent color like an unclipped fuchsia hedge. I had slept through an interview date with a head of state. I was twenty-five. I would be fired by the network. With luck, the Libyans would shoot me first. I had just betrayed every woman in the boiler rooms of television news.

How, after my long climb to the Oasis suite, after maneuvering and cajoling and probably risking rape, could I stand up Qaddafi? Who would believe I simply overslept? The dismal Mediterranean Hotel had no wake-up call. My roach-infested cell had no windows to see daylight. Not until 3 A.M., too late to rouse my NBC colleagues, had I received the message that the interview hour was fixed. I had been out most of the night sipping warm Pepsi and sweet almond milk with other members of the Middle East press corps roving the dry Islamic port, pining for the prerevolutionary days of King Idris, when banquets were spread on priceless carpets laid end-to-end on the beach.

With Qaddafi's man frothing before me, I snapped. I was never limbered up to do combat on a Sunday morning. I was fed up with officials. The shower was cold. What was worse, the Beach Hotel housing the delegates had little soaps and a pool. I interrupted the stream of abuse.

"I'm leaving the country."

The official continued his offensive, repeating that the "exclusive" interview granted to NBC was now canceled.

"I'm taking the next plane."

He paused, sucking the air like a spawning salmon, and blinked. "I am sorry. That is not possible. The Colonel is expecting you."

"You said it was canceled."

"Wait one moment, please."

The official scurried to the phone. After much haranguing in Arabic, the Colonel's man returned.

"Madame, His Excellency will see you at midnight."

Along with this sharp grinding of gears, the small man informed me breezily that Idi Amin was en route to the capital. The thought of the Butcher of Kampala arriving to confer with the Lion of the Desert was too rich to digest at that moment, so I agreed to the midnight date, left messages high and low for the crew, and repaired to the souk. I felt light-headed. I would not be fired. I had not betrayed the women of my profession. I was saved by a game of chicken.

There was little to buy from the market stalls but poor-quality carpets and oversized copper pots. I was happy wandering through the narrow alleyways of the old city just for the smell of camel hide and cumin.

That night, two black sedans pulled up at the Mediterranean, and the NBC entourage piled in, along with a *Time* magazine photographer I had befriended. Olivier Rebbot begged me to bring him along. Rebbot was talented, witty, and resourceful. "You're going to be a great journalist," he teased. His own brilliant career was cut short when he was raked with gunfire in a dusty street in El Salvador.

We tore through the shuttered capital following a wildly circuitous route to Qaddafi's barracks. It was a maneuver either to confuse us or to lose an unwelcome tail. The barracks were brightly lit and swarming with security men. We were directed to a wing that served as Qaddafi's study and sitting room with a floor-to-ceiling bank of television sets. I thought of Lyndon Johnson, who insisted on watching all three network news broadcasts at once. The difference was that in Libya the government-controlled channel devoted the news almost entirely to the movements and pronouncements of their leader. Thus Qaddafi was forever critiquing and admiring himself.

When he walked in, still wearing Levi's and a polo coat from his meeting with Idi Amin, he dashed over to show me his state-of-the-art video equipment, at a time when networks were just switching from film, and asked with boyish enthusiasm what I thought of his television image.

"How do I look?" He studied my face. Libyan television technique left much to be desired. Qaddafi looked like an extra in *Ben-Hur*.

"You look terrific," I assured the Colonel. He beamed at himself appreciatively.

The Libyan leader had more questions. He wanted to know whether the IRA, whom he liberally supplied with weapons, was close to victory. At the time, IRA bombs were exploding regularly in London streets (I still cross the road out of habit when I see garbage bags on the sidewalk), but it was a war of gruesome incidents, harassment, and skirmishes, without winners. Qaddafi was strangely naive. He assumed that Redgrave's fringe group, the Workers' Revolutionary Party, was the leading party of the British left. He was optimistic that Enrique Berlinguer and Georges Marchais, leaders of the Italian and French Eurocommunist movement, were poised to take over Europe. I began to have serious doubts about the talents of Libyan intelligence. No doubt they were telling the Colonel what he wanted to hear.

Before 3 A.M., awash in sweet tea, Qaddafi invited me to stay for another week. "I'll take you to the desert." Before I could discern whether he was inviting me to have an affair, he added, "And I would like you to meet my wife."

Mrs. Qaddafi was tall and formidable. She was a keen advocate of women's rights. There were no veils in Tripoli. One of the Colonel's entourage confided to me with mirth, "Everyone in Libya knows he is henpecked."

I made my excuses and left the country, sated with almond milk and, for the moment, heads of state. In the grand scheme of things, the interview was unimportant. One sound bite ran on the news. My triumph was a blip on the airwaves. But I was now backstage with the actors in world events, watching them at close range. I had wandered onto the set of a black comedy.

THREE

The Island Bureau

ZANZIBAR opened its doors across from the Masonic Temple on a side street off Covent Garden. It was a small but elegant club that attracted the London literati and café society. David Hockney often had a booth or Harold Pinter and Antonia Fraser. At the opening party Martin Amis and Christopher Hitchens were shoring up the bar. Mary Furness, later Countess Chewten, was holding court. My date, John Head, was visiting from New York, where he and his partner Lorne Michaels had dreamed up a comedy show for NBC called *Saturday Night Live*. John introduced me to a tall, exceptionally pale man who was wearing dark glasses at midnight. He had broken his regular "spectacles." I asked my future husband for a light.

Andrew was an investigative journalist who specialized in the arms trade and American politics. We had a great deal in common. He made programs for a British news documentary series called *World in Action*, which constantly ran the risk of being banned under the Official Secrets Act. Andrew was shooting a story on American weapons sales to Italy and Japan. Defense contractors were under intense congressional scrutiny in Washington for overseas bribes. After that story, Andrew would go on the campaign trail of the governor of Georgia, Jimmy Carter, who was then running for president.

Here was a fellow journalist, raised in Ireland, whose mother had walked across Africa, mapping the languages of the Congo Basin in the 1930s for the Royal Geographic Society. His father, Claud Cockburn, was a British journalist whose exploits at Oxford and in Berlin (his first wife was the real Sally Bowles of *Cabaret)* were legendary. He covered the Wall Street crash of 1929 and interviewed Al Capone for the *London Times,* fought in the Spanish Civil War as a communist, and founded *The Week* and *Private Eye.* Claud's cousin Evelyn Waugh had written what I regarded as the seminal work on journalism, *Scoop.*

I invited Andrew to stop by my boat, *Orpheus.*

"Just go to World's End," I said, "and head for the river."

I had no idea if he would ever appear.

Still wearing dark glasses, he arrived on deck one evening an hour before a dozen dinner guests. The little fishing boat with its Deco glass captain's cabin overlooking the Thames was rocking on the swells of a turning tide. By nine the river was calm and the saloon was packed with people. Just as dinner was served, Andrew lay down on the banquette and fell asleep. He snored. The guests exchanged looks. It was impossible in these cramped quarters to avoid the body in their midst. It was a scene out of Flann O'Brien. When the last guest left, Andrew woke up refreshed. He insisted that we go dancing. We stayed up and watched the sunrise over the Chelsea Bridge. He asked casually whether I would like to come to County Cork for Christmas.

The twenty-foot ceiling in the hall of Andrew's family house in Ireland was painted a deep coral pink, a color found in Chinese silk embroidery and Etruscan terra cotta. The damp seeping in through the walls created the effect of frescoes after centuries in volcanic ash. There was a black ebony chair from Zanzibar inlaid with mother-of-pearl and a black marble pillar for rock roses and meadow grasses. The hundred-foot stretch of hall served as Andrew's hurley field when he was a small boy.

I fell in love with Brook Lodge at first sight. The scale of the Georgian house in East Cork was much like the house where I grew up. But Brook Lodge was centuries older. One wing containing my bedroom had been inhabited for over five hundred years. Undressing to bathe in that wing was like ice fishing. The unfortunate John Huston managed to lock himself in that same bathroom for an entire day while he was working on the screenplay adaptation of Andrew's father's novel *Beat the Devil*.

I checked the weather listings in the *Herald Tribune* and found the temperature in the hall was two degrees colder than Moscow's Red Square. The doors of each room were slammed shut to trap the warmth from roaring fires.

At Brook Lodge, there were indoor and outdoor cats who stole into the kitchen to curl up next to the Aga. Horses, dogs, and chickens filled the stable yard and a donkey grazed contentedly in the front field. A huge black cat called Malkin plagued the dining room, nudging the sturdy silver covers over the cold ham and spiced beef to the table's edge until everything crashed to the floor. Andrew's mother, Patricia, claimed an old gray ratter had passed on the skill to Malkin. She described interrupting a seminar one day as Malkin watched with scholarly attention when the elder cat capsized the cold lunch.

The stone walls on the edge of the field had been repaired by a Texan houseguest, Bill Broyles, Andrew's best friend from Oxford. Bill was absorbed in resetting the stones, laboring in muddy hip boots and tweed cap, when a tour bus full of Americans came to a halt outside the front gates. The passengers piled out and trained their cameras on the typical Irish farmer. The scene was being watched with interest by an intelligent white donkey called Jackie, who posed obligingly with Broyles.

Everyone who arrived in Ireland seemed to beat a path to Brook Lodge. A jumbo jet load of New York policemen landed at Shannon and a delegation appeared at the door. A mounted policeman marched in with his guitar and a repertoire of songs about lonely nights in Central Park. His girlfriend was from Queens. When I asked what her job on the force was, the girlfriend shrugged. "I used to be on bomb squad, but I switched to hostages. Some Croat nationalists planted a bomb at Kennedy and it blew up in my face." On closer inspection, I could see the massive repair work that had been done. We all sang carols and drank poteen, 90-proof Irish moonshine.

We spent Christmas Eve down the road at Myrtle Grove, where Andrew's mother grew up. The house, behind massive walls in the medieval town of Youghal, had changed little since Sir Walter Raleigh lived there. I stood in the grove of ancient yews where Raleigh smoked the first pipe of tobacco brought from the New World. Upstairs in the drawing room, the alcove of leaded glass was where Edmund Spenser wrote the first lines of *The Faerie Queene*. Spenser worked on the book for a month in Myrtle Grove and finally decamped to finish it elsewhere. Andrew's father, wrapping his impossibly long fingers around his cane, assured me that all writers suffered the same difficulty with finishing books in the Blackwater Valley. Claud called it Blackwater fever, the desire of the inhabitants to do nothing but fish, ride, and drink.

I wandered through the house full of loot shipped back from the Far East at the end of the nineteenth century, when Andrew's great-grandfather Sir Henry Blake was governor of Hong Kong. Blake opened up the New Territories for the Crown colony. His wife, Edith, raised the British flag that came down ninety-nine years later in 1997, when the lease was up and Hong Kong reverted to Chinese rule. The flag raised by Lady Blake was at Myrtle Grove.

Back in London, Andrew proposed. We were married in the spring of 1977 in a San Francisco wedding that lasted for seven days. Planeloads of guests arrived from Ireland and New York. There were lunches, dinners, cocktail parties, the endless changing of dresses. Patricia compared it with St. Petersburg before the revolution.

My house dated from the Roaring Twenties, when San Franciscans imported painted beamed ceilings, wood-paneled libraries, and black and white marble floors from Florence. The kitchen stove was a 1927 Wedgewood. We played show tunes on the player piano and raided the wine cellar in the vault behind the bar, with its carved Bavarian gargoyles. Californians like my father regarded wine as a kind of religion. He bought the rights from small vineyards to an allotment of cases each year. "The best California wines," he said with satisfaction, "don't travel." My sister had her own label. She threw grape-stomping parties where everyone's feet were stained purple.

The massive walk-in vault was also a humble shrine to the Cuban Missile Crisis, when it doubled as a bomb shelter. It was still stocked with Campbell's soup and Hershey bars.

On the walls were photographs of my mother and father shooting ptarmigan on Alaskan glaciers and catching sailfish in Mexico. Their love of adventure was infectious. We had sailed together through the Grenadines, hunted in the San Juan Islands in the Pacific Northwest for old Civil War block houses, ridden rickshaws in Macao to the Red Chinese border. We had explored Greek islands and watched the Shinto temple deer bow low in Kyoto. They regarded my interest in the world as simply an extension of my childhood. My choice of profession was, however, dubious. The only journalist regarded as respectable in my house was Herb Caen, the columnist for the *San Francisco Chronicle*, as much a part of the city as Coit Tower or Alcatraz.

Among the guests was a flaxen-haired Minnesota native, Sarah Pillsbury, who had roomed with me at Yale and trekked to my village in Kenya. Now she was a Hollywood producer. At the rehearsal dinner, Sarah toasted the missing eighty-eight goats, my forfeited African bride price. Andrew's brother Alexander raised his glass to one relative, Admiral George Cockburn, who torched the White House in the War of 1812, after polishing off the cabinet's dinner and stealing First Lady Dolley Madison's cushion.

The morning of the wedding, I had a crushing hangover. The aisle was a carpet of lawn, framed by flowering magnolias. The receiving line was in the rose garden, where plane trees stood as sentries around the boxwood beds. My grandmother, who had once willed her piano teacher to fall through a crack in the earth only to find her wish fulfilled in the 1906 earthquake, stood by my side. Mabel Agnew was fourteen years old when she watched San Francisco burn.

My grandmother was a true California pioneer and my earliest inspiration. Her own grandparents had moved West from Virginia in 1865, impoverished and defeated by the Civil War. The Tomblins had been farming there for over a hundred years before the Revolution. But my grandmother herself was molded in the California frontier. Her family cleared land in the foothills of the Sierras along the American River. They planted the hills with fruit trees, and as children we played in the gold mine.

My great-grandfather was a mining engineer who ran the Borax mines in Death Valley as well as mines in the Sierra mother lode.

My grandmother told stories of riding her giant tortoise across the desert and shooting rattlesnakes. Her father brought his grand piano tied down in a wagon to the mining camps. The rough-hewn miners were assembled to attend concerts. In towns like Candelaria that are now ghost towns, they listened to Mozart and Chopin.

Andrew and I found maps of the old wagon train routes of the Nevada wilderness, followed them until the roads disintegrated into boulders and crevasses, and camped in the Ruby Mountains outside Elko, where the meadows still supported Basque shepherds.

We exchanged vows in a lattice arbor under giant redwoods. Judge Jerry Dunn, who performed the ceremony, was so moved by the occasion that he forgot to have us sign the license. So, as four hundred guests bade us farewell, we were not legally married.

Three days later, it hit me that we were, in fact, living in sin.

"Did you sign anything?" I asked Andrew.

"No. Did you?" We spent the day on the phone. We had forty-eight hours to do the paperwork or the marriage was invalid. We flew back to London in the midst of Queen Elizabeth's Silver Jubilee, celebrating the monarchy at a Linden Gardens party where two hundred guests, for some inexplicable reason, danced the hokey-pokey.

Marriage gave me a partner in crime, someone who understood the shorthand and inside workings of journalism. We both traveled. We spent roughly 70 percent of our first year of marriage apart on the road. We enthused about each other's stories. Our phone bills were equal to the gross national product of a small country.

Less than a year after our wedding, I was asked to join *60 Minutes*, the CBS News broadcast then in its prime and hosted by Mike Wallace, Dan Rather, and Morley Safer.

In the spring of 1978, the NBC News bureau was undergoing shock treatment. Irv Margolis had been notified he would be recalled to New York. The staff was informed they would be moved to dreary offices in the shadow of the London telephone tower. These were cost-cutting measures. The London bureau, which had discretion over international stories, what to pursue, what to "offer" to New York, was being downgraded. Henceforth, decisions would be made by the New York executives at Rockefeller Center. Morale plummeted. Irv quit. His replacement offered me a raise.

The inducement to stay was tempered by what I regarded as poor judgment on New York's part, interfering with a smooth operation. I was wary. I thought it signaled a decline. By sheer good luck I heard that *60 Minutes* had an open slot.

Each *60 Minutes* correspondent had his European team for overseas stories. Morley Safer's producer, John Tiffin, was an impeccably dressed Englishman with a taste for classic cars, croquet, and sheepdog trials. He wore a distracted air behind slim glasses that slid down the bridge of his nose. Tiffin was hunting for an associate producer. Over a bottle of Sancerre at Chez Victor in London's Soho, I accepted the job. It entailed digging up stories, flying to Africa, Asia, or Europe, spending weeks on the road, setting up interviews, finding scenes we needed, and field-producing the minor shoots on my own. This was a quantum leap from Irv's bureau.

By 1978, *60 Minutes* had become a national addiction. The program had a voracious appetite for stories. There were ample budgets and huge audiences. Each piece ran for roughly ten to fifteen minutes. Each was a very satisfying polished film. I would be working under the most talented people in broadcasting. I packed up my St. James's Street office overnight and migrated to a back corner of the CBS News bureau on Brompton Road, overlooking the Harrods pet shop.

The structure of *60 Minutes* was fiercely territorial. The broadcast's creator, Don Hewitt, a television genius who cut his teeth in the CBS studios when a piece of cardboard and a lightbulb could make a set, encouraged competition. A story idea had to be typed up and fired off to New York as a "blue sheet." After approval from Hewitt, the Wallace, Rather, or Safer unit that proposed the story owned it, though there was a danger of raids by rival *60 Minutes* producers until the story was shot. This kept everyone alert.

Soon after I signed on, Hewitt appeared in London for a flying visit. He asked me to lunch, along with Safer and Tiffin. Hewitt had a boyish enthusiasm that brought to mind Mickey Rooney. He grabbed the floor. "Okay, I want to try something out on you," the vaudeville trouper primed his audience. "I've got an idea for a new *60 Minutes* correspondent." He paused for effect. "A Chinese Canadian woman. What do you think?"

Tiffin made approving noises. But then, Hewitt could have sold the table on a Chinese Canadian husky. Tiffin worshiped Hewitt because the *60 Minutes* creator had *made* television news; he was on the set behind Edward R. Murrow and had invented words like "anchor." Hewitt admired Tiffin because the former cameraman had a remarkable eye for a shot and assembled films with great style and timing. He was the Jacques Tati of news documentaries.

Morley Safer, the weather-beaten Canadian, who had educated himself and made his mark with a story that featured an American soldier casually flicking his Zippo lighter to ignite a village in Vietnam, was Tiffin's best friend. Morley could write, cook, paint, and stay up until dawn drinking Courvoisier and smoking Rothmans. They shared cigarettes and the same dry sense of humor. Morley chafed to come out on a story to flee "the dairy" in New York, the windowless maze of offices at CBS News headquarters on West 57th Street. He was bullish on the Chinese Canadian, I suspect for nationalistic reasons, to add to the ranks of "the Canadian mafia" in New York.

John Tiffin in his pin-striped suits and spectacles, mulling over a camera angle, pondering an edit, was meticulous to a fault. He taught me how to use a slow pan, how to zoom, when to use quick cuts, when to let a scene "play." I learned the value of "straight cuts," not depending on flashy dissolves and "wipes" to move the film along. He drilled me on the importance of sound. Our soundman approached the job with such dedication that he kept an archive of several dozen variations of waves breaking on a shore. Inside *60 Minutes*, we became known as the Island Bureau, because of our affection for the tropics.

The first story I suggested was a profile of Sam Cummings, an American arms dealer who specialized in supplying both sides in small wars. The little conflicts raging around the globe had captured my imagination, for in the cold war, backwaters of every continent were crawling with armies funded by one of the superpowers. The two sides would clash in some godforsaken place and Sam Cummings, a cherubic fifty-year-old teetotaler, was there with crates of Kalashnikovs. Sam had boundless charm, warehouses in Manchester, factories in Virginia, a chalet in Switzerland, and a suite in Monaco. He wore dark suits and traveled economy-class. War was his business and guns did not make decisions. Sam washed his hands of responsibility. With his CIA background and long history of negotiating with generals and guerrillas, Sam was determined to teach me how the real world worked. "Madame Leslie," he would say patiently, "it's not a question of morality."

I took the train to Manchester for my indoctrination into Sam's world of small arms for small wars. Manchester was a grim city of gray housing estates and Victorian row houses that ended abruptly where they met the wrecking ball. The birthplace of the Industrial Revolution, where the great textile fortunes of the nineteenth century were made, had grown old and feeble with the empire. Sam chose Manchester to house some six stories of weapons, 300,000 of them, the largest private arsenal in Europe.

We toured the rifle range and stepped over the machine-gun mounts, making our way to lunch at the pub. The arms dealer had his English manager, Mr. Spense, in tow. Dressed in black, the two of them looked ready for a funeral. "Madame Leslie," Sam said with the quiet intensity of a good southern preacher, "the arms business is founded on human folly. That is why its depths will never be plumbed and why it will go on forever. All weapons," Sam warmed to his sermon, "are defensive, and all spare parts are nonlethal." Sam had a stockpile of aphorisms to go with his guns.

Sam's office was the first place I saw an RPG-7, a rocket-propelled grenade. This was a handsome weapon with a long barrel capped with an onion dome like a Russian Orthodox church. Fired from the shoulder with a satisfying rush, the RPG could explode a jeep or blow a hole in an embassy. Sam's RPG came from a cache with Arabic markings captured in Northern Ireland. It was a gift from Muammar Qaddafi to the IRA. In the Manchester Interarms warehouse I saw British Enfields used by the United States in Vietnam when that war was still a covert operation. There were old Garand rifles, Springfield rifles, and Mausers used by General Chiang Kai-shek in 1949. There were M-16s from Chile and Brownings from the Dominican Republic. I got a crash course in arms laundering, using arms made by your enemy, purchased in a neutral country for use in a third country's war. Who would know you were the sponsor? Sam saw every war as an opportunity. The world's leading private arms dealer was itching to get his hands on the arsenal abandoned by the U.S. in Vietnam, $5 billion worth of weapons, enough to fuel ten small wars. There were, he said, 800,000 M-16s and 600 M-48 tanks. He could salvage 100 artillery pieces and 73 planes.

At the pub we agreed to set up a date at Sam's Swiss chalet for the interview with Morley. On the balcony of the picture-perfect arms dealer's hideaway, with the Alps in the camera frame, Sam talked about his trade. He got his start in Latin America supplying the Guatemalan government of Castillo Armas that staged the 1954 coup. He supplied Trujillo in the Dominican Republic with machine guns and Vampire jet fighters. In Cuba, he was reputed to have supplied Castro before the revolution and anti-Castro forces for the Bay of Pigs.

Sam felt no attachment to causes or remorse for the consequences of sales. I was fascinated by his fatalism. Men waged war. War was good business. His motto was *Esse quam videri*—to be rather than to seem. "World peace," Sam liked to say, "would give me the chance to build up my inventory."

Tiffin let me roam alone with a camera team from the Cummings empire headquarters in Monte Carlo to Sam's arms factories in Virginia. I was now working with top cameramen like Jan Morgan in London and Robert Peterson in Washington. The piece was a success.

My next port of call was Singapore. It was September 1978 and I was pregnant. My first memory of impending motherhood was sitting with Prime Minister Lee Kuan Yew wondering if my stomach showed. I was two months along, feeling queasy after a party for the Chinese monkey god the night before. (In a steaming open air temple reeking with incense and melting candles, a monkey priest fell into a trance and slashed his tongue with a sword.) Lee was at his desk at Istana, the magnificent old governor's mansion from which he ran his tiny but prosperous empire like the godfather. "I'll take care of him," the small fastidious boss scowled at the phone receiver. "What do we do about the other one? I'll shake him up."

Lee Kuan Yew wanted to talk about the Singapore miracle of productivity. Singaporean workers could build computer circuits and service American corporations like no one else in Asia. They were housed right next to the factories. Not an inch of space was wasted. Not a moment was misspent. We adjourned to Lee's private golf course. The visionary leader played nine holes in unbearable heat. The full-dress band on his lawn for the evening reception, wilting in the humidity, was hopelessly out of tune.

Outside the gates of Lee's palatial compound, things were under strict control. Space was tight. I went out with government inspectors who patrolled the crowded housing blocks, unfit for lab rats, to police birth control. "Are you taking your pills?" inspectors asked each woman with Orwellian efficiency. I saw drug addicts slung into airless, common cells in Changi prison for cold turkey. Lee believed in order. Dropping a cigarette butt was against the law. Even the sampans in the Singapore River were scrubbed. The Cricket Club was dull. The sterile spirit of the place was expressed by the Overseas Bank of China building, a giant calculator hogging the skyline. This was the model for Asia. The senior cadres of Chinese party men, the Burmese generals from SLORC, would one day come and drool.

At the Palm Court of Raffles Hotel, that had once housed Rudyard Kipling and Somerset Maugham, I sat in a deep depression studying the silent progress of a gecko up the wall. A waiter scurried over to say that I had a call from the Comoro Islands. It was Bob Denard on the line, a legendary French mercenary who had just seized control of the spice islands in the Indian Ocean. He would be happy to do an interview, but only in French. The network demanded English. I explained to Bob that the *60 Minutes* audience did not speak French. The international outlaw who had just overthrown a government was understanding. He went back to counting what was left of his mortars, rockets, 7.62 AK ammo, and his men. I ordered a Singapore Sling.

If a trip to Moroni to see Denard was off the itinerary, there was another story in the region that suited Morley perfectly. A young German couple on the "hippie trail" had ventured from India to a necklace of islands off Sri Lanka called the Maldives. In a guesthouse in Male, the dozy capital, they injested quantities of psychedelic drugs, and after a quarrel, the German stabbed his girlfriend. He locked himself in with the body for seven days. The murder was ruled a crime of passion by the Maldivian court, who sentenced the distraught killer to banishment in paradise. Joachim Bloem was transported to an island called Furudu.

The verandah of Raffles Hotel was a fitting place to plan the voyage to the condemned man's island. Joseph Conrad sat in the same spot, gazing at the rubber brokers along the quays and the Malays in the kampongs who inspired the story of Lord Jim. I contacted the German ambassador in Colombo, Sri Lanka. He seemed amenable to our coming, and noted that the only tool the convict had been allowed to take along was a fishhook.

At 2 A.M. on October 7, a three-masted schooner called the *Dhandehelu* set sail from Male to Furudu in the Baa atoll. I had bargained the merchant owner down to a ridiculously good price to charter the antique cargo vessel, and Morley Safer, John Tiffin, and crew were sleeping soundly belowdecks. Eight Maldivian deck-hands, all tiny, sat chewing bark and leaves in their berth under the bowsprit.

The water, in daylight the color of a Ceylon aquamarine, was alive with bonito tuna, mackerel, and flying fish. Sea turtles were lumbering across our path and the coral ranged from white to deep raspberry to black. Fishing boats carved from coconut bark floated silently without light under square rigged sails. There were cones and cowries of every size and color, the same cowries dumped on the garden paths at Myrtle Grove in Ireland when the Maldivians sent tea chests full to the British governor in Ceylon, Andrew's great-grandfather, as tribute.

In the hot night my porthole refused to open. I drowned a cock-roach in the sink and emerged on deck, dimly lit from the saloon. Old charts and compasses cluttered the wheelhouse. I navigated the stacks of coiled rope and saw bodies sprawled everywhere, refugees from the insufferable heat below. That night Morley managed to pry open his porthole only to be drenched with a gallon of sea-water.

There were vague outlines of islands on the horizon. We did not know precisely where we were going. From the nautical charts, Furudu could have been one of three islands. The next day, as we dodged the reefs in the relentless equatorial sun, we arbitrarily chose the middle one, a confection of white sand, pink coral, palm fronds, and sapphire sea. With the camera rolling, Morley would hop off first and whatever happened would be recorded on film. We had no idea whether Bloem, assuming we found him, spoke a word of English. We knew that for the first six months of banishment, the islanders had rejected him utterly, refusing to speak to him. They were repulsed by him. Violent crime was an anathema here. Locals racked their brains for details of the last case, either during World War I or three centuries ago, depending on the informant.

Morley climbed into the skiff with the camera trained on him, and as we approached the shore of "murderer's island," we saw an astonishing sight. Dark-skinned natives, half-naked, came pouring onto the beach. In their midst was a white blond head. Bloem, bare-chested and burned brown, with a sarong wrapped at his waist, approached Morley and in perfect English welcomed him to Furudu.

Bloem had lived on the tiny island, sustained by fish and coconuts, for a year. He had strangely bleached blue eyes and two stab wounds in his brown stomach from attempting suicide after the murder. He seemed gentle and resigned. The islanders now considered him one of their own. He had married a twelve-year-old child bride and learned their language. He led us to his hut of coconut leaves. The German had taught the islanders how to play checkers and chess, with rooks and pawns carved from bark. They taught him how to build a sailing dinghy called a *doni* and how to fish their waters with a drop line.

Bloem showed us a freakish bird with bat wings and a monkey's face called a flying dog. Inside his hut, he offered us coconut japatis, flat pancakes, and played a tape of *Down and Out in New York City*. The child bride flipped through a year-old *Zeit* magazine full of pictures of blondes in electric kitchens. Breadfruit was handed around, filling the hut with its heavy perfume.

The prisoner swore to us that he would never go back to Germany to stand trial. He was happy with Maldivian justice. He was reconciled to being an islander in this Crusoesque existence and would stay for life.

As we boarded the skiff and headed back through the reef to the *Dhandehelu*, Bloem suddenly untied his *doni* from the trunk of a coconut tree. He unfurled the sails and tacked toward us with deliberate speed. His child bride was on board. As we were waiting to climb the schooner's rope ladder, in the flat noon sun, the *doni* cut across our bow. The convict was hard to see with the light glinting off his port side. He shouted, "Is there a possibility of coming aboard?" There was silence, then murmuring in our skiff, confusion as to what he had said. Would he come about? Try to board? Bloem did not return. He and the child bride glided back to the shore of paradise and disappeared through the palms, without an answer.

The silent deckhands hoisted sail and the *Dhandehelu* ran with the wind. We were escorted by dolphins. The outlines of Furudu evaporated in the heat.

I waited to disclose the news that I was pregnant until I had to shed my cotton skirts for a bikini and was convinced that my figure now resembled an armored personnel carrier. Someone would notice. In fact, at the end of month three, there was nothing to see. "So, can you tell?" I asked the mystified Safer and Tiffin as we prepared to dive down to admire some giant mushroom coral. They reacted to my news with equanimity. Both expected me to quit.

Four months later I was booking a ticket to Monrovia, the Liberian capital nestled on a coast christened last century as the White Man's Grave. The story was the precarious rule of the Americo-Liberian elite. Morley and John, both with impeccable manners, said nothing about my condition. Another *60 Minutes* producer, Bill McClure, went wild. "How," he bellowed at the reticent Tiffin puffing a Rothman, "can you allow a woman seven months pregnant to go to Africa?" Grisly hospitals, contagious diseases, bad roads, were we out of our minds? Tiffin was polite but firm. The decision was mine. I saw no reason to cancel my reservations. My stomach showed, but being six feet tall and in excellent shape, I could carry the weight without complaint. I felt physically fit. My views were summed up by Jessica Mitford in *The American Way of Birth*. It was a perversion to regard pregnancy as a sickness.

As an Africa hand, I knew that millions of mothers managed to give birth on the continent. I also knew how to watch out for conditions that posed a danger, malarial mosquitoes and typhoid-rich dirty water. Driving into jungle ruts and stony riverbeds, I shifted my weight as though I were slalom racing.

The Liberians considered my condition very becoming. President William Tolbert, not long before he was executed in the coup that began Liberia's decade-long slide into civil war and unspeakable horror, reached into the drawer of his ornate desk and presented me with the old republic's distinguished medal of honor.

Tolbert's doomed country was born in the "back to Africa" movement that swept the United States in the nineteenth century. An independent republic was declared in 1847, and American colonists settled in Liberia determined to build an enlightened society unencumbered by the glass ceiling of race. They were educated, relatively affluent pilgrims with Jeffersonian ideas of government.

When they landed on the disease-ridden coast, hundreds of miles in most cases from where their own families had been kidnapped and transported, they migrated up magnificent rivers, the San Pedro, the Sewa, and the St. Paul, much like the Mississippi, to escape malaria. The early settlers cleared the riverbanks, building graceful plantation houses, churches, and red schoolhouses. They named one county Maryland.

By the time I arrived in 1979, younger generations had abandoned these early settlements, planted with willows and magnolias, draped in Spanish moss. Emma Knuckles, the oldest inhabitant, invited me for iced tea on her screened porch. She proudly opened the family albums, pointing to president after president of Liberia, Roberts, Barclay, Cooper, Tubman, all relatives.

Emma vividly recounted to me her American father clearing the land in the 1880s, with his "indigenous" laborers. They braved crocodiles, puff adders, *Pandinus imperator*, gigantic scorpions more than six inches long, that infested the forests. Surrounded by colobus monkeys, potto lemurs, and *Hysignathus monstrosus*, fruit bats with monstrous heads, the founding fathers toiled to re-create a genteel world that looked eerily like a replica of the antebellum South.

By the time Emma was thirty, she explained to me, caressing the old photographs, there were about fifteen thousand settlers and 2 million tribespeople, Vai, Gbandi, Gora, Kru, Kpwesi, Buzi, and Mandingo, to name a few. The Americans married each other. Emma's grandchildren's generation summered on Martha's Vineyard and were educated at Harvard and Yale. Their families held every powerful position as senators, judges, diplomats. When Firestone rubber set up its vast plantation, the contract was signed with the American upper crust. The rubber tappers, quartered in the neat cabins beneath the massive trees stuck with spigots, were drawn from the tribes.

I attended a tea dance just outside Monrovia, in a well-appointed villa on the beach. All the best families were there. There were quantities of linen and lace, wide-brimmed hats, and cucumber sandwiches. The president arrived from his plantation in the interior. In a country with few passable roads, he had built a broad highway to his front gate. I had been to his commodious country seat for lunch. The main attraction of the estate was the president's private zoo, where he nurtured his prized pygmy hippos. The president and the other distinguished guests seemed completely unaware, as they sipped champagne, that the country was coming apart. A year later, the cream of the guest list would be dragged onto that same beach, tied up, blindfolded, and shot.

The "indigenous people," as the rulers insisted on calling the tribespeople, wanted schools, roads, a Senate seat. The upper 1 percent was growing insular, decadent. As they closed ranks, hid behind the smoke glass of an air-conditioned Mercedes, dark forces seeped into the rarefied air. The best families were obsessed with black magic.

A scandal broke, a gruesome murder. A famous Liberian singer was invited to a polite barbecue with scions of Americo-Liberian families. The singer was stabbed, quartered, and grilled. The assembled guests ate the heart first, to absorb the singer's power and charisma. When asked what they hoped to gain by this act of cannibalism, they replied, "Ambassadorships."

I realized the extent of the fixation with *juju*, or black magic, when I was asked to lunch with the president's son, Abie Tolbert, who mounted his white pony and rode around the garden for me to admire. Tucking into fish soup with Abie, we turned to the subject of black magic. He said everyone was dabbling in it. Spells were becoming as essential to government as astrology later became to the Reagan White House. Spells were spreading fear, eating away at the civilized veneer of the rulers. The barbecued celebrity was a case in point.

Sitting alone one day with the president in his cavernous office, I got the strong impression he believed himself invincible. What spell had convinced him a bullet would never graze his flesh? It was an ordinary army sergeant with the innocuous name of Doe, who months later shot President Tolbert and took possession of his comfortable chair. The country, propped up with recycled dollar notes flown in by Brinks and Reagan administration loans to secure our secret cold war listening post, began to die. Society was ripped to shreds. With the departure of the last American ambassador, James Bishop (whose next post was Mogadishu), the lights were turned out in Liberia. In January 1995, a dispatch in the *New York Times* revealed the shocking news that at least one faction in the civil war that bled the country to death was practicing cannibalism.

Who remembers how to make cucumber sandwiches? What happened to Emma Knuckles' priceless family albums? Nowadays it is unwise to admit you are related to a president.

Two months after flying back from Liberia, I gave birth in West London Hospital. I danced until well after midnight the evening before with Christopher Hitchens. My doctor was a famous obstetrician who was "in the country," unavailable for a Friday night birth. His replacement was a reserve Royal Navy officer. He appeared late, after a banquet, in full-dress naval uniform complete with epaulets. Fortunately, I was attended by an Irish midwife. After a lot of "ho ho huff huff" to ride out the contractions, the agony of drug-free labor subsided into euphoria and champagne. Streams of visitors appeared with more bottles and I was politely asked to discharge myself early. Chloe, drinking mothers' milk laced with Moët, as recommended by the English doctors, seemed content.

Three days later, I deposited Chloe, swaddled in hand-knitted blankets and Italian booties, in a carry cot in the corner of my office. I was anxious to show her off and thought it perfectly natural that she should be with me. I began making calls on my next story, a piece on the highly secretive brass-plate law firms of Liechtenstein. After three weeks of breast-feeding, I left Chloe in London with Andrew and Willis, a graduate of the Norland school for nannies. I flew to Vaduz, capital of this lucrative kingdom that sheltered a wealth of corporate enterprises from the scrutiny of the FBI, MI5,

Interpol. Legal work in Liechtenstein was a family business. Fathers passed their confidences to sons. They lived contentedly in a capital that boasted of one stoplight and the affable prince of Liechtenstein's medieval castle that housed one of the great art collections of Europe and an elegant princess with hereditary Transylvanian fangs. Unbeknownst to my colleagues and the lawyers who offered me their services, my blouses were soaked through with mothers' milk.

There was a myth pervasive in the seventies that women could never be as "reliable" as their professional male colleagues because of childbirth. How could you depend on them? The myth kept women in the barrios, the research pools, the secretarial jobs, and was never far from the surface in contract negotiations. I was determined to break the mold. If I did not, the options were stark: quit, go without children, forget about promotion. There were many childless women "married to the network." This seemed perverse. Male colleagues doted on their children. So would I. This was not my last pregnancy.

Accomplishing this required stamina, and a husband who shared responsibilities. Andrew warmed bottles, changed diapers, woke up at all hours. He believed that the words "father" and "mother" had equal weight. He also regarded my work as important journalism.

Tiffin allowed me to move my office to Cape Cod for two months that summer to a cottage we had rented at Agawam Point. There were bell buoys offshore, horseshoe crabs and devilfish. Chloe could don her red gingham sun bonnet on the beach and I could research my next story.

I was dispatched in September to find an island, a remote speck in the Pacific, which the U.S. Army had just declared off-limits to humans for 24,000 years. The forbidden island was called Runit. Its unfortunate position as part of the Enewetak atoll in the U.S. trust territory of Micronesia meant that Runit had been used throughout the 1950s as a testing ground for atomic and hydrogen bombs. The signature mushroom cloud in a blood-red sky had sprouted above Runit routinely for a decade. The island was ankle-deep in deadly plutonium.

The U.S. Army launched a $100-million "cleanup" of the irradiated atoll, in response to mounting lawsuits from natives of the islands, whose forced removal at the time of the tests left them wards of the Interior Department in Washington. The people of Enewetak, Enjebe, Bikini, and Ujalang had spent years in listless exile, living in flimsy "temporary housing," receiving medical benefits for thyroid cancer, a product of the blasts. They were showered with welfare, Great Society programs dating from the Johnson administration, warehouses full of spoiled school lunch milk, which the island children would not drink. The regular shipments of USDA canned beef were so foul, I watched displaced Bikini islanders feed it to their pigs. There was a curious assortment of Wall Street lawyers who washed up on the islands to represent them. The Bikini islanders' spokesman was a hairdresser.

En route to the army cleanup, the Island Bureau assembled on Kwajalein, a closed military atoll that might have been invented by Arthur C. Clarke. Every futuristic device the Pentagon could afford was shipped to the edge of Kwajalein lagoon, where MIRVed missiles (MIRV was Pentagonese for multiple independent reentry vehicle) designed to knock out Soviet missile silos in a nuclear war, were tested for accuracy. Launched from Vandenberg Air Force Base in California, the multiple warheads soared across the Pacific and landed in the turquoise waters inside the reef. It occurred to me, watching this exercise, that when the president of the United States was handed the "football," the briefcase with the top secret codes to launch an attack, all the missiles, out of habit, would head for Kwajalein.

Phased-array radars (which fried the casual observer who stood in the wrong spot), whitewashed tracking domes, and electronics-stuffed pyramids sparkled in neo-Pharaonic splendor in the Pacific sun. They logged, monitored, and assessed the impact at "ground zero" and watched the Soviet subs watching them just offshore. The island was a military Disneyland, with tidy streets for bicycles only, the "Kwaj" Lodge for guests, the nightclub serving exotic tropical fruit drinks with plastic mahimahi spears for pineapple chunks. The residents had Macy's West for Nestlé's Quik, Ban Roll-On, and Hershey bars shipped from the "mainland."

This missileers' dream sat on the site of one of the bloodiest battles of World War II. I was relieved to find that the base commander, unlike the blow-dried Huntsville contractors in starched white shorts who jogged past his window, had stormed the beach. Most of his unit was decimated. He showed me photographs he took as they landed, climbing over jagged barbed wire, huge twisted sheets of rusty metal, bloated bodies. He and his fellow soldiers had defeated the Japanese here at horrible cost. The Japanese fleet lay at the bottom of the Pacific, perfectly preserved, in the Truk lagoon. I had floated over the battleship funnels, like underwater skyscrapers. In the depths, first-aid kits and skulls were still in place. In the jungles of Yap, where betel-nut-chewing islanders still traded with two-foot-high stone money, I found a perfectly preserved Japanese Zero fighter plane entombed under a canopy of creepers. On Kwajalein, every sign of the devastation had been wiped clean. They were busy thinking about the next war, played out again and again, as the alert sounded and the missiles crashed down.

On Kwajalein there was no crime, no slums, no disease. It was a plum posting. All of those unsightly realities were parked offshore, on the island of Ebeye. This was the service island for the base, the native quarters. Sewage ran in the streets. The hospital was famous for its amputations. The dour priest was a double for Spencer Tracy. On the day USDA food shipments arrived, young girls sat astride the crates of fruit cocktail sipping Pepsi.

The old chief of Ebeye was paid by the Department of Defense. He was allowed to shop at Macy's West, dressed in an ill-fitting American general's uniform, complete with stars. He was tolerated as local color, though the Macy's staff complained that he shoplifted snacks and abused customers. No one on Kwajalein seemed bothered by the festering sore next door. Few residents had occasion to ride the ferry to Ebeye.

We boarded a C-130 Military Airlift Command flight to meet the nuclear cleanup team, housed in a trailer encampment on Enewetak. Helicopters transported troops to the surrounding islands in the atoll where they donned surgical masks and scraped the sand with bulldozers. Their mission was to haul away the plutonium, so toxic that a single particle lodged in their lungs was courting death.

The heat was punishing, 120 to 130 degrees at midday. The soldiers were pouring with sweat. When their superior officers were distracted, they stripped to the waist and yanked down their masks. The plutonium dust was stirred up in clouds by the earth movers. Once the plutonium was collected in piles, it was removed to Runit, where the army was building a colossal dome, worthy of Cheops, to house it.

The Runit beach was covered with painted cones, spotted cowries, conch. The old residents of Enjebe next door used to come ashore in canoes carved out of breadfruit trees. The beach was now "hot" with radioactivity. Runit would be left carpeted in hot dust, the great dome only sealing in the poisonous nuclear waste from other islands. We walked up the beach, so idyllic, into the decontamination hut. We were fitted with yellow moon boots, each of us issued with a clean surgical mask. Approaching the dome was like standing at the foot of a Mayan temple, a pyramid from Giza, some ancient relic of a lost civilization, an eighth wonder.

Fifty generations from now, the concrete slabs weighing tons will be analyzed by archaeologists. They will puzzle over what sort of culture worshiped here. The signpost announcing that the island is quarantined for 24,000 years is hand-painted, made of wood. How many typhoons can it stand? Who, passing this way in a breadfruit boat, can read English?

The army was merely guessing that the dome might last as long as the plutonium. When I asked to meet the architect of this monstrous temple to the cold war, to get some hard facts on the materials and design, I was informed by the army commanders in Hawaii that he was dead. "Gee," they said with feeling, "we're sorry." Outside estimates predicted it could last a few thousand years at the most.

We were scanned for radiation before leaving the site (if we were irradiated, the information would be classified) and proceeded to the next island in the poisoned chain to admire some of the relics of testing. On Enjebe there was a black scar of a building custom-built to be blasted apart by the "Mike shot," the first hydrogen bomb, the culmination of Project Panda. The ruin was known affectionately as the Enjebe Hilton. The only life that flourished on the abandoned island was rats and cockroaches. There were rats everywhere. It was unsettling to know that in the postnuclear world, the 9 million rats in New York City would reign supreme. The tall coconut palms bore fruit that was laced with radioactive strontium and cesium, a problem the military had not been "tasked" to fix.

We flew by chopper to inspect what had been a neighboring island, evacuated in 1952. When the ten-megaton H-bomb exploded on November 1 that year, two months after I was born, the island of Elugelab was vaporized. The explosion, said one Los Alamos bomb designer, was "so huge, so brutal—as if things had gone too far." The blast left a lapis-colored pool two hundred feet deep and a mile-wide gash in the reef that looked as though it had been cut with giant wire clippers.

Back at the Enewetak trailer park, the navy contingent was throwing a toga party. Officers appeared at our trailer and invited me to come in period dress. It was a command performance. Safer and Tiffin helped me turn a bedsheet into a vestal-virgin costume. I was the only female in attendance and the tunic was a huge success. The next morning officers turned up again to accuse me of inciting a riot. I had inspired the party, they grumbled, to drive a jeep into the swimming pool.

A delegation of nuclear experts arrived from the Department of Energy in Washington. They had come to meet with the old inhabitants of Enjebe, the island with the melted Hilton. We traveled by boat with the experts to the refugee camp where the islanders had lived for nearly thirty years. The entire community was ushered into the meeting hall. Translators prepared for the discussion. Bonhomous introductions were made. The government scientists and bureaucrats, men with complacent faces tinted beet red to bronze, had come with jarring news. Once the army bulldozers had packed up and left, the island of Enjebe would be safe for resettlement.

Half the crowd was under thirty. Enjebe was a mythical place for them. They had been raised with stories of the apocalypse, the great migration. The excitement attached to "the return" caused confusion, shuffling. Everyone was whispering. The nuclear bureaucrats in their open-necked cotton shirts were ready to answer any query, clarify any point. They spoke as though everyone in the room was *au fait* with the abstruse terminology of the Department of Energy. When they thought everything was crystal-clear, that the briefing charts measuring rads, the unit of radiation, had satisfactorily explained the risks, there was a pause. A question from the floor was translated. Everyone had the same question in mind.

"How big is a rad?" the translator's voice boomed. "Is it as big as a rock?"

The assembled islanders had not understood a word. Their coconut palms would be toxic for two generations considering the half-life, the time it takes for radiation to decay, of strontium-90. I imagined them back on Enjebe, with the mysterious Runit dome a canoe ride away. Could they resist climbing it? What happened when children or lovers snuck over to the luxuriant plutonium-encrusted sand? Would they obey the sign for twenty thousand years? No one asked or answered the question.

The experts left the same day, pleased the matter was resolved. The file on the Enewetak atoll could be closed or shredded. The people had been sufficiently advised of how things stood, the "risk factor," and had chosen, freely, to go home.

Before leaving the atoll, I became friendly with the U.S. government shark specialist, who had come to study the behavior of feral gray reef sharks who fed on irradiated flora in the lagoon. Sharks entered the reef through the yawning hole left by the H-bomb. The specialist offered to take me diving to observe them, promising that if I avoided jerky movements and followed him closely, there would be no danger of attack. His cool assurances were somewhat offset by the chunk of flesh that was missing from his arm. He saw me gazing at the scar and promised that the bite was the work of a different breed of shark.

We took a dinghy out laden with scuba gear and flipped over the side into a popular feeding ground. Amidst the hot-pink and iridescent-green fish, we descended to the base of a wall of coral. We were encircled by gray shadows. Normally at this moment, I would have suppressed panic and moved smoothly out of the area. My guide pulled me up to his side and we were within a few feet of the weird snouts and sawteeth of a foraging school of radiation-rich sharks. They did not, as it happened, glow in the dark. My companion would not tell me whether he was watching for sickness, erratic behavior, sudden lashing aggressiveness. The data he was collecting, to be cataloged and banked in some Pentagon computer, no doubt part of an assessment of whether a nuclear war was "winnable," was classified.

Later in New York, I ran into the shark specialist by chance, walking down Fifth Avenue. It was a brief encounter, an exchange of pleasantries. But somehow his presence flooded the city's canyons with images from the atoll. For a split second, I saw postwar Manhattan, the melted silver candelabra at Tiffany's, the boiling rink at Rockefeller Plaza, the 9 million sewer rats emerging victorious, gnawing on strontium sumac. Survivors somewhere were telling their children about the apocalypse, the great migration, and the Department of Energy's upbeat news.

FOUR

War Games

THE LESSONS of Enewetak were lost on the U.S. Army. A year after taking in the horror of the plutonium dome, the poisonous monument to the twentieth century, I found myself sitting in Adolf Hitler's former command post in Heidelberg watching nuclear war games. The U.S. Army was gearing up for World War III. American soldiers in gas masks and nuclear-protection suits in secret, raw Defense Department footage of a recent "European theater" war game projected on the big screen were working a Xerox machine. They were training for nuclear "war fighting." The footage was declassified at my request. The masked men, stumbling through their bizarre drill, keeping the command post paperwork in order in the midst of a nuclear holocaust, played like Monty Python.

The Führer's great hall in what was now Campbell Barracks, headquarters for the U.S. Army in Europe, could hold five hundred comfortably and I was alone. I sat with the ghosts of the last war while watching a demented scene from the next. The film had been stamped secret not because the men in gas masks were tripping over each other, jamming the keys of their manual typewriters with pencils as the nuclear gloves were too clumsy to peck the machines, but because I was looking at the secret command post for the next European war. It was a revamped Third Reich breeding camp.

I stared in wonder. What could they conceivably be typing in the middle of Armageddon? Who could possibly want a Xerox at a time like this? Every branch of the military demanded a role in the nuclear war "scenario" that envisioned Germany as the flash point. Most startling was what the U.S. Army had in mind. They were incorporating nuclear weapons onto the battlefield as artillery and land mines.

This was footage I needed for "The Nuclear Battlefield," a one-hour broadcast that would air as part of the *CBS Reports* series "The Defense of the United States."

It was the winter of 1980. Andrew, Chloe, and I had moved to New York City and were settled in one of the great Upper West Side buildings, 333 Central Park West, where the landlord screened tenants for creativity. Mr. Sheldon chose writers, composers, filmmakers, actors. "Over the Rainbow," originally "Somewhere on the Other Side of the Rainbow," was composed at 333. The crank elevators were operated by hand and Chloe would ride up and down ceaselessly with Benny, the Dominican who acted as chief of staff. My office was in one of the CBS buildings on West 57th Street. I had landed a job at *CBS Reports*, the hour-long documentary program that was famed for Edward R. Murrow's classic film on migrant labor, "Harvest of Shame," and the recent "Selling of the Pentagon." *CBS Reports* was "the jewel of the Tiffany network." Producing and directing *CBS Reports* hours was a coveted position in television news. This was the height of television journalism. Each documentary was a substantial and beautifully edited film that took nine months to research, shoot, and cut. We shot *CBS Reports* on 16-mm film and edited on Steinbeck flatbeds. I was now a director and writer for the broadcast, in Europe to research and film our nuclear army. I spent much of the winter freezing in the Bavarian woods.

CBS poured resources into the Defense series, to be broadcast on five consecutive nights. Dan Rather was the host. The executive producer was Howard Stringer, a Welshman who read history at Oxford and volunteered for Vietnam, with a promise of citizenship. He landed a desk job in Saigon. At CBS, Stringer rose precipitously from researcher to president of news and then scaled Black Rock, CBS headquarters, to run the network. As he paused to executive-produce *CBS Reports*, Stringer made the documentary series the most desirable berth at CBS News.

One of his lieutenants on the Defense series was Andy Lack, a New Yorker who had grown up on the stairs of the "21" Club and had a résumé that included inventing the slogan "Fill it to the rim with Brim." Lack was a salesman and raconteur. He had boundless energy and a Philistine's view of news. It was a product. There was money in it. CBS management was clueless. Yet, contrary to the opportunism he affected, Lack devoted countless hours to difficult and incendiary stories, checking every detail, badgering the news division to promote them. He is the only television executive I have ever heard say, "I don't *care* what the *New York Times* says. *We go with our story.*" Lack balked at pressure, even from the White House. He would eventually decamp to 30 Rockefeller Plaza, to become president of NBC News.

The senior producer was Judy Crichton, niece of composer Richard Rodgers, a sophisticated New Yorker who started her television career as a booker for quiz shows like *I've Got a Secret.* Twenty years my senior, she was a devoted reporter, surrounded by stacks of files, congressional hearings, and obscure documents that maddeningly concealed whole packs of cigarettes. She was the first woman hired as a *CBS Reports* producer, had raised four children, and was married to Bob Crichton, a brilliant and successful writer whose novels flung themselves onto the best-seller list. Judy supplied the gravitas of the network, pushing stories on the African National Congress, the war in Angola, Three Mile Island, the CIA's army of anti-Castro Cubans in Miami, and now the nuclear "Triad."

She became my mentor. It was Crichton who had hired me onto the series and who made the supreme effort to convince the Secretary of Defense and the Joint Chiefs of Staff to cooperate. They succumbed to her timeless arguments about democracy and the public's right to know.

With the rapprochement of Russia and the United States, it is difficult to conceive of the power of the nuclear theologians who murmured their incantations in the E-ring of the Pentagon. Crichton and I, in our well-cut suits, paid calls on most of them. We listened with rapt attention to discourses on first strike, megatonnage (size of the bomb and destructive power), circle error probable (how close an intercontinental ballistic missile could get to its target), retaliatory strike. Damage assessments were computed the way Vatican mystics count the angels on the head of a pin or the ayatollahs contemplate Islamic deportment in other planetary systems, a subject to which the Ayatollah Khomeini devoted considerable energy. Dr. Strangeloves, with soft pale skin and terrifying imaginations, sat in offices built inside impregnable vaults. They plotted targets for thirty thousand weapons. There were not enough cities, towns, military bases, tank parks, or rail yards in the old Soviet Union for all the missiles. Two, three, ten warheads were trained on one spot.

We fanned out in the wilderness, to White Sands missile range in New Mexico, a large swatch of the state where missiles could be fired at dawn without waking the neighbors; Cheyenne Mountain in Colorado, where, in the name of national security, the mountain was dynamited to accommodate a "command and control" center deep in the cavern; and Port Canaveral in Florida, the venue for nuclear submarine missile tests. (Crichton broke the story that our nuclear sub commanders were supplied with the launch codes, that a commander on his own could incinerate Murmansk or Kiev.)

I spent a long day at sea off Port Canaveral waiting for a Trident submarine commander to launch. The Clinton administration's Secretary of Defense William Perry, then a Carter-appointed technocrat, was on board as well. The sub carried more firepower than was dropped in all of World War II. Its multimillion-dollar profile was sleek, black, sharkish. Here was the ultimate weapon of mass destruction.

Unfortunately, on countdown, the missile tube hatch covers refused to open. The shoal of VIPs darted around nervously. Another countdown ended with the call to abort. The sub was lost. There was a twenty-minute lull while the sub, with the aid of an observation boat's navigation gear, found its bearings. When all the coordinates matched up, another countdown miscarried with the wrong hatch opening. Adjustments were made, VIPs were offered more instant coffee. At last we filmed the fiery launch. The naval component of the nuclear war-fighting machine needed work.

My primary focus was the "nuclear battlefield." Before the strategic forces were launched from the Dakotas and Omaha, before the subs prowling the waters off Madagascar and the Sea of Japan released their "city-busters," before the F-111s took off from the English countryside, before the bomb-laden A-4s and A-5s fired up their afterburners on the decks of aircraft carriers in the Mediterranean, before the carriers used their stash of nuclear depth charges, the army intended to "go toe-to-toe with the Russkies" on the ground in Germany.

They would arm their tactical nuclear weapons as a "trip wire," a first stage of escalation. Nuclear land mines, in the thousands, were on hand to blow up enemy patrols and tanks, small mobile Lance nuclear missiles were disbursed along the East German border, eight-inch guns packed nuclear shells for short-range artillery, larger Pershing nuclear missiles were on twenty-four-hour alert in Geilenkirchen to shell behind the lines, vaporizing Warsaw Pact fuel and ammunition dumps.

In the host countries of Eastern Europe, in what is now the Czech Republic, Slovakia, and Poland, the enemy was set to unleash nuclear-tipped short-range Frog missiles, more hefty Scud missiles, SS-20 missiles to wreak havoc behind the lines, and their own briefcase-packed version of the atomic land mine. (Though as the Russians did not trust their allies, warheads were guarded jealously by the mysterious Twelfth Department of the Soviet Ministry of Defense.) A great many nuclear weapons were cluttering up the European landscape, and the residents, vaguely aware of it, did not appreciate the devastating plan. Army Training and Doctrine, TRADOC, told the troops that a nuclear blast was little worse than an ordinary incoming rocket. Thus, troops I met in the field were set to ratchet up the kilotonnage fast, lobbing nuclear artillery all over West Germany. The chain of command that was meant to zing codes and instructions down the line through NATO's SHAPE, AFCENT, and USAFE was vulnerable to electromagnetic pulse. Communications would be the first casualty of war. Nuclear missiles batteries trundling through the woods expected to find local pay phones to check their orders.

I discovered that the war games for the nuclear battles against the armies of the Warsaw Pact were played on giant "battle boards" at Fort Leavenworth, Kansas. A fairy-tale valley in Hessen was selected, thirteen miles from the West German border near the Fulda Gap, a mountain pass where the Russian hordes were expected to pour through en route to London. Army teams arrived in the valley, surveying, sketching, photographing. In the valley of Bad Hersfeld, farmers showed me the precise spot where the army stood in the steep pasture, checking the angle of every house, every steeple in the villages below, so picturesque they looked like carved and painted children's toys.

The surveyors mapped the correct proportions of every stand of pines, every barnyard and duck pond. Then an exact-scale model was fashioned on the board, meticulously colored, complete with cows dotted around to make it look just right. Army officers stood around the board like a pantheon of gods. "Okay over here." A colonel, his thin face drained of color, taps an eighteenth-century church in the village of Hattenbach with his pointer. "We have a ten-KT detonation. This is ground zero." His voice, clipped and cold as a meat locker, assesses the damage in the concentric rings emanating from the explosion. The church is pulverized.

I arrived at the church door early on a winter Sunday and found it unlocked. The organist was absorbed in a Bach chorale, and the sound from the 180-year-old pipes soared into the eaves. It was the sound of the Enlightenment, sacrificed in a Kansas war game. The organ was the town's treasure. Everyone showed up for the service as much to hear the breathy pipes as to hear the sermon. I stood transported, and asked permission to film. The organist was delighted someone wanted to record his music. He had been playing in this church loft for sixty years. His arthritic hands were forcing him to retire.

When the fine cut of the hour was broadcast, the voice of the army officer vaulted over from the war room at Fort Leavenworth to the congregation pouring out of ground zero. In the winter sun they filed through drifts of fresh powdered snow, exhilarated by the blasting pipes. Bach echoed through the valley, in concert with the omniscient officer's assessment of death and destruction.

The German government erupted with fury. They demanded to know what the U.S. Army was doing blowing away German villages, even in games. There was an international incident and demands for the removal of several thousand tactical nuclear weapons from German soil. "The Nuclear Battlefield" was run dozens of times on German television. German documentaries were made about the documentary. Film crews appeared at CBS News head-quarters on West 57th Street for comment. Vice-presidents were called upon to vouch for the film, including Roger Koloff, whom I nearly killed in an ice storm on the autobahn when he joined me in Hattenbach to "get his feet wet" in the field.

There was a moment in the film when General Niles Fulwiler, responsible for army nuclear war-fighting doctrine, was asked by the late Harry Reasoner how, with all of these nuclear weapons flying around the battlefield, he avoided hitting his own troops. "Well, Harry"—General Fulwiler paused reflectively—"that's a real problem."

Out in the Bavarian woods, in waist-deep snow, American troops in chemical suits and gas masks were maneuvering tanks through the drifts. With the camera rolling, everyone got mired in rivers of churned-up mud. In a clearing, two soldiers with frozen fingers rolled what looked like an oil drum into position. This was the centerpiece of the day, a simulated nuclear explosion. After detonation, the troops were drilled to react as though it were a real flash in the meadow. For painful minutes the jerry can bomb refused to go off. The fuse was wet. The officers cursed this idiotic duty. Finally, there was a *pop* and a mushroom cloud. The tank commanders shouted to their men to hop inside with lightning speed and batten down the hatches. The hatch doors were iced over and sticking. One refused to open, another failed to shut. There was general chaos, and the troops, glum and soaked through, retired from the battle.

We repaired to the bar of the local Bavarian inn outside Hohenfels. Stiff with cold and desperate for a hot drink, I was surprised to find all of the German men dressed as drag queens. They wore bodice-ripper dirndls and petticoats, red lipstick, rouge, and wigs. It was Fasching, a German cross-dressing holiday on the eve of Lent, and we danced all night to the accordion and the tuba. It seemed a suitable end to a day of nuclear war.

The Defense series' executive producer, Howard Stringer, wanted an "act" in the documentary on nuclear proliferation. His idea was to highlight one case of potential "regional conflict." Looking at the map, my choices were India–Pakistan, where subcontinental atomic tensions were running high; Argentina–Brazil, showing signs of a Latin race for the bomb; South Africa, where the clandestine program was the circled wagons of the Afrikaners; Libya, where the Colonel was ever flirting with producing or buying the bomb; and Israel–Iraq, where the Baathist regime in Baghdad was using Saudi millions to build an arsenal to match Israel's. It was the specter of the "Arab bomb."

I flew to Washington to consult a self-effacing spy I had befriended in the Pentagon's Defense Intelligence Agency. Of ordinary height and complexion, wearing an ordinary suit and raincoat, his modus operandi was to blend in. He disclosed in an offhand way that the Israelis were planning to knock out the Iraqi nuclear reactor.

It was eight months before air. The unknown factors were dissuasive. Was it true? If so, when would they strike? Such intelligence was seductive but dangerous. Disinformation was a perennial hazard, particularly in the light of the relationship between the U.S. and Israeli intelligence services, allies who shared some very sensitive intelligence but also spied on each other. Did some faction at DIA stand to gain? I had to make up my mind to press ahead or drop it. To include the story in the film required shooting in France at the nuclear center at Saclay, where the Iraqis trained at the Osiris reactor, the model for the reactor in Baghdad. It meant plaguing Israeli military intelligence generals to "confirm or deny," in a country where the one taboo subject was anything related to the word "nuclear," from their own Dimona reactor in the Negev desert (where cameramen were forced to steal shots from fast-moving cars and smuggle the footage out of the country) to their silos, on alert in the '73 war, and certainly their plan for a preemptive strike. It meant trips to the Middle East. I pitched it cautiously to Howard Stringer. With all of the variables, he said yes. Stringer had a Fleet Street instinct for a good risk.

Eight months later, the night before the CBS Defense series went on the air, two Israeli Air Force bombers flattened the Osirak reactor in Baghdad. I was able to give *CBS Evening News* their entire piece instantly and had a polished story, complete with rare Israeli footage and an interview with the newly retired head of military intelligence, General Schlomo Gazit. Perhaps the air force had planned it that way. Dan Rather called to say he was impressed.

I won an Emmy and the Writers Guild Award for "The Nuclear Battlefield." The series as a whole swept the awards for 1981. Stringer was promoted. Andy Lack took over *CBS Reports*. Judy Crichton was forced out. They had played a game of musical chairs and Crichton, who conceived of the series and lobbied for the mantle of executive producer, was outmaneuvered. She spoke bitterly of "the poker game," a regular old-boy network gathering where relationships were forged, a kind of CBS News executive club. Women were not invited. (As late as 1973, women at CBS News received a terse memo from management banning trousers at work. The women protested and broke the dress code.) Crichton packed her bags and moved to a younger, rival documentary unit, *ABC Closeup*. She eventually migrated to PBS, founding a much acclaimed series called *The American Experience*.

The following year, in the spring of 1982, I was promoted to *CBS Reports* producer and director and promptly took on the tobacco lobby. Big tobacco was not yet caught in a snare of public revulsion. The Tobacco Institute, the industry lobbying arm in Washington, exuded confidence. Its spokesman, Walker Merryman, treated the antismoking lobby as a nuisance more than a threat, a few zealots with a phone and ambitious schemes for persuading restaurateurs to set aside nonsmoking sections. Still, the institute dispatched a blow-dried tobacco advocate to the smallest radio station or Rotary Club to put out brush fires.

My interest was in the tobacco lobby's power, and how the cigarette kings operated in Washington. I was intrigued by the man who had declared himself their champion, Senator Jesse Helms. The senior senator from North Carolina was tall and courtly with eyes that spoke of untold grudges. The prophet of the right-wing fringe, Jesse was a master of the filibuster. He droned on hour after hour. Jesse had years under his belt as a local television commentator. His detractors found the message racist and homophobic. His on-air catchphrase for Martin Luther King, Jr., was "sham, agitator, fellow traveler."

When Jesse entered the national spotlight, the transcripts of his ripe views grew scarce. Racist campaign posters from the 1950 Senate race of Willy Smith, who brought Jesse to Washington as his top aide, disappeared. Jesse's critics in North Carolina said he had them destroyed, erasing his telltale past with the thoroughness of J. D. Salinger. In fact, they were not all out of circulation. We found a private archive and filmed one of the posters that read: DO YOU WANT NEGROES RIDING BESIDE YOUR WIFE AND YOUR DAUGHTER IN BUSES CABS AND TRAINS? Another screamed: WHITE FOLKS WAKE UP! Helms told me it was a "canard and falsehood" to accuse Willy Smith of racism. "He was the kindest, most compassionate man I ever saw."

At a time when the suggestion that Jesse might become chairman of the Senate Foreign Relations Committee would have astonished the Senate, I was already riveted by this brilliant politician. We met at dawn in a parking lot in Fayetteville, North Carolina, as the senator strolled into a roadside diner for a breakfast meeting with a Japanese delegation. I stopped Jesse to say that his staff had not given me a straight answer on whether or not we could do an interview on tobacco, that an interview with the senator was difficult to arrange. Jesse stared at me. "Not when they bait the hook with you, honey."

Jesse had a way with words. He was a southern gentleman. He adopted our camera team. We piled into the backseat of his car and caught him onstage flanked by Tobacco Queens, who caressed the senator like a favorite uncle. On camera, Senator Helms defended our freedoms: "Well, you put a ban on tobacco, there goes sugar. There goes whiskey." Inspecting the bales of pungent leaf to the rhythm of the incomprehensible auctioneer, the senator left no doubt that he was pledged to stand by cigarettes. R. J. Reynolds was his constituent as much as the small farmer who inherited the cash cow of a tobacco allotment. If there was a congressional urge to eliminate the subsidy or a threat to force the tobacco companies to regulate or indeed disclose what goes into a cigarette (how much arsenic, for example), Jesse Helms was there to defend the companies' interests. Tobacco for Jesse was "as sweet as mothers' love."

One broadcast was not enough to do justice to the political prowess of the man known in some Washington circles as the Prince of Darkness. When North Carolina Governor Jim Hunt challenged Jesse for his Senate seat, I was there with Bill Moyers to cover the race. Helms was apparently moved by the broadcast. Soon after air, he proclaimed his intention to buy CBS. Moyers called me into his office to state plainly that Helms's rattling of the corporation was in part our fault. I took it as a compliment. Bill brooded.

I assumed Jesse took exception to the poster about Negroes on the bus. Perhaps it was the senator's views on Martin Luther King. Helms had a campaign to roll back the King national holiday, citing the Reverend King's "communist associations."

"I've got to tell you," the senator confided on-camera in his office, "anybody who has traveled with communists in this country of ours, I don't know that we ought to have a holiday for 'em. I think Congress made a serious mistake." The fact that Helms embraced the bourbon-soaked rhetoric of Senator Joe McCarthy (whose regular diet was whiskey and Wonder bread) was popular in Jesse's North Carolina, as were Helms's "free enterprise" friends abroad. Roberto d'Aubuisson, a prominent Salvadoran death squad patron, who during the guerrilla war in the 1980s counted Catholic Archbishop Oscar Romero among his squad's victims, was a man of "principle" in Jesse's view. D'Aubuisson's ARENA Party, the presentable face for the late Major Bob's rough conservatism that drew the spotlight away from his less salubrious activities (the dead were found mutilated by the side of the road in the mornings or chucked among the skulls on the town's body dump), had become one of Jesse's causes. "You would think," the senator said with indignation, dismissing the mountain of allegations against d'Aubuisson, "that the ARENA Party consists of the crazies of El Salvador. Actually, they are the business leaders, the Chamber of Commerce types." D'Aubuisson's sobriquet in Central American circles was Major Blowtorch. Jesse waved this away as malicious talk. "Now," the senator added to cover his flank, "I don't say that there aren't some wild guys in any political party."

Jesse rallied the faithful to buy CBS stock in order to "be Dan Rather's boss." Bill Moyers drew on his political training as Lyndon Johnson's press secretary and retreated from the fray. It was the second time we had taken on powerful figures in Washington. The first was a Pentagon story I produced called "The Pentagon Underground," so embarrassing to the Reagan White House that the president watched the July 1983 broadcast (perhaps with TV dinner as was his habit) and promptly called Defense Secretary Caspar Weinberger over to 1600 Pennsylvania Avenue. The president asked Weinberger to explain how and why we had been given access. The film juxtaposed the secretary and his generals conferring in his baronial suite, with the activity directly below in the River Entrance parking lot. Documents were being hustled out of the building courtesy of military reformers known as closet patriots. The documents contained real test results for some of the most prominent "big ticket" weapons systems, endorsed by the gentlemen above. The upstairs/downstairs approach was electrifying television.

The day after "The Pentagon Underground" aired, I was in the international arrivals hall of Logan Airport in Boston waiting for my mother-in-law's plane to land. The airport hall was jammed with summer travelers. A phone rang on the desk in the center of the melee. It was for me. In fact, it was a conference call with one crisp voice belonging to Van Gordon Sauter, president of CBS News. It seemed the Pentagon had thrown a fit. As I shouted over the throngs, the executive roundtable at the other end of the line questioned me about issues raised in the film like the finer points of the M-1 tank. To change the oil, the tank engine had to be removed, cooled down, and replaced.

The airport inquisition turned to cruise missile guidance. The Pentagon claimed that the reason the cruise guidance system could not be tested in rain or cloud cover, essential for a realistic test, was the chaser planes' safety. As Aer Lingus announced the plane from Shannon had landed, I pointed out that the air force did not need chasers to monitor the missile's telemetry readings. AWACS planes or high-flying C-130s could do the job. The air force claimed its F-11 aircraft were "all-weather." Taxpayers shelled out hundreds of millions for that "capability." Why not use them?

I met the plane. A memo went out from Weinberger's office to all government agencies informing them that I was formally banned from the Pentagon. I was also blacklisted at other agencies. The Reagan administration played rough.

Having invested so much time walking the corridors of the Pentagon, I was not ready to retire from defense. If I was locked out of the building, I would go into the field. Central America, in early 1985, was swarming with arms dealers, politicians, and generals. It was the sort of place you might meet Sam Cummings, Jesse Helms or one of his lieutenants, or a Pentagon general with an alligator shirt and no stars. I was heading for my first war.

The Dirty War

M ASAYA was a storybook volcano, like the steep cones fancifully painted behind dinosaurs locked in combat, with the pterodactyl screeching through a darkening sky. Volcanoes defined the landscape of Central America. It was possible to stand on the rim of the crater, not far from Managua, and stare into the steamy abyss in complete silence. A flock of emerald-colored parrots would emerge from the depths, circle the volcano's gaping mouth, and trill like a section of piccolos in the Hollywood Bowl. Then more silence as the mist puffed skyward and the exquisite birds took another turn. How could they bear the sulfurous smell? Invisible and noxious gases belched up by the earth would surely suffocate them. Nicaraguans shrugged. The green parrots of Masaya were a fact of life, like the miraculous Virgins in the cathedrals who sweated blood and cried salt tears.

When I first peered into the volcano, it was April 1985. I had flown into Managua on the last Nicaraguan Airlines flight to load passengers in Miami before the airline was barred from U.S. soil, as part of a congressionally approved embargo against the outlaw state. When the flight attendants cranked shut the heavy forward and aft doors, there was a sense of finality. The Reagan administration was intent on stamping out the nasty outbreak of revolution in Central America, and quarantine was an effective weapon.

The "spooky old couple in the White House," as senior U.N. diplomat Brian Urquhart once described the Reagans, consulting their astrologer before making up the presidential schedule, detested the Sandinista leadership in Managua. The Sandinistas had Russian engineers picnicking on their beaches, Cuban doctors relaxing at their baseball games. But the virulent hatred seemed to reach beyond the freshened-up Red Scare. It was generational, a continuation of the war between Lester Lanin and Mick Jagger, neat Scotch and rolled joints, the domino theory and sit-ins. The Nicaraguan leaders were thirty years younger than Ron and Nancy, they wrote magical realist poetry and danced the frenzied Palo de Mayo until they were practically having sex on the dance floor. They scorned TV dinners, Frank Sinatra, face-lifts, and B movies, the staples of Reagan style. They had a resistance patina, having destroyed the little kingdom of Anastasio Somoza, whose rank force of national guardsmen stole the blankets and food airlifted in for the victims of the Managua earthquake and blew up buildings to save the trouble of rescuing the wounded inside. They could notch their guns while the president made up sad lies about his personal odyssey liberating the death camps in World War II, when in fact he never left the back lots of Hollywood.

The Reagan White House missed Somoza and his kind, the cigars and gold chains, the bevy of "señoritas," the Miami bank accounts, the white and dark rum Nica Libres, and obsequious bows to the gringos. "Our backyard," Manifest Destiny, "our son of a bitch," the legacy of empire, was not something the Reagan administration wanted to forfeit.

The night drive from Sandino Airport, named after a totemic guerrilla who fought the U.S. Marines, following the cold embrace of an airport security bureaucracy infatuated with forms (one slip of the pen and I was ordered to start again), was a revelation. The enemy was destitute. The capital was a dimly lit shantytown. The city center was a blank, an empty space where the earthquake leveled it. I harbored subversive thoughts. These people were not what the Pentagon liked to call "a credible threat." Managua made Nigeria look like imperial Rome.

The shabby Hotel "Inter" served as an international press club. Hotel rooms converted to news bureaus lined the hallways. CBS had a corner suite with panoramic views, mounds of equipment, and a well-stocked fridge. The drivers rushed in and out with wads .

79

of cash from black market currency deals. The bureau manager was Cookie Hood, a gregarious beauty who was forever helping someone down the hall through a cocaine hangover. Cookie was half Nicaraguan oligarch, half American southern belle. She favored skinny tops and skating skirts with mirrored shades. By class, she should have been an enemy of the revolution, but in Managua, half the Sandinistas were children of privilege. Cookie was well "wired." She remembered birthdays. I recall sitting on a Matagalpa sidewalk in the baking sun waiting patiently for Cookie, wearing a slash of red lipstick and hot pants, to track down the local military commander and deliver a beautifully iced cake.

My intention was to get out of the capital and into the remote countryside where the war was being fought. The "contras," thousands of Nicaraguans and Miami Cubans on the U.S. payroll, led by former officers of Somoza's National Guard, were billed by Ronald Reagan as freedom fighters. His speechwriters outdid themselves with the phrase "the moral equal of our Founding Fathers" to describe the rabble roaming the mountains. Reports filtering out from priests and nuns in isolated communities suggested a systematic use of classic terror tactics, to sever the tenuous links between villages and the government. New clinics, stocked with Cuban medicine, were blown up. Volunteers carrying vaccines into the jungle had their throats slit. Even American nuns were kidnapped and threatened with rape. I wanted to establish at what level the tactics were sanctioned by Washington, whether the contras' CIA minders encouraged them or turned a blind eye. I was determined to make the backbreaking journeys to find the witnesses and victims of the attacks and question them directly, with a camera.

Cookie was game. Her translating skills were essential because she spoke the archaic peasant Spanish prevalent in the countryside. Ask any farmer how far the next village was and he would answer cheerfully, *"Dos leguas,"* two leagues, as though we were passing conquistadors. Our on-camera "talent" was Jane Wallace, an athletic freckled brunette with a deep smoker's laugh and the mouth of a Raymond Chandler dame. "How many bricks of hundreds are we talking about?" she would ask a hardened criminal about his take. "Could you fit 'em in a bread box?" Jane had spent months across the border in Honduras covering the buildup of the "secret war," which meant attending "dog and pony" press junkets to contra camps where camera-ready recruits shimmied across ropes suspended over gorges and crawled, whooping war cries, through obstacle courses. Neither Jane nor Cookie had ever ventured into the battle-scarred provinces where I proposed to go.

For one thing, it was difficult to get there. Two of my destinations, Siuna and Río Blanco, were ostensibly cut off. Río Blanco was the setting for a major military operation; a large chunk of the Nicaraguan Army was there trying to flush out and corral the contra units. The region was off limits to journalists by order of the Nicaraguan minister of defense, Thomas Borge. There were roadblocks on every access road. Siuna, in the heart of the gold-mining region, was on the far side of a wide band of forbidding terrain in Zelaya Province controlled by the contras. Traveling by road, our jeeps would be hit with grenades and plundered of expensive camera gear at the very least. Planes were not flying there due to antiaircraft fire and attacks on the mountain strip.

I asked Cookie to arrange a meeting with the defense minister. Borge, a squat Napoleonic figure with brusque manners and a deeply cynical view of the world, suggested lunch at his officers' club. Cookie, Jane, and I arrived to find ourselves ushered into a private dining room with a well-appointed table set for six. It seemed Borge, infatuated with Jane, had thoughtfully brought two friends in tow. I was paired off with a well-traveled, bookish ambassador. Cookie was assigned a rakish general. We survived this absurd lunch without disgracing ourselves, and by the time we returned to the CBS bureau, a dozen roses were waiting for Jane.

There was also a note saying my urgent plea for access to the war zone in Río Blanco was denied. I called the defense minister demanding a good reason why. Borge laughed. "I couldn't possibly send you there. It's too dangerous." With that, I alerted Cookie, Jane, and crew that we were heading for the mountains papers or no papers. I made a valiant effort to alter the stamped and signed documents for another zone to read "Río Blanco." The paper was so thin, my botched retyping punched a large hole in it. Wheels up, I announced, was first light regardless.

Our gear included hammocks, mosquito nets, first-aid kit for gunshot wounds or snakebites, army-issue mosquito repellent, bottled water, and military rations. The triple-canopy jungle was full of unspeakable parasites. *"Animalitos"* meant creatures that crawled in your ear and eventually exited through the eyes, voracious worms, beetles, furry tarantulas. The *animalitos* were just as terrifying as the prospect of jaguars, land mines, or the sudden burst of machine-gun fire.

We collected gallons of rationed gas and mended tires and set out on the torturous journey. The rutted, washed-out roads were so bad, the jeeps could only travel five to ten miles per hour, leaving us battered and bruised. After ten hellish hours, we were at last approaching the military roadblock. We needed some ploy, some distraction, to slip through. Our opportunity presented itself. A military convoy rumbled by with dozens of troops, all with red bandanas, packed like cattle in flatbed trucks. We hailed one of the flatbeds and asked if we could jump aboard to film the soldiers. The commander apparently thought three women in shorts would be good for morale. We dove into the middle of the troops and our jeeps followed as part of the convoy. At the roadblock, there were shouts and whistles and salutes and we were through. Two miles down the road, we climbed back into our jeeps.

Having entered the danger zone, I felt abandoned now without our escort. Each of us took masking tape and spelled out TV on the sides and roofs of the jeeps. We stripped our pillows of their cases and held the white "flags" out the windows. In the clouds of grimy dust, the white cotton was streaked with dirty brown. Two more hours of bashing our heads against the roof pitching over the bumps and we were engulfed in the tropical dusk. Traveling in the dark was suicidal.

We spotted a small *finca* off to our left and stopped to see whether we could spend the night. The farmer was agitated. He wanted us to move on *"rapido."* *"Vaya veloz!"* We would surely attract the contra guerrillas who were hiding in the surrounding hills. He then gave us the unsettling intelligence that the last jeeps to attempt to go through were savagely attacked. He was unable to tell us precisely how far we would have to drive under these nightmarish conditions. It seemed absurd that we should be cowering before a force armed and paid for by our tax dollars. I imagined the conversation. *"Compadre, soy una amiga de su patrón, el Presidente*

Reagan." We all agreed that moving out was our best chance. The soundman, a fastidious vegetarian, was demented with fear. He wanted to stop *now*. We finally convinced him that he would certainly be killed if he mutinied here, while down the road, our odds of being attacked were fifty-fifty.

In the next hour, our jeeps were easy prey for an ambush in the black soup beyond the headlights. The thought of who was waiting in the darkness flayed my nerves. No one spoke. Being here at all, against the express orders of the minister of defense, was entirely my fault. I had six-year-old Chloe and one-year-old Olivia to think of. Cookie had a son. I steadied myself, breathed deeply, and let Bonnie Raitt belt through my headphones. When we came over a rise and saw the lights of Río Blanco, the fear that pressed on me like a yoke of ice lifted. The pain in my stomach retreated. The mood in the jeep dissolved into bad Latin jokes.

The hotel on the adobe town square was a seedy dormitory with cardboard partitions. The temperature indoors hovered around 100 degrees. We carted speakers and chairs onto the sidewalk and unpacked the Flor de Cana rum, attracting a crowd of black Cuban military advisers. Local civilians also gathered around to demand Marlboros. One slender man in jeans chose his moment to reveal that he was in fact a contra, in town to gather intelligence. Our Miami Cuban cameraman questioned him. It was common for contras to cross the lines. He mumbled that there was a large, semipermanent contra camp a few miles into the dense vegetation and added that he would be honored to act as guide in the morning. Careful instructions followed: turn left out of town and take the left fork. Our informant would meet us at a rendezvous point. We thanked him discreetly for the tip.

An emissary appeared from the regional commander who was dining across the square. Cookie, Jane, and I were summoned for a drink. The regional commander was hunched over a bottle of rum with his officers. It was within his power to arrest us or send us back down the road we had just traveled, so it seemed prudent to radiate charm. Unfortunately, we outdid ourselves, for the whole party piled into jeeps, sweeping us along, in a convoy heading for the main military camp. Stumbling over sleeping soldiers, we were hustled along to what I realized with horror was the commander's tent.

In one harrowing moment I grasped that we were the evening's entertainment. If we crossed the barrier of German shepherds guarding the entrance, they could knock us flat if we tried to retreat. I reversed course, and in tandem the three of us began gently backing down the narrow path through a sea of snoring bodies. We faded into the ink-black night and fled on foot. Our hosts were mercifully too drunk to hunt us down.

The morning was clear and hot. I ordered the drivers to the hospital, where victims of a fresh contra attack were bandaged. A middle-aged woman, Elba Molina, greeted us with a bullet hole in her breast. Her children and parents died at roughly eight o'clock the night before from shots fired into the house. Her son was shot in the legs and the mouth. Her father had been a career soldier, which seemed to have condemned three generations of her family to death.

Out on the road, some of our party were anxious to follow the lead of the contra informant the night before. I was torn. I had come here to find an American Catholic priest, whose tiny village of Paiwas was reached by the right fork, veering away from the advertised contra camp. Father Feltz was at least two hours down the secondary dirt track. I insisted we reverse and make a hairpin turn to pursue our original mission. That evening, we learned that the first vehicle to drive down the left fork, the route mapped out by our friend in the square, exploded. The road had been sown with mines. Had he known?

Before we understood that the road we had chosen was providential, everyone was grumbling. Fording a river, the jeeps sank. Wheels spinning, engines flooding, we filmed the catastrophe. Hours later, with jeeps resurrected, we found the priest at home on his verandah. He was middle-aged and gaunt, with bad teeth and the disquieting air of shell shock. His whole person conveyed an overfamiliarity with the heart of darkness.

Father Feltz offered us refreshments and told us he had heard President Reagan's lines about the "freedom fighters" and "Founding Fathers" on his shortwave radio. "I've gone from township to township, picking up bodies," he said dryly of the victims of contra raids. "They just kill them and slit their throats. Rape a fourteen-year-old girl because her father was a member of a [government] committee. Cut off her head and put her head along the trail so that the rest of the campesinos get the idea." Father Feltz adjusted his baseball cap and remembered his friend the judge, a father of ten, riddled with bullets and dumped outside the chapel. He bled to death in the priest's arms in the pickup truck en route to find a doctor in Río Blanco. "This was my first contact with the contradiction"—Father Feltz' gaze was like the beam shot by a magnifying glass catching the sun—"of my government supporting the contras." He sipped tea. "One fellow was hanged from the ceiling of his own house. Another fellow had his throat cut, his eyes gouged out. Whether it be a teacher or [a volunteer] carrying the polio vaccine to remote areas. Anybody who was in any way collaborating with the Sandinistas would be a victim. The more gruesome the death or the torture, it's simply to spread the terror. The fear." The priest's lips looked permanently parched.

He told the story of Christina Borje Díaz and her miraculous recovery. "A girl of eleven years old, visiting her uncle. I was only able to get out to see her fifteen days after she was shot. She was used for target practice." The wound in her chest healed with household remedies. Her head wound was infected and her hand was swollen from the bullet lodged there. "They finally got her down to Managua where they could operate on her skull."

We climbed into two canoes at the river's edge and paddled across to find Christina. She was exquisite and almost pathologically shy. She pulled her frock off her shoulder to show us the scar above her breast where a bullet pumped into her back had exited. Christina remembered the band of contras torching three houses, including her own. "They sent me to another house. They made me lie facedown. Then they shot me." The man pulling the trigger never said a word. Asked how she felt about it now, the little girl shrugged. "I don't feel anything."

The Espinales twins, Pedro and Felix, had moved to Paiwas after their farm cooperative was destroyed and most of its members massacred. The boys witnessed a number of killings the night of the attack. The dead left piled in the co-op's defensive trench included militiamen and their children. When the twins found their father among the dead, he had been mutilated. When we asked exactly what had been done, the boys turned away. Felix spoke in a reedy, almost inaudible voice. "They peeled the skin off his face and his feet."

I scoured Managua for a charter flight to take us to Siuna, the besieged mining town in the highlands where an American nun, Sandra Price, was stationed in the middle of the fray. Only one aircraft was available in the entire country, a Russian biplane. I hired it, paying a fortune for the privilege. I called Andy Lack in New York for permission.

"Do you really need a Russian biplane?" he asked.

I assured him I did.

"Fine. *Bon voyage.*"

Siuna was a bizarre throwback to the nineteenth century. The collection of wooden shacks on stilts thatched with palm fronds was a frontier gold town made up largely of descendants of Chinese mine laborers. Sandra was expecting us. The sister had a warm, Celtic face with celadon eyes and a sturdy build. Her hands were chapped and red from four years in these primitive conditions, four years, she said sadly, of "death, destruction, kidnapping, and rape. Disappearances of people, whole families, whole communities. When we first came here, we visited forty-eight communities. Now we only visit thirty-eight. The rest have been wiped out. The single most frequent thing that happens here with the contras is massive kidnapping. Men, women, and children. They take everybody. Animals. Everything goes." Villagers were driven, she said, on foot toward the Honduran border, where they were used as forced labor on abandoned *fincas* and as mules to ferry weapons. The sisters were nursing a newborn whose family had been shot. Sister Price rocked in her chair. "We listen to the Voice of America and the lies. It's a wonder we haven't pulverized the radio."

A priest and sister from the next parish were kidnapped for two days. "They are close friends of ours. They were taken to a camp. The entrance was strewn with human bones and skulls. They had blood-drenched uniforms hanging on the trees." Sister Price was herself kidnapped by contras. "I spoke for about four hours with the leader of the group. We talked about, I guess, everything. Who I was. What I was doing in the area. That day, as we were coming up the river, we saw the planes drop supplies to them. Money, batteries, cigarettes, walkie-talkies. The *comandante* was saying that everything they had came from the United States. And he made a play on words, saying, 'We don't call him Ronald Reagan, we call him Donald.' Don, *donar*, 'to give.' "

The sister took us through Siuna to Guadalupe Davila's house. Guadalupe was a frail little girl with brown eyes one could swim in. One night five contras arrived with guns blazing at the thatched hut perched on stilts. The contras fired up through the flimsy, rush and slat floor, killing her four-year-old brother. They hauled her uncle and father out of the house, shot her father five times and slit his throat. Her mother had a bullet wound in the head.

"They choked her and then they took her clothes off," said Guadalupe, swallowing hard.

"And then?" we asked. "*Y después?*"

"They burned her clothes and then they peeled off her face."

All of us felt ill.

"Jesus, this is awful." Jane lit a cigarette.

When Guadalupe appeared on television in August 1985, dozens of people called to adopt her.

Guadalupe's haunting story was the last thing the administration wanted on national television. Eliot Abrams, the Reagan point man for Latin America at the State Department, said her testimony was impossible. We must have fed her the lines. Coupled with the defection of a civilian director of the contra forces, who confirmed the hideous tactics in a bombshell interview, the State Department was frantic.

Edgar Chamorro was inordinately handsome, well born and disgusted. After we finished filming in Nicaragua, he agreed to meet with us in his tasteful house in Miami, where the contra leadership kept property, bank accounts, and wives. He wore a white summer suit. We sat in a fragrant garden with frangipani and bougainvillea in bloom. We told him in frank terms what we had seen. Chamorro began to talk. Neither Jane nor I expected him to be nearly so forthcoming about the contra army he had helped to run. "The tactics are what we call terrorist tactics," said the former contra director, hired and paid by the CIA. "They are not military tactics. They're tactics of using terror for the purpose of making people respect or follow you. The policy," he said, meaning Washington's policy, "gives a green light to defeat the enemy by any means." A

CIA field manual was the bible of the camps. "With the manual, they [the CIA] were condoning the practical use of terror." Chamorro seemed overwhelmed with guilt and pain. "Our atrocities towards prisoners, towards civilians, were routine." Reagan's hyperbole astounded him. "Their actions are more similar to the Founding Godfathers than the Founding Fathers."

The contra commander, Enrique Bermudez, received us at his headquarters in the suburbs of Tegucigalpa, the capital of Honduras. The border camps, where volunteer and press-gang recruits were put through their paces, were too rustic for the *comandante*. In Tegucigalpa, or Tegoose, as the carpetbagger suppliers just in from New Orleans and Miami called it, Bermudez was close to the proconsul of the region, the American ambassador. Military hardware, ostensibly shipped from the United States to the Hondurans, could be quietly transferred, right in the heart of the capital, to the contras.

Enrique Bermudez had a cruel face, with sharp edges and scars. He had served as a henchman in the Guardia of the deposed dictator Somoza. Bermudez had vendettas. He threw his weight around among the upper ranks, notifying one and all that he did not tolerate dissent. He threatened to kill Edgar Chamorro for washing the contras' dirty laundry in public.

The *comandante* was chivalry itself when Jane and I came to call. He playfully deposited his monkey on my shoulder who nuzzled the back of my neck. We realized as the session got under way that the contras' military commander had never faced a tough interview. In fact, he told us, this was the first time he had been asked to sit down to talk. The fact that the questions were not the gentle "How do you see the future of your country?" variety or "Could we have your comment on . . . ?" shook his equanimity. His thuggish lieutenants, who closed in around us as the questions grew hostile, glowered. Bermudez knew enough about public relations not to have us shot.

"There have been reports of your troops attacking civilians," Jane said as the camera rolled, "mutilating civilians, murdering civilians."

"That's not true. That's not true. I won't say"—he paused judiciously—"that we have not committed at least one atrocity. There were some, out of our control. But we don't use that tactic. We have no use for terrorism." His unshaved accomplices nodded. "And we *could* use it." His thoughts returned to some phase of his training, in Washington or Buenos Aires. "To start an insurrection, two important elements are terrorism and sabotage. Of course not indiscriminate but *discriminating* terrorism and sabotage. It is considered by the intellectuals in insurrection that those two factors have to be used if you are going to accelerate the process. But in this particular revolution"—he smiled broadly—"we have been very romantic. We are very respectful of the population." He had not found cause to discipline one commander, not one common soldier, for abuses.

We raised the prickly subject of a series of photographs published in *Newsweek* and aired by us on CBS, of Enrique's men forcing a suspected spy to dig his own grave. The executioner unsheathes his massive "commando knife," issued by the CIA, and slits the man's throat. In what looks like a ritual murder, the offender is then gruesomely cut open.

Bermudez, drawing a handsome covert salary from the White House, was unmoved by the photos. "Well," he said blandly, "it wasn't necessary for them to do it the way they did it. He could be shot."

We asked Edgar Chamorro, on his Miami patio, if the White House knew the true state of affairs. "Well, you know, we only talked to high people in the CIA." His voice dropped to the volume of discretion from habit. "Those people used to say that the White House knows very well what's going on."

Commanders, whose excesses were a threat to their superiors, had been secretly court-martialed and shot. Yet, "If the soldier is close to the *comandante*"—Edgar smoothed his white linen cuffs—"nothing will happen. He could even be promoted." There was talk of instituting a code of conduct. Chamorro was bemused. "A code of conduct in a Mafia results in more suffering for people who are not loyal to the system. So who is the one who will put the code of conduct to the godfathers?"

Their CIA minders only seemed troubled, said Chamorro, himself appointed to his directorship by the CIA, by *comandantes* mistreating their own men, "like keeping somebody without enough food. Or tying people to trees. We found that people had been treated like animals. Also, I would call rapes atrocities. Some *comandantes* raped women, not only on the enemy side but also women who were our own fighters, who didn't want to give in to a particular *comandante*. Using a knife, you know, threatening a woman so she will give in." Chamorro was groping for some understanding of why his war of liberation was hemorrhaging. "These people are sadistic. Borderline psychotic. Sick people. People who have endured a wild life in guerrilla war. It's very dirty. People go crazy. Some of the fighters are so into killing, it's hard to stop them. People who are sadistic become more brutal. More cruel."

When "The Dirty War" aired in 1985, the State Department blacklisted Jane and me, another government agency to add to my list. One of our key sources inside the administration warned us that senior officials planned to lobby the president of CBS News to have us fired. Forewarned, we mobilized support on the CBS end and the tense situation was defused, for the moment.

The following spring, in 1986, I made a call from CBS to the White House National Security Council. I asked for a colonel called Oliver North to confirm or deny that the White House was running a covert operation, not authorized by Congress, to sustain the contra war in Central America. North responded through one of his minions. He said the allegation was preposterous and absurd.

There had been leaks in the field, disgruntled trainers and gun-runners who told a fabulous tale of White House spookery. They told it with precision and apprehension. After the first film, I was determined to stay on the story. Andy Lack gave me months to build up sources and dig in Washington. Finally, he turned me loose to go back to Central America. I convinced one of Oliver North's operatives to go on camera. Two defectors from the operation also agreed to talk and lead us to secret border camps.

I arrived back in May 1986 with Jane and camera crew. We found ourselves in the rain forest of northern Costa Rica, creeping along jungle paths that marked the Nicaraguan border, sweating over land mines and the unmistakable caterwaul of a jaguar. Chattering cabo blanco monkeys in the trees screamed at us, betraying our position. We had plenty of enemies here, Sandinistas who could mistake us for contras, contras who did not care for our curiosity,

American operatives who stood to lose if the White House gambit was exposed. We were on the trail of a training camp, our skin coated with army mosquito repellent so strong, it burned the lettering off our pens. The camp was in a clearing, with evidence everywhere of use: ashes, rations, spent cartridges.

The film was explicit and damning about the White House operation. We ran the official White House denial as a "tag" in the studio close of the piece. Howard Stringer, then president of CBS News, was chuffed to be ahead on the story. We offered to share our material with other CBS units to push the evidence further. No one else at the network expressed more than passing interest, until the day six months later when Attorney General Ed Meese stood at the podium and announced that there was indeed trouble at Pennsylvania Avenue.

Comandante Bermudez was shot once in the head in front of the Intercontinental Hotel in Managua in February 1991. The shooting took place, after the war was over, in the wake of the parade of administration witnesses chauffeured to Capitol Hill to recall or not recall what they had known about the "Iran–Contra Affair," where monies from arms sales to our purported enemies the ayatollahs were salted away in Swiss accounts by Colonel North and funneled in cash and kind to the late Enrique and friends. There was barely a ripple of interest in the disturbing news that the beneficiary of the White House's Byzantine system of dispensing largesse was now a corpse.

Once the "scandal" broke, there were so many names and faces to learn, such a rogues' gallery of players to keep straight, so many hundreds of thousands of pages of depositions, testimony, exhibits, tape transcripts, computer messages, secret bank account records, flight manifests, in short, so much dross (I am one of the few people who read it), that the conduct of the war, where the dollars and bullets were raining down on the landscape, was forgotten. The contras, as wards of the U.S. government, were deep-sixed. I witnessed one of their handlers in Washington telling commanders on the phone there would be no first-class tickets to Miami. No green cards. The final curtain came down heavily. The *comandante*'s death was an obscure footnote.

There were plenty of jokes about the last person to leave Central

America turning out the lights. When the Bush administration shut the door, the story, for the networks, was wrapped up and the bureaus in Managua and Tegucigalpa closed. Cookie Hood landed a job in a video arcade in Virginia. Jane Wallace moved on to host a cable TV talk show. It is hard to say what was gained by the sound and fury along the Río Coco.

Covering that war was a watershed for me. I saw the imperative of the fourth estate as the camera. We needed checks and balances on what was done in the name of American interests. After seeing Christina and Guadalupe, I knew that the urgency to get their story out overrode the danger. What is eerie for me now is that I have seen the horror in that fetid jungle endlessly replayed in other wars, some already fading from memory, in the years since. Does it signify nothing? Perhaps there is a Bosnian–Serb defector, an Edgar Chamorro, grappling now on a patio in Pale with the corrosive effects on an army and a cause of a wild guerrilla life.

SIX

The Leopards

W HEN CBS DISPATCHED ME to Haiti in the first days after Baby Doc's hurried departure, blackened corpses of Tontons Macoute set on fire by vengeful crowds lay curled up in the streets in the bright tropical mornings. Jean-Claude Duvalier, known with mock affection as Baby Doc, had fled his wedding-cake palace, with rooms deliciously chilled so the ladies could wear their furs, and boarded a U.S. military transport bound for the Côte d'Azur. It was February 1986. For days the U.S. Embassy staff had been coaxing their testy ally to leave. The pain of exile was cushioned by the spoils of office. Baby Doc was thought to have $60 million in foreign bank accounts. His legacy would linger. His defiant words "I am the tail of the monkey" were borne out by the fact that two of his closest cronies would take power. This was to be a carefully managed revolution.

The euphoria of the crowds in La Saline and Carrefour, dancing to the Ra Ra bands, hailing the Dechoukaj, the smashing of the old order, was premature. Still, the man who was given his first machine gun as a child had failed as a hereditary dictator. When Baby Doc's BMW hurled onto the airstrip, his weak face etched with a tepid smile through the bulletproof glass, twenty-eight years of dynastic Duvalier rule came to an end.

His twisted father, the illustrious Papa Doc, had worn black. Black hats, black suits, black shades, gave him the signature of a demonic *loa*, a voodoo spirit called Baron Samedi who haunted the island's graveyards in black top hat and tails, smoking a cigar. Baron Samedi needed henchmen and Papa Doc rounded up the riffraff of Haiti, gave them wide-brimmed blue denim hats and menacing shades, and called them his Tontons Macoute, his Bogeymen. When Papa Doc died, the Macoutes transferred their affections to his son.

As soon as Baby Doc landed in France, the brutal force of some 25,000 Macoutes, twice the numbers employed by Papa Doc, melted into the countryside with their weapons to avoid being burned or hacked to death. All Port-au-Prince was whispering that their sadistic leader, Madame Max, had escaped to Miami dressed as a nun.

I drove up through the steep streets of Pétionville, the same streets Baby Doc had often used as a racecourse for his Ferrari, on the road to the cool mountain resort of Kenscoff, to Madame Max's walled villa. Halfway up the mountain, a set of wrought-iron gates sported a Tontons Macoute hat. It was Rosalie Adolph's scarlet letter. Rosalie was Max. I scaled the padlocked gates.

The abandoned villa had been looted the night before. Furniture was overturned. Engraved invitations to formal dinners and dances were strewn on the marble floor. The guards and servants had fled. The pool, sparkling like an opal in the glare of the Caribbean sun, was fed by a fountain cast as a bronze shark. I knew, looking at it, that she reveled in her cruelty. This is where Madame Max relaxed after her sorties to the Catholic cathedral, wearing jackboots and carrying a bullwhip.

As the bishop said mass, Max stood before the congregation. She surveyed them slowly, from behind her shades, as though they might be edible. She said nothing, fingering her whip, and departing in silence. Everyone knew she had a taste for torture. Her presence in the cathedral, a sanctuary from the dark terror and abject misery of Port-au-Prince, was calculated to impress upon the flock who was omnipotent in Haiti.

"She became a crime addict," mused an old Adolph family friend. "She used to enjoy torturing personally—especially women."

Before leaving her villa, I took a souvenir, Madame Max's false teeth. I imagined her roaming Miami's Little Haiti district in a voluminous habit, clutching a fake passport, and sucking her naked gums.

I had come to Haiti for CBS to assess what was taking shape in the wreckage of Duvalier rule. While I was shuttling between New York and Central America, discontent under the dictatorship had boiled over into the streets. In the blighted landscape of central Haiti, one of the world's most destitute countries, a rebellion broke out in the shabby market town of Gonaïves. Gonaïves was famous for its revolutions. In its dusty streets, the first successful slave revolt in this hemisphere in 1804 drove Napoleon's men from the island. When I walked through those same streets, I was told that the rebels fighting the Duvaliers' army had supernatural powers. Bullets stopped short of their bodies.

Trouble spread north to Cap Haïtien, a sleepy port city of brightly colored villas favored by cocaine traffickers. Riots broke out over the price of cooking oil. Rage spread over First Lady Michelle Duvalier's looting of the treasury, her trips to Paris, the children's charity that she used to launder funds. Michelle brazenly imported Mother Teresa to praise the charity and its benefactress while she was busily skimming cash. When the Catholic priests and the voodoo *houngans* finally threw their weight behind the movement to "uproot" the regime, there was elation and systematic pillaging. Haitian crowds targeted the Duvaliers' thugs and ransacked their houses. Everything was ripped out and carted away, including the bathtubs and the sinks.

I had vivid memories of the old Haiti they were so desperate to exorcise. When I first flew into Port-au-Prince in March 1974, Baby Doc had only recently inherited the mantle of his father and was as yet under the iron fist of his mother. He was slow-witted and frivolous. The country was blanketed with posters enjoining the populous to celebrate the birthday of their "Leader," a strange and potent foreign word for speakers of Creole French to lend stature to Papa Doc's offspring.

I walked through the steamy Port-au-Prince customs hall as a twenty-year-old student, straight into the pages of Graham Greene's *Comedians*. There, waiting for me in his immaculate white suit, was the fey figure of Aubelin Jolicoeur, Greene's Petit Pierre.

Here was the ultimate survivor. Aubelin fussed over me, ordered boys to shoulder my bags, escorted me in his car to the residence of the American ambassador. He prattled in the car, his fine-boned face breaking into an elastic grin like a West African mask. The few words that I had said were printed in full the next morning on the front page of the Haitian newspaper. It was the recurring experience of Greene's owner of the Trianon hotel, the forbearing Mr. Brown. The American ambassador, Hayward Isham, teased me for my innocence. The seasoned ambassador lay on his back in a small sitting room of the grand residence and laughed. *"La jeunesse Américaine."*

Like Brown, I also fell under the spell of the "Trianon," the gingerbread hotel with its fanciful turrets and balconies, its regulars playing backgammon and louche clientele awash in rum punches. The Trianon was the Oloffson. Its owners and impresarios were an American pair, Al and Suzanne Seitz. They created the illusion of an ongoing house party, with the piquant magic of Jolicoeur, fluttering around the hurricane lamps, whispering gossip about a famous voodoo priest or a lady of fashion spurned by the Duvaliers. Just beyond the party and the luxuriant gardens there was always the terror of the Tontons Macoute. Suzanne kept a voodoo priest in residence to ward off evil. People took such things seriously in Haiti.

There was an air of decadence at the Oloffson, like the heavy perfume of jasmine. We dressed for dinner. The waiters served lambi, rich conch, always slightly tough. The band played until well after midnight, when the crowd was leavened with politicians, generals, drug traffickers, and the inevitable spy at the long bar. Suzanne put her foot down when a CIA contract gunrunner tried to recruit her sons with tales of his dark missions and a present of a bomb.

When I returned as a journalist in the choppy wake of the Duvaliers, the backgammon players had fled. Al Seitz had died. Suzanne, her commanding figure striding across the painted wooden floors, was stepping over camera gear and typewriters. With the dusk-to-dawn curfew, the Oloffson terrace was packed with stranded revelers. The reporters downed their drinks and raced to the telex machine. There was always one figure crouched on the stairs, bellowing copy or an update into the only telephone. The caliber of journalist varied from table to table. One English "hack" asked me the color of the presidential palace down the street on the Champ de Mars. It was famously white, like icing sugar. I was tempted to say pink to tip off his editors that he was covering events from a haze of Babancourt rum at the Oloffson bar. He was afraid to go out.

The sound of street battles wafted on the breeze from the port, which smelled of salt and night-blooming flowers. A periodic rat-a-tat of automatic-weapons fire ricocheted through the city.

Suzanne gave me *"chambre onze,"* the coveted Gielgud Suite. These were the same rooms taken by the touchingly naive American presidential candidate and his wife as the Barrymore Suite in Greene's novel. (The candidate had run on a vegetarian platform and was determined to improve conditions in Haiti with vegan reform.) Edwardian mahogany, paintings like childhood dreamscapes, rush mats, counterpanes with embroidered *vèvè*, the delicate tracery of the voodoo signs to summon the spirits, filled the rooms. There was a smell like the inside of a camphor chest and an open-air gallery as broad as the bedroom.

I slept in an outdoor bed draped in mosquito netting where the clamor of Port-au-Prince at dawn sounded like a breaking wave. The verandah formed a corner of the hotel, and where the ends met, there was a cupola, just wide enough for one, suspended over the pool. It was the pool where Greene placed Philipot's body, curled up in the empty deep end, his throat slit. Philipot, a fictional minister under Papa Doc, killed himself rather than face the rough justice of the Tontons Macoute. Now the tables were turned, the Duvaliers and their men had fled. I visited one Tonton Macoute in hiding in Jacmel who had been savaged by a crowd with machetes. He was a minor villain, an extortionist. He would be allowed to live, but the situation was unstable. The Macoutes had burned their denim uniforms but had kept their arms. There was a sizable arsenal at large.

Beyond the pool was the sprawl of city, its architecture frozen in a late Victorian daguerreotype. There were roadblocks on every avenue at night and outbreaks of fighting in daylight. Across the water from the deserted port was the Île de la Gonâve.

In the chaos of the rebellion, cocaine traffickers, who regularly used Haiti as a transshipment point, flew duffel bags stuffed with cocaine over la Gonâve and dropped them on the island. It was a routine drop, except that their coordinates were off and the mysterious powder landed on a rural village with no experience in such matters. When I landed in Haiti, word had just gotten back to the Drug Enforcement Administration regional office in Puerto Rico and its Haitian counterpart in Port-au-Prince that the enterprising villagers were marketing their windfall *trouvaille* of drugs. At first, they thought it was a suitable whitewash for houses. The cocaine's performance was mixed. They then experimented with cocaine foot powder. Again, so-so. Finally, by chance, they found its true purpose: to soothe baby rash. Sales of cocaine baby powder were brisk. The authorities were debating when to move in.

The jubilation that swept Haiti after Baby Doc boarded the C-141 Starlifter turned to restlessness and anger. Where were the trials, the prosecutions of the Macoutes? What were General Avril, an old Duvalier family friend (said to have lavished $150,000 to decorate a bathroom in his villa), Haitian Army chief General Henri Namphy, the "president" of the provisional government (a deal brokered by the U.S. Embassy), and the former minister for public works, Monsieur Cineas, Baby Doc's handpicked heirs to the palace, doing about elections? The walls were painted with patois graffiti, CHAK 4 ANS, every four years, a demand for an election cycle to mirror that of the United States. The city filled with the acrid smell of burning tires.

When the rest of the CBS team arrived, including Jane Wallace and Ingrid Arnesen, a fluent patois speaker with family in Pétionville, the street violence was growing ugly. Truckloads of shock troops armed with suspiciously new weapons and shiny truncheons invaded the neighborhoods. Their uniforms marked them as an elite force, distinct from the regular army. We stood next to the flames of a barricade of burning rubber and watched the mood swing to terror as the trucks appeared and the safeties clicked off the M-16s and Uzis. The crowd began to run. As the troops began to fire, figures stole down alleyways, were snatched into doorways, leapt over walls, crouched under anything that could stop a bullet. We ran. Complete strangers yelled to us, "This way, quickly," and we were guided through the labyrinth of the slums. I asked whose bullets we were dodging. "Leopards!" "Lay-o-pard!" in patois French.

An appraisal of the Leopards' state-of-the-art equipment gave me the sinking feeling that here was a jackbooted force designed to fill the vacuum left by the Duvaliers' departure, and American taxpayers had unwittingly supplied it. I marched into the American Embassy and demanded answers from two State Department officers who had accompanied me to a fashionable Pétionville brasserie the week before. They feigned ignorance. "We have no idea," they swore impassively, "what's going on out there." Their office was minutes from the trouble. All of us knew it was a lie.

At the morgue, I found some of the bodies. One badly wounded man bled to death on the floor in front of me. I was sure there were more casualties. Near a town aptly named Bon Repos, there was an unmarked graveyard known as Titanyan, which had long been used for discreetly dumping *camocan*, troublesome opponents of the regime. Bleached skulls and human bones littered the dust. The skulls rocked in the wind. The only sound was the buzzing flies. There were signs that fresh graves had been dug, possibly paupers or, as I suspected, victims of the Leopards.

Among the political exiles flocking back to Haiti from New York in the wake of the Duvaliers' demise was Jean-Jacques Honorat. With the blessings of the Lawyers Committee for Human Rights, Honorat was determined to open a human rights office near Sacré Coeur church. This was a more dangerous undertaking than he had expected, considering the ongoing bloodshed downtown. Honorat appeared on the capacious verandah of the Gielgud Suite as the Oloffson band was serenading me with their latest composition, "Macoute Mange Ka Ka" ("The Macoutes Eat Shit"), a celebration of the new and fleeting openness.

Jean-Jacques knew Titanyan, the dumping ground for bodies, well. He compared the Tontons Macoute, officially known as the Volunteers for National Security, with the SS under Hitler. Honorat spoke languorously, giving weight to each word. He hissed SS. "Jean-Claude Duvalier used to tell them in rallies, 'You are the backbone of my government. You are entitled to do whatever you want.'" Honorat estimated that fifty thousand civilians had been killed under Papa Doc. One hundred thousand, he thought, had died under "President for Life" Jean-Claude, the dutiful son. "Killing was the only way for the regime to maintain what they called *peace and stability*"—he spat out the words—"the peace and stability that exists in a cemetery. Haiti was a cemetery."

He felt it was an insult to the American Embassy down off Harry Truman Boulevard to suggest that they did not have all the facts about the brutality under the Duvaliers and the Leopards now patrolling the streets below. Haiti was America's best-kept secret, Honorat observed soberly, with the full support of the administration. Baby Doc's government received roughly $100 million a year from Washington, a good portion of which was skimmed by the First Family and friends. Honorat savored the Reagan administration's use of the word "democrat" to describe the young Duvalier.

The very public American betrayal of Baby Doc, in the face of the maddened citizenry in revolt, clawing through the cement walls of a CARE warehouse with their bare hands to loot the flour and cooking oil, was swift. "They are artfully taking credit," laughed Honorat, for the seventh of February, the day of liberation. Given the provenance and loyalty of the Leopards, the public posture was a gesture.

"The Leopards," said Honorat with a faint smile, "were trained by the American military mission, equipped by the American military mission." Their purpose, he said, was to replace the Tontons Macoute. Baby Doc himself was trained as a Leopard. The elite corps was a force of occupation, "to keep the population in peace and tranquillity."

There was shooting that night in Carrefour in the shantytown along the bay-front road that turned west to Léogane. In the morning heat, we threaded our way through the *tap-taps*, the overflowing buses painted with garish scenes of voodoo *tonnelles*, cockfights, saints, old market women smoking their pipes, the snake spirit Dambala, the voodoo maiden Erzulie. Carrefour, normally heaving with humanity at this hour, was silent, like an empty set. The action came moments after we arrived. Truckloads of Leopards roared toward us, enveloped in dust. They were wild-eyed and rigid with tension, as though they were gripping an electric fence. They lurched to a halt, jumped down, and fired round after round into the air. The camera was rolling.

As the soldiers fanned out into the alleyways, the cameraman stuck fast at such close quarters that I waited in horror to see if one would reel and shoot him in the face. His boldness captured arresting footage of savagery. Cracked skulls, bloody limbs, wanton shooting. Ingrid, her face knotted with tension, clutched his back as a shield against the *thwack* of a rifle butt. The thought kept running through my mind: Why are they allowing us to witness this? There was no rational answer. Just by chance they spared us, like insects one decides on a whim not to squash.

I called the *Evening News* foreign desk from the Oloffson and fed the pictures by satellite for that evening's broadcast. I also got through to Ty West, a CBS researcher who was a crack investigator, and gave him the name of an American company involved with equipping the Leopards. The company was called Aerotrade. It could have been in any city, active or defunct. West had a week to find it.

The next morning at dawn, we drove north into Haiti's back country, far off the tarmac Route Nationale No. 1, through villages that could have dotted the West African interior. Houses were roofed with palms and flamboyants, fenced with cactus. We were once more enveloped in dust, careening around deep gashes in the dirt roads from flash floods. Everyone was bad-tempered. Why exactly was I dragging everyone over backbreaking roads into the bush?

"Leslie," the cameraman said, wiping dust-caked sweat from his face, "you always take us to the nicest places."

I was looking for another priest, in a village at the epicenter of the land wars that had ravaged Haiti's Artibonite Valley, the country's rich farm belt. I wanted to see exactly what U.S. policy was protecting, whose interests and why. It was hard to imagine that America had major interests here. The industrial showpiece had been the baseball factory, which was now closed. The Haitian countryside had been stripped of lush forests, the once magnificent stands of mahogany, satinwood, rosewood, cinnamon, cypress, and sassafras, logged for export and hacked down for bags of charcoal sold for pennies by the side of the road. Whole plains were given over to Barbaresque deserts, with giant yucca. The one swath of verdant green was the Artibonite Valley.

One prominent American with an interest in that land was the scion of an expatriate family whose fortunes flourished under the Duvaliers. Butch Ashton was a lanky, strawberry-blond fixture in the fashionable Canapé Verte set, where the villas of the mulatto aristocracy overlooked the American ambassador's pool. His business interests ranged from the Toyota dealership in the capital to Haiti Citrus, an expanding fruit operation targeting ten thousand acres in the Artibonite. Butch had run into stubborn farmers who refused to sell or lease their land. The problem was efficiently resolved by the Tontons Macoute.

This was a region of Haiti uncharted by journalists. I stopped our convoy to film a Ra Ra band snaking through a village, blowing conch shells, playing long hollow *vaccines*, petro drums, and hand-beaten tin horns. We moved off to reach the Catholic church in time for mass. It was Palm Sunday. Through the open windows, we could hear the children singing a Creole hymn set to an African rhythm. Inside they danced, in spotless white muslin dresses, twirling palm fronds. Their priest, Père Grandoit, with the face of a conquistador, perhaps an imprint of a Columbus voyage to the island, was the man I was looking for. Above his starched cassock and neatly trimmed goatee, his eyes were electric blue. Father Grandoit had witnessed the treatment of small farmers who refused to yield their plots to Butch Ashton. We waited until everyone in the overflowing church had taken Communion.

Père Grandoit walked with us into the garden and found some chairs in the shade. He was not accustomed to interviews but began to quietly detail the conditions in his parish under Baby Doc's regime. The peasants, he said, were jailed. They were beaten and "jacked up," a special torture invented under the Duvaliers. "They tie you up. You become like a punching ball. They beat you up all over your body." The priest explained that the Macoute commander of the region had been hired by Haiti Citrus. "The commander was on the payroll," said Father Grandoit. "He was paid every two weeks by Haiti Citrus to keep tight control over the situation. To intimidate and to torture."

We filmed in the citrus groves and talked to local farmers before confronting Butch in his Port-au-Prince office next to the old base-ball factory. Jane asked if he had ever hired Tontons Macoute.

"Never!" swore the American entrepreneur, pounding the table in his office compound. "There have been people"—he paused to select his words carefully—"the mayor of the area, who *happened* to be a Tonton Macoute, who was, in fact, not on the payroll, but he was on a consultant basis."

I thought it was very "eighties" to have a Tonton Macoute consultant.

"You hired Tontons Macoute to protect your fields?" Jane pressed him.

Butch scowled. "Absolutely not."

"Except this one mayor, who was a Tonton Macoute."

"The mayor was a Tonton Macoute, a known Tonton Macoute, agreed," Butch conceded. "But he was the mayor. We were aiming at the mayor. We were looking at the judicial system. Now, if part of the judicial system at the time involved the Tontons Macoute, I don't think we can be responsible for that."

Ashton lamented the passing of the Duvaliers. Even though you had a corrupt regime, he said, you knew where you stood. Today, you don't know where you stand. You don't know what's going to happen tomorrow. You're living day-to-day. Ashton told us he had a lot of U.S. customers and was doing the best he could to convince them to continue to keep the faith, to hang in there. "It's not very easy."

He had arrived in Haiti when he was a year old. All of his eggs, he told us, were in this basket. All of his money. All of his time. He had never stopped to try to count how much he had put in. He was afraid he would commit suicide if he did. Why did he choose Haiti? It was chosen for him by his family. His father came here as an explorer. He came here in 1940 with the State Department. Haiti, insisted Butch, had always looked toward the United States for guidance. Always followed in the United States' footsteps. Always did what the U.S. wanted Haiti to do. "We put Papa Doc in power. We kept him in power."

Ashton remembered the American training of the Tontons Macoute. He told us that in 1961–62, a U.S. naval mission here was supposedly training the army. At the same time, they were knowingly training the militia, the Volunteers for National Security, the Tontons Macoute. "Our weapons, our M-1s, our rejected weapons, were given to the militia, and our new weapons were given to the army. We knew this. We had the actual marines training these civilians. I was here during the whole period. We had something like forty or fifty men, officers of the U.S. Marine Corps in Haiti at the time. And a great part of that was used for training the Tontons Macoute. It was not hidden. It was done right on the palace grounds and in the army training camp, Camp d'Application."

Ashton remembered that the Tontons Macoute were ex-army men, retired or fired, who were used to enforce the laws. Most of them were just the average guy on the street. You had a handful that were very scary. Very. There's no question about that. "Where does the responsibility lie? Should not the United States be prosecuted? We're the ones who put this whole thing in power. We're the ones who set it up. We enforced it. We bankrolled it. We armed it. So, shouldn't we have some responsibility in it?"

I had never heard anyone speak so frankly on camera about the U.S. role. The fact that we had tracked down his own dark secret in the Artibonite seemed to have unleashed this torrent of raw candor that you normally only hear at a cocktail party behind high walls. Ernest Fitzgerald, a famous Pentagon whistle-blower, had an expression for it: committing truth.

Back at the Oloffson, I called CBS in New York. Ty West had found Aerotrade, the company I had been told equipped the Leopards. Aerotrade was in Miami. West had also convinced the owner, James Byers, to talk to us. We flew to Miami with the crew and drove to a middle-class neighborhood with well-tended ranch houses. Byers was surprised we had found him. He volunteered that he had trained and outfitted the Leopards. He had done it, he said on camera, under contract to the CIA.

Everyone seemed in the mood to confess.

"We supplied them with everything," Byers said in a deep lazy voice that flowed like swamp water in the Everglades. "Toothbrushes, handkerchiefs, underwear, socks, shaving equipment." He smiled at his thoroughness. With his meticulously groomed black hair and exposed chest, Byers was the seasoned contract operative. He displayed perfect manners and genuine affection for his work. He had trained them as a counterinsurgency group. "Ex-Marine Corps drill instructors really did a good job on these people. They had a parade after Jean-Claude had become president. When the Leopards came by, it was really something," Byers remembered. "All the foreign ambassadors were there and damned if they didn't stand up and clap."

When we asked whether they were really a first-class counterinsurgency unit, Byers's tone became confidential. "Let me put it this way." He leaned in close. "They were a hell of a lot better than anything else they ever had down there. But now what they are is palace-controlled terrorists. Killing and beating people. That's not what they were trained for. They've taken over what the Tontons Macoute were designed to do. Scare the hell out of the people and keep the people under control."

Byers's companies, Aerotrade International and Aerotrade Inc., had no trouble exporting massive quantities of arms. The State Department signed off on the licenses, and the CIA had copies of all the contracts. M-16 fully automatic weapons, thousands and thousands of rounds of ammunition, patrol boats, T-28 aircraft, Sikorsky helicopters. Thirty-caliber machine guns. Fifty-caliber machine guns. Mortars. Twenty-millimeter rapid-fire cannons. Armored troop carriers. "Supposedly, that stuff was for the so-called threat of invasion." Byers smiled. "But to any nation like that, they're toys. All the dignitaries touch it and look at it and play with it. They were toys." He paused to reflect. "Unfortunately, the so-called toys that we sent and trained the Leopards with were used against the people down there."

The chief executive of Aerotrade delivered expensive gifts to Baby Doc as part of the covert military aid package. One birthday toy for the dictator was a twenty-eight-foot Magnum speedboat. Byers remembered it fondly as one hell of a boat. The dictator, he said, had a ball.

We left the arms trader lost in reverie somewhere in the heyday of the Duvaliers, the era when I first landed in Port-au-Prince, when the elite packed the casinos and clubs, fell giggling into the Ibo Lele pool, played backgammon on the giant board of inlaid wood in the floor of the Habitation Leclerc.

Back at the Oloffson, Jean-Jacques Honorat rested his head on the white wicker and sighed. "The regime hasn't changed. Only Duvalier is absent." The brutal tactics, he believed, would only get worse. "Why?" He smiled playfully. "Peace and tranquillity."

The Haitian human rights activist was so jaded by the alliance of the Haitian military with the Pentagon and the CIA that when a former CIA operative, General Raoul Cédras, fronted for a military coup five years later, Honorat accepted the position of prime minister. His justification was realpolitik. Reform from the inside. Honorat had also used this logic to extract a grant from the Ford Foundation to teach human rights to the Haitian Army. I asked him in his office near Sacré Coeur what he could possibly accomplish. "If I convince one soldier," he said, "not to beat someone to death. Is that worthwhile?"

When the film titled "Haiti's Nightmare" aired on CBS April 30, 1986, the issue of U.S. responsibility raised by the Leopard shock troops crushing skulls at close range was hotly debated in Congress. The film ran again on the congressional closed-circuit television, and the Black Caucus demanded that U.S. military aid to the post-Duvalier regime be cut off. In spite of the tempest, Ashton's fears that Washington was recklessly dismantling the edifice of Duvalierism were, in the end, unfounded. The Leopards shouldered the burden through various military juntas until the resurgence of a militia dubbed the Attachés, who found their mission brutalizing the followers of the populist priest Jean-Bertrand Aristide, Haiti's first democratically elected president.

In the falling light of a spring afternoon in 1986, on the verandah of the Gielgud Suite, the future was as plain as the pattern of a voodoo *vèvè*. We had just extricated ourselves from a teeming mob in the streets, hoarse with rage that the promises of democratic reform from the wedding-cake palace had been smashed by black-booted Leopards. The mob held aloft a Leopard victim whose head had been expertly split open. Blood gushed over his entire face like a ghoulish red Mardi Gras mask. He glistened in the sun. We forced our way through the bodies to an outdoor staircase and climbed for a higher vantage. There was a roar from the crowd below and around us. The eyes behind the river of blood spotted us and fixed on the camera. The crimson arms rose slowly in the air like a crucifix.

SEVEN

Dinner with the
Drug Lords

I N THE SPRING of 1987, I sat in my CBS News office, flooded with sunlight, on West 57th Street in New York. I had a floor-to-ceiling picture window, overlooking the CBS "dairy" across the street and a panorama of the Hudson River. I could see King Kong, the massive inflatable gorilla, clutching the Empire State Building.

I had just returned from Lyon, south of Paris, where Steve Kroft and I were dredging up the terrible history of Klaus Barbie, who was awaiting trial for Nazi war crimes. Everyone in Lyon of a certain age had an exceptional memory for who was a collaborator and who was in the Resistance. I found Barbie's torture victims and convinced two survivors to return to the dank basement, with its slick stone steps and warren of cells, where they had endured unspeakable pain and humiliation, right in the center of the city. I still dream about that place. We collected old photographs of the children of Isieux, orphaned French Jews, and drove back to the farmhouse where they were sheltering from the Nazis before they were hauled away, on Barbie's orders, and murdered.

Poring over interview transcripts with my feet on my desk, I got a call from David Fanning, executive producer of *PBS Frontline*. Would I consider trading CBS for *Frontline*, where I could both produce hour-long documentaries and appear as an on-air correspondent? I accepted the job without a second thought and immediately set about getting CBS to release me from my contract. Andy Lack, my executive producer, gave me his blessing.

Since the *CBS Reports* series was quietly canceled in the wake of the Westmoreland trial (General William Westmoreland sued CBS for a broadcast that charged the general's men with manipulating intelligence estimates in the Vietnam War and withdrew the suit when CBS assured him they had not intended to impugn his patriotism), I had been agitating to restore an occasional slot for prestigious hour-long broadcasts. The truncated "magazine" format stories we were producing were a source of endless frustration, like squeezing an epic into a short.

There was no more appetite for broadcasts like the famous "Harvest of Shame" or "The Defense of the United States." CBS had lost its edge. What was once a stubbornly independent news division had become a tame subsidiary of the CBS corporate empire at Black Rock. Documentaries, in spite of the public relations value of Edward R. Murrow, were a nuisance. If they were good, they caused trouble, an uproar in Congress and editorials in the press. Ratings were famously low, but if the broadcast was controversial, everyone claimed to have watched. This, along with the often direct cause and effect of changing the status quo, was how one measured success. CBS, at this low ebb in the eighties, wanted no part of documentaries. The form was compared with a dinosaur. *Frontline*, based in Boston, was its only permanent habitat.

Defecting to PBS had its drawbacks. The *Frontline* brass lacked the confidence of "network" executives. On the other hand, they were not turning news hours into quick-cut music videos, which was the devastating industry trend. *Frontline* looked to British television for standards and began a partnership with England's Channel 4. My films could air in London as well as in the United States.

The other advantage of the move was that Andrew could join me as a coproducer. A husband-wife team was rare in journalism. We could travel together and double the breadth of any investigation. The most striking consequence of our merger was its effect on interviewees. Hardened criminals, spies, black marketeers, secret police, would appraise the two of us, pause, and ask tentatively, "You're married, right?"

"Yes."

"So, what's it like working together?"

A married couple on hazardous duty was a curiosity, conducive to confidences, intimacies, secrets.

Our children reserved judgment. Chloe was now eight and Olivia three. We traded a Central Park West apartment for a comparatively spacious house in Georgetown and transformed the basement flat into an edit room.

Reconciled to her new surroundings, Chloe expressed her doubts about our career move. "What happens if you both get killed?"

It was not the sort of question you could answer by saying, "Everything is in order."

All the practical arrangements were in place, the doting aunts and uncles who would take charge, the grandparents who would offer ballet lessons and new bicycles. We took precautions. Traveling in a region where an ambush was a real possibility, we never rode in the same jeep. But there was no guarantee of security. Our life was not "gated."

When I was a child, my neighbors booked a cozy stateroom on the first-class deck of an ocean liner. They chose not to fly in the fat Stratoliner that plied the Atlantic route. Flying was risky. A ship was the way to travel in style. The ocean liner was called the *Andrea Doria*. After it sank, investigators pored over the wreckage piecing together the tragic events of the collision off Nantucket. They found the bow of the other ship, the *Stockholm*, had crashed directly into the cozy stateroom. I have never really believed that a sheltered life guaranteed protection.

"We'll be fine."

Chloe regarded us as eccentric, mildly deranged parents. Hearing of each new destination, she would narrow her enormous green eyes and say censoriously, "Don't you know there's a war there?"

"Well, yes," I would say. "Just a little war."

Interestingly enough, while people often ask me if I am worried about leaving my family, no one has ever asked Andrew that question.

When we announced our plans to head for Colombia, to film the inside story of the cocaine cartels, Chloe and everyone else we knew no longer questioned our sanity. They simply changed the subject. I found I could no longer discuss my work at dinner parties. I built a moat of polite conversation.

In 1989, the cartels of Cali and Medellín were locked in a vicious war. At the same time, one ruthless faction of the drug lords had declared war on the state. Colombia was being shredded. Foreigners had fled the country. The violence was triggered by Colombia's acquiescence to the Bush administration's demand to extradite the capos of the cartels to the United States. The "Extraditables" struck back with breathtaking cruelty and firepower. Colombia was a very scary place indeed.

As we dispatched our last will to our lawyer, Michael Kennedy, we were battling with the insurance industry to give us and our film crew protection. "This," our broker said, laughing, "is the kind of coverage we talk about for years at office cocktail parties. I regard this as a personal challenge." Somehow he succeeded. That October, an American journalist traveling to Colombia was the definition of high risk. Andrew was lucky to carry an Irish passport.

Our first stop was Miami. We called Bill Moran, a member of the white powder bar, the high-flying Miami lawyers whose taste ran to Lacoste shirts and crocodile boots. Moran's notorious clients depended on absolute discretion. He invited us to the office. Moran's golden hair and meticulously trimmed beard had gone gray. His watery blue eyes, bloodshot, betrayed his fear. Moran represented the Ochoa brothers, a family of Medellín ranchers, popular in the Colombian region of Antioquia, who controlled a large share of the cocaine business. Moran's partner, whose old desk was in the next room, had been blown apart at point-blank range for an indiscretion.

Moran, adjusting the clean white cuffs of his powder-blue shirt, urged us to exercise the utmost caution. We were entering a carnival fun house, where nothing was what it seemed and no one could be trusted. He was skeptical that we would make it out of Colombia alive.

That night in Miami, Andrew and I decided that Moran's theatrical response to our plans was overblown. He was influenced by his partner's murder. If we ran into trouble, he did not want to feel responsible. We would get cooler advice in the morning from George.

George Morales was a Colombian cocaine trafficker who had the bad luck to land in Miami's Metropolitan Correction Center, the vast prison complex south of the city. George was more often than not in solitary for making bootleg wine and decanting it in the water cooler. He was a champion speedboat racer, a sports idol. He also controlled a drug trafficking organization from prison with a hundred men who would kill at his command.

I had befriended George while covering Central America because of his charitable involvement with the contras on the southern front. He was also heavily involved in the Haiti transshipment end of the drug business. The square, well-built Colombian with his handsome broad face and meticulously clipped beard had been my tutor on the intricacies of the cocaine business. Now Andrew and I hoped George might give us a contact in Bogotá, someone inside this business which was organized like a complex molecule. We had to see him in person; this was not something we could discuss over the telephone.

In a sterile cubicle off the crowded main reception room where convicts huddled with women in tight jeans and spiked heels, George blanched when we told him we were boarding a plane that afternoon for Bogotá. "This is very dangerous," he warned in a cold voice I had never heard the "narco-trafficker" use. "It is the worst possible moment to go as journalists like you." He studied us without expression. "You're a prime target for the *sicarios*," the death squads then engaged in an orgy of killing throughout Colombia.

I told George we did not intend to cancel our flight. "Give us protection," I said, fishing for a response. I knew that, affiliated as he was with the Bogotá cartel, he did substantial business as a subcontractor with the men then terrorizing the country from Medellín. He worked with them, affording us protection, but he was not *of* them. That nuance could save our lives. It meant the sworn enemies of Medellín in Cali would not immediately mark us as part of the enemy camp. The second we set foot at Colombian immigration, the cartels would have detailed intelligence on our movements.

George asked for paper and a pen. He wrote down a Miami phone number and handed it to us. If the phone in our Bogotá hotel room did not ring by eight the following morning with a voice announcing himself as "William," we were to call the number.

We were the only foreigners boarding the Colombian Avianca flight that afternoon, and we were watched with intense curiosity. I was wearing a fuchsia silk jacket and short skirt with green dark glasses rimmed with tortoiseshell. Andrew wore a perfectly tailored Armani suit. An educated guess would have marked us as "in the business," which was the impression we were hoping to convey. If a *sicario* had to pause thinking, "Will I get killed for kidnapping them?" that hesitation gave us enough time to move out of harm's way. In Colombia, you counted the seconds of exposure, from doorway to car door. There was no question of lingering on the street or going out for a breath of fresh air. It was discouraged to leave the hotel Tequendama to walk ten paces to the travel agency next door.

The Tequendama was an Intercontinental in midtown Bogotá, with a wide, very public entrance on a broad boulevard. The advantage was that gunmen could not discreetly shove you into the backseat. The disadvantage was, all Colombia knew precisely where you were going, when, and with whom you were fraternizing. The hotel staff seemed bemused by our appearance. The place was deserted. The emerald dealers were shut.

The call came at eight sharp. "William" dispensed with formalities. He said briskly that he had assigned "one of my men" and a driver to be with us *at all times.* They would appear at noon and would find us. End of discussion. We had just entered the fun house.

Who was William? Was that his name? Why not Guillermo? Were we deluded to trust George? Frankly, on reflection, we had little choice. Contact with the U.S. Embassy, a fortress in Bogotá, was not advisable. The slightest whiff of association with a U.S. government agency, the CIA or the Drug Enforcement Administration, was catastrophic for a journalist trying to penetrate these circles. The Colombian government was helpless to protect us. It was porous, infiltrated at every level by the cartels. Before William's men arrived, we attended a meeting at the presidential palace with one of President Virgilio Barco's young technocrats, an American-educated aide called Gabriel Silva. In the elegantly appointed chambers, the suave Silva looked small and vulnerable. We talked about the bombs, exploding like kettledrums in the city. Silva seemed very nervous for us. "Please," he said with a pitying smile, "take my car."

We slid across the black leather seat of the presidential limousine and sped back to the hotel. There, waiting on the steps, were our cartel escorts, bulging with firepower. We stepped out of the palace car into the backseat of a deliberately nondescript Bogotá cartel sedan. The government was at war with our companions. We had just crossed the front lines.

Our bodyguards were large, fit men who spent their time scanning the streets for danger. They were scrupulously polite and oblique about their associations. All we could discern was that they had been ordered to protect us with their lives. If they failed, they would pay—dearly, it seemed, if their devotion to the job was any indicator. Before making our rounds to find a door behind the mirrors, we stopped back at the hotel room. A bouquet of two dozen Tropicana roses bore the note: WELCOME TO BOGOTÁ. GEORGE MORALES. The "Patrón" had somehow ordered the flowers from inside the Miami prison while he was locked in the "hole," solitary confinement. No phone. No visitors. Incommunicado.

That evening we drove through the deserted streets to the base of the cliff that acts as the town wall of Bogotá and climbed into an aerial tram. The angle of the funicular was eighty degrees up the mountain to Monserrate, a luminous church on the cliff. The tables at the candlelit San Isidro were empty. As we drank neat *aguadiente*, Colombian "firewater," there was a massive explosion below. The sound rolled over the rooftops and ricocheted against the rock face at our feet. We searched for the smoke curling up above the skyline in the city of 6 million. Bogotá stretched for miles with untidy blotches of impoverished barrios, ever expanding its limits, packed with refugees from the guerrilla wars in the Magdalena Medio. Surveying the glittering lights, I realized something was very odd. It was the dead silence, the vacuum of sound. Even the dogs had gone quiet. Tonight, the drug war had extinguished the life of the city. The bomb that had ripped a hole in a city block near the center was the work of a swashbuckling drug lord called Gonzalo

Rodríguez Gacha, known as El Mexicano for his love of a good mariachi band.

Gacha was lashing out at his enemies, both the Colombian government (excluding those on his payroll) and the formidable Cali cartel. By chance, we had a key to the outer gates of Cali. We had befriended a Colombian astrophysicist, a temperate man who thought of little but the origins of the universe. He in turn introduced us to a filmmaker whom I shall call Eduardo. We had much in common including a number of Hollywood and New York friends. Eduardo happened to be a schoolmate of the chief of production of the Cali cartel. The chief of production, he laughed, was a dead ringer for Andrew.

Before setting out for Cali, we had breakfast with Eduardo at the Dann Colonial Hotel in Bogotá's old quarter. Tile roofs the color of burnt sienna, wrought-iron balconies, adobe walls washed with white, ochre, and turquoise, framed the narrow streets. As our bodyguards made camp on the sidewalk, we noticed another set of gunmen bristling with Uzis and AKs. It turned out they were the escort of a Colombian senator who was joining us. The senator was a member of the Unión Patriótica, whose senior membership was being decimated by death squads composed of both Rodríguez Gacha's men and the right-wing vigilantes who trained with them at army camps in the Magdalena. The senator, Pedro Alcantara, came from an old-guard Colombian family who traced their roots to the conquistadors. (Such families, Pedro explained, always adjust their arrival date on the new continent to coincide with the appearance of the first boatloads of Spanish women. The real founding fathers married Andean natives, whose children were of mixed blood.) Among his ancestors were presidents, judges, and the gifted chemists, two brothers, whose discoveries in German labs had revolutionized the processing of cocaine. Pedro was also a *maestro*, a celebrated painter. His works embodied the *violencia* that plagued the country. The ghoulish images of the *desaparecido*, the disappeared, were sprinkled throughout the collections of the Cali cartel, known for their generous patronage of the arts.

The senator offered to introduce us to the Cali cartel's cultural adviser, who schooled cartel executives, including the Rodríguez Orejuela brothers, in art history. This cultural adviser commanded a fee of $2,000 per hour and a Lear jet taxi. When one Rodríguez brother landed in jail in Spain, the cultural adviser was rushed to Madrid to continue his lessons.

The portly tutor was called Alvaro. He had smooth brown skin, almond eyes, and a snowy-white mustache. Alvaro guided the Rodríguez brothers and the Santa Cruz Londono family in making their investments. They bought impressionists, cubists, Picasso, Van Gogh, and a healthy selection of Colombian painters. "The gentlemen of Cali," as the senator referred to the cartel men, had reportedly managed to acquire a Titian from an impoverished Italian Mafia family who paid a business debt with the picture.

The common view in the capital was that the Cali capos were civilized, upwardly mobile bootleggers, whose children—educated at Oxford and Cambridge—would join the oligarchy. Unlike the crude *campesinos* in Medellín who were their hated rivals, the Cali men eschewed violence unless the dispute was a business matter. Cali preferred not to murder politicians, generals, judges, and journalists, on the grounds that the attention was bad for business. If at all possible, Cali bought them. We hoped, as we boarded the 7 A.M. Avianca flight to Cali, that the cartel's reputation for enlightenment and restraint was deserved.

On board we were joined by the senator, his mass of receding white hair suggesting a disheveled Mark Twain. He and his bodyguards, along with everyone else on the plane, placed their Uzi machine guns and Kalashnikovs in the overhead compartments. Having settled in (the squat Uzis fitted snugly in the overheads), the passengers popped corks on bottles of Geneva gin and guzzled it down before landing. There was no one demanding that we place our seatbacks in the upright position and stow our tray tables. Fortified for the uncertainties of a Colombian day, everyone reeled off the plane.

The senator offered us a ride to the Intercontinental, which we gratefully accepted. Having left our armed escorts in Bogotá (they would not enter Cali), we found ourselves in the care of the senator's small militia, being bundled into a silver bulletproof sedan as heavy as a tank. The windshield glass was so thick, the sheets of rain from a cloudburst left the driver completely blind. He roared into town at eighty miles per hour, clearing traffic with a police siren.

Cali was a low-built city with lush gardens and neighborhoods that might have been plucked from Beverly Hills, surrounded by rich coffee and sugar plantations. The oligarchy lived in vast compounds with tall electrified gates and personal armies. They drove dull aging compacts from their homes to the Club Campestra to avoid the constant danger of kidnapping. A few miles toward the Andes from Cali was the town of Santander, famed for being both the pop-up book capital of the world and the kidnapping capital of the world. I suggested to one Cali matron that the kidnap victims might be needed for the pop-up book assembly line, to satisfy the demand.

Once at the club, the elite watched with satisfaction as their daughters displayed their dressage skills on some of the most magnificent Arabians coffee and cane profits could buy. The Mafia, as the Cali aristocracy called the cartel men, were not members. They had been socially ostracized from the Club Colombia as well. Chepe Santa Cruz Londono responded to the snub by building a house that was a replica of the club.

The poor barrios of Cali bred young guerrilla fighters like mosquitoes. Conditions were wretched in Agua Blanca, where a black river of sewage sludge wound its way through shanties on stilts. There were vultures on the banks. Walls were covered in graffiti, FUERA YANQUIS ASESINOS DE COLOMBIA ("Get Out of Colombia, Yankee Assassins"). EPL, M-16, and FARC, all thriving guerrilla groups, were represented. The misery bred restless teenage boys who haunted the open-air pool halls listening to the music of Carlos Gardel. They wore baggy jeans and soft cotton shirts open down their chests. They were *sicarios*, hit men for the cartels, and they died before they saw twenty-one.

As we rumbled in the armor-plated sedan into the Intercontinental, we found ourselves fighting our way through a convention of Colombian beauty queens, the Reinas, stopping over en route to Cartagena. They were a blur of red satin, gold lamé G-strings, and gold leaf headdresses with tropical feathers. Accompanied by their watchful mothers, the queens preened and strutted, hoping to be chosen by one of the cartel men who used the Intercontinental terrace and coffee shop for business meetings. The Reinas'

G-strings sparkled next to the breakfast display of fresh pineapple and crispy bacon.

We set out to find the cultural adviser Alvaro, who lived in a tasteful *casita* with a rare set of John Lennon's erotic drawings on the wall. Alvaro fondly described his patrons, the Rodríguez family, who had amassed billions in the cocaine trade, as a simple proletarian family. Their father was an itinerant billboard painter. He carried a sign that read: PORTRAITS PAINTED. AUTHENTICITY NOT GUARANTEED. The boys took what jobs they could, a delivery boy in the pharmacy and an Avianca mechanic. He described the birth of their business enterprise in Queens, New York, where the brothers sold their cocaine like Avon. "The United States," Alvaro warmed to his theme, "should render homage to those heroes who were able to start what is now the biggest business—bigger even than the oil industry—by selling door-to-door."

They fought their Medellín competitors, the *paisas* from Antioquia, for markets in New York and L.A. The bad blood had thickened into the full-scale war. Cali and Medellín were like medieval Italian city-states, ruled by intractable Montagues and Capulets. Anyone entering Cali was marked by the cartel. Hit men and saboteurs shipped in by El Mexicano and the other Medellín godfather, Pablo Escobar, tried regularly to breach the defenses. When they torched fifty Rebaja pharmacies, one of the legitimate businesses owned by the Cali cartel, they were hunted down and executed.

We were already being closely watched. The cartel was using its efficient intelligence organization in the United States to do a security check. Their concern was any possible link to the DEA (Drug Enforcement Administration) or American intelligence. As I had just written a book revealing that the CIA's hands were not clean on the drug front and together Andrew and I had produced a *Frontline* detailing the marriage of convenience between traffickers and covert operations going back to the Kuomintang in Burma, they were satisfied that we were not agents.

We did, however, make a mistake. Lulled by the hospitality of those on the cartel's fringes, we were coaxed into an unwise intrusion. It was a perfect Sunday. We had joined Eduardo the filmmaker, with his face out of a Goya canvas, at Cali Viejo, an old hacienda that served spicy *ajiaco* soup and *aguadiente* with absinthe. Eduardo stroked his black beard and convinced us to pay a casual, unannounced call on the chief of production of the Cali cartel. We would drop by his home. It was not far.

The impregnable fortress walls told us we had arrived. Eduardo was in a jocular mood. He told us to wait in our car while he went in to announce us. We could hear children and men kicking a soccer ball inside the compound. Our first inkling that something was dreadfully wrong was the odd behavior of our driver. He had covered his head with a cloth. He seemed reluctant to move from a cringing position as he slowly sank in the front seat. His sweat was seeping through the cloth. Four angry-looking gunmen had emerged from the gate. They stood sentry, without moving for several minutes, before Eduardo emerged from chatting with his school chum.

Eduardo, the bon vivant, had lost all color in his face. He looked gray and appeared to be in a state of shock. Our driver was still under the tea cloth.

"Bad news." Eduardo gulped for breath like an asthmatic. "He's going to kill you if you don't leave town in twenty-four hours." More gulping. "He's also going to kill me for bringing you here."

Andrew directed the hooded driver to step on it, and, watched by the killers at the gate, we all thought hard about this nasty turn of events. The chief of production was known to be a man of his word.

We drove to a deserted café and ordered espresso. We smoked. We apologized to Eduardo, who had lost his ability to speak, for invading his town and causing so much trouble. We had put him in such an awkward position. His fate was suddenly tied to ours, mere acquaintances, foreigners, strangers. We had all been sentenced to death. We ordered more coffee. In a wilted state, we retreated to the Intercontinental.

The prospect of being shot the following afternoon made me feel physically ill and then giddy. I reached into my past for the answer to this mess. What would Emily Post, the arbiter of manners, do under threat of execution? She would write a letter, I decided. A self-effacing letter displaying the best etiquette. I would extend my most profound regrets at having disturbed the family gathering and would plead graciously that Eduardo should not be blamed. It was all my fault. And as a token of our esteem, I would send along cassettes of one or two of our documentary films.

I wrote the letter, packed up the cassettes, and sent the peace offering by messenger. We waited. There was one faint hope, which was that the cartel's chief of production wanted to direct. He longed to direct feature films. His hacienda was equipped with the finest home studio cartel profits could buy. If he liked our films, which were beautifully shot and cut, he might give us a reprieve.

Night was falling. We had to plan our next move. Both Andrew and I agreed that if we fled Cali, our film project would be finished. Our fear of death was replaced with fear of failure, which seemed marginally worse. Our mood was black.

Before midnight, we received a message. The chief of production wished to retract his death threat. He extended an invitation to visit his studio on our next trip to Cali. (I had told him we hoped to return to film in December.) "You are," he added with the gallantry that Colombian men fire like a quick mortar round, "always welcome at my house."

Before making contact with the chief of production's reclusive superiors, we would have to wait until December. By then, circumstances had changed dramatically. Cali's sworn enemy, El Mexicano, had launched an offensive so reckless that in spite of his generous gifts to generals and politicians, he had to be stopped. Cali crouched in the shadows while the arc lights were turned on the man with the passion for mariachis. That December, he ordered half a ton of dynamite delivered to the headquarters of the Colombian secret police. The explosion at morning rush hour tore a city block in half. Sixty-three people died. Two hundred were wounded.

It was the first time I had seen an office block with its face ripped off. General Miguel Maza, the chief of the Departamento Administrativo de Seguridad, known as DAS, invited us in to film the damage. On the upper floors of the nine-story building we wandered at will through the rooms without walls. The wind was whipping through the corridors, past staircases hanging in midair, blowing stacks of top secret documents like confetti into the street below. I stood on the edge, dodging glass shards sailing into space, looking down at the convulsion of twisted metal and churned-up concrete that had been morning traffic. Only later did I realize that the pillars supporting the floor I was standing on had been pulverized.

General Maza, with his wide Andean face and parched lips, had been the drug lord's target. The general had a reputation as the only man in Colombia who could not be bribed. He had been probing the insalubrious relationship between Rodríguez Gacha, El Mexicano, and the Colombian Army. In the last assassination attempt, the army had provided details of his motorcade route. Maza was ambushed and survived.

He told us in his slow, thoughtful voice that in his office the blast felt like a small atomic bomb. The bulletproof plate-glass window behind his chair was torn out of its frame and landed on his desk. He had been inches away from being instantly crushed. Two weeks later, the general's men hunted down and killed Rodríguez Gacha, his bodyguards, and his son Freddy. They left a scene of raw carnage. The general found Gacha's bank records, detailing multimillion-dollar payoffs to whole brigades of the Colombian Army.

Cali erupted in celebration. As Colombian television ran pictures of the languid fingers of the corpses being rolled in ink and fingerprinted, the Cali cartel, having emerged as the clear victor in the drug war, rejoiced. The Cali men had not been sitting on the sidelines waiting for General Maza. The cartel's intelligence was better than the secret police. We were told that a go-between called the Navigator shared intelligence with the general.

We received a call from the Rodríguez Orejuela brothers, now the undisputed capos of the cocaine business, welcoming us back to Cali. They guaranteed our security and extended an invitation.

That night, we were collected from the Intercontinental and driven at top speed to a leafy neighborhood of Cali. Our escorts tried to shove a gun in my purse. I had to forcefully object, explaining that journalists don't carry guns. Once armed, you are more likely to be shot. I was determined to behave as though I was a guest at a dinner party like any other. The butler opened the door of the white house with soaring ceilings and a gold Salvador Dalí sculpture in the sunken living room. Our little party was escorted through the Japanese garden to the gazebo. There were a half dozen other guests, all watching a portable TV set with rapt attention. One of the Colombian soccer teams was playing that night in Tokyo.

The guests sipping their Scotches were men you did not want to cross. I flashed smiles at everyone, not knowing which one was my host. The wives wore emeralds. The rustic and expensive gazebo had small figurines scattered around, like children's toys. On closer inspection, I realized that they were rare Inca artifacts.

Suddenly, the air crackled with cherry bombs, let off by soccer fans somewhere beyond the tall hedge. Everyone jumped, including a well-armed knot of gunmen hiding behind the bonsai trees.

Our host was disarmingly young and soft-spoken. The others spoke deferentially. The host called them by their cartel noms de guerre, "the Hindu," "the Black." Our elegant hostess chatted and fussed. She had a turkey flown in from Miami for the occasion, the occasion being the death of Rodríguez Gacha.

A delicate little girl appeared with her nanny and demanded her television set back. Her parents gave in, and moved the party inside, up a spiral staircase to a cozy alcove with another set. We were in a tasteful bedroom with a massive four-poster bed carved from solid white marble. There were shouts and catcalls as the Colombian team lost the match. Andrew and I expressed our condolences. The gentlemen of Cali laughed. They were delighted with the outcome. They had made a lot of money. The team was owned by the Medellín cartel and was therefore, like the corpse with its fingertips smudged with ink, their enemy.

We were asked repeatedly if we wanted to "take a break." It was slang for a snort of coke. We declined. The cartel men did not, as a rule, indulge in their own product. They drank heavily, partly because the butler materialized whenever a glass was half-full, snatching the glass and pouring fresh whiskey into it. This peculiar way of freshening a drink may have been due to the inexperience of the butler, only recently promoted from hit man.

Dinner was served at half past one in the morning. There were rowdy toasts with Lalique glasses raised to commemorate the dead. The guests told "Freddy" jokes, for the son of the deceased drug lord had been pudgy and slow.

Our host reminisced about his last trip to the United States when he had served time for trafficking. He talked thoughtfully about the business, as though we were discussing Exxon or AT&T. He confided, watching us intently, that the cartel's biggest problem was finding "good middle management." It was difficult to teach employees handling millions in cash not to be foolish, buying Mercedeses and New Jersey mansions. We wondered whether he was making a job offer.

In the days that followed, there was a cartel barbecue, a cartel symphony concert and benefit for factory employees, traditional Caleño food at a jammed cartel restaurant, and salsa till dawn at a cartel disco. When we announced we planned to spend an evening in the Amazon and needed to charter a plane, our cartel host offered to find us something. It was only at the airport that we realized we were staring at the handsome pilot and sleek personal jet of the Rodríguez Orejuela brothers.

We had arrived late, thinking that our rented plane would be waiting. There was confusion. The dispatcher explained that the plane had another passenger to collect in Bogotá. We protested that this was our charter. We were paying for it. The pilot realized that we did not fully appreciate that this was a cartel jet. He kindly ushered us to a hangar next door where there was a plane, run by a legitimate commercial outfit, for hire.

While we were socializing with Colombia's most dangerous men, they were ostensibly on the run. The entire Colombian Army was looking for them. Some of their Cali villas had been occupied by troops and stripped of their contents, including the paintings. The general in charge of this operation, famed for his ruthless campaigns against the guerrillas in the mountains of Cauca, was an art connoisseur. General Manual José Bonnet melted at the sight of a Van Gogh. For him, the cartel manhunt, having yielded so many good pictures, was a great assignment. The general, making his inventory, telephoned Senator Alcantara, the Unión Patriótica painter, and teased him about being so "well represented" in the cartel collections.

One day we received an urgent message at the hotel. General Bonnet wanted to see us. We were alarmed. Did he know what company we had kept for the past weeks? Would we be interrogated? Expelled? At headquarters, there were thousands of soldiers in fatigues milling around, some just in from bloody skirmishes in the mountains. We were shown straight to the commander's suite. The general, with his lean, taut face and long aquiline features, looked like something from a frieze on an Inca temple. He shook our hands firmly and directed us to sit down. Before he could speak, there was a blackout. The three of us stumbled around in the dark, looking for matches. The light illuminated his face like a death mask. "I have asked you here because I want to show you something." The generator was switched on and the general lost no time in producing a photograph. It was a handsome building in a town in the banana-growing region of Santa Marta. It was the town hall in the place where the general was born.

The general explained he had a dream. He wanted to found a great library, with thousands of books. He had used his military clout to force the mayor to vacate town hall. The first floor, he said softly, fingering the photograph, would be set aside for folkloric dancers. It was to be a tribute to his father, and the people of the town who had worked for the foreign banana company. When the company had pulled out, they left nothing. No clinic. No school. No books.

Would we be so kind, he asked, to send him some books? He wanted our own books, autographed, and anything else we might recommend. As we sat in the headquarters of the military commander for a vast swath of Colombia, in the middle of the drug wars and the search-and-destroy missions against the guerrillas, hearing about the general's dream of the great library, I thought of Gabriel García Márquez. In Colombia they say he is not a brilliant writer of fiction. He is just a good reporter.

We arrived back in Washington with mounted tarantulas and piranha fish from the Amazon for the girls. The film "Inside the Cartel" was a success. Elaine Shannon, then covering the drug beat for *Time*, called. "One of my DEA guys told me he fell out of his chair when he saw what you got."

This was not our last expedition to Colombia. Two *Vanity Fair* stories would take us back into the labyrinth. Eventually, we became pen pals with the Medellín don, Pablo Escobar. When Pablo was on the run, before he was gunned down by *sicarios*, the Al Capone of his time signed his letters to us with a thumbprint.

124

EIGHT

The Emerald Buddha

W E SPENT CHRISTMAS of 1989 in Ardmore, the Irish fishing village where our bowfront eighteenth-century drawing room sat on the headland like a stone tiara. Its massive walls rose twenty feet above a sheer cliff. From the Georgian windows, one could scan the bay as if from a captain's bridge. On a ledge below was a pre-Christian wishing well of remarkable potency and the ruin of one of Ireland's earliest churches. The thousand-year-old place of pilgrimage was built by St. Declan, who tried in vain to convert the local worshipers of the pagan fertility goddess Brigit before St. Patrick judiciously converted the king.

Ardmore Bay opened to the south, where the treacherous Irish sea met the Atlantic. The cliffs of Ardmore Head were littered with ancient wrecks. Cormorants patrolled the jagged rocks. A mile down the electric-green head, gorse and brambles wound their tendrils around the castle of Ardo, where the ghost of a horseman was sometimes seen riding off the cliff. Ardmore was a place of wild beauty.

Our house was sadly empty, as Andrew's mother had died in the fall. Her Border collie and ginger cat guarded her memory, and Rock House was kept exactly as she had left it.

I had lost a friend in the war in El Salvador, where the fighting ravaged the capital in November that year, counting among the casualties six Jesuit priests and David Blundy. David was a British

125

journalist with handsome beetle brows, the frame of a scarecrow, and a taste for life on the edge. He liked convertibles, late nights, and pranks. David once shoved a hooker through the front door of the Cosmos club, a retreat of the Washington establishment, to kidnap Andrew's brother Patrick. This barely clothed Amazon swept Patrick off his feet, to the astonishment of the members, and carried him out to David's car.

David wrote stories of shocking massacres like the *operación de limpieza,* the "cleaning operation" at Las Aradas on El Salvador's Sumpul River in 1981. He recorded the plight of the abandoned lions and bears in the Salvador Zoo. He stepped, at the wrong moment, into the middle of a deserted street in the capital and was shot by a sniper. His last words in the unforgiving dirt were GET ME OUT OF HERE.

I thought about him as I packed my mosquito net. My next destination was a dank, malarial jungle with exploding butterfly mines sown in the trees. The strain of malaria that had reached epidemic proportions had no treatment and no cure. The chloroquine dispensed by well-meaning tropical clinics was as effective as the quinine in a gin and tonic.

Having just decompressed from Colombia, I was heading off for ABC News to Cambodia, to produce an hour broadcast with Peter Jennings on the resurgence of the Khmer Rouge. With three *Frontline*s on the shelf, I was ready for the comparative luxury of a network production, a pride of assistants, a publicity machine. I was free to choose my subject.

ABC had flown me to New York to "pitch." Jennings welcomed me into his modest fishbowl of an office adjoining the newsroom on West 66th Street. The Ottawa-born anchor, with the build of a Canadian Mountie, ferociously chewed a stick of gum in lieu of a cigarette. He had been converted by a Boston hypnotist.

"So. What exactly do you want to do?"

I ferociously inhaled a Sobrani, a cigarette without floor sweepings. I had been to the same hypnotist.

"Cambodia."

There was compelling evidence that the United States was lending covert support to the Khmer Rouge (whose atrocities while in power in the 1970s ran to killing anyone who wore glasses on the grounds that the offender was an intellectual) in a marriage of convenience so vile it was akin to resurrecting the Nazis. Jennings was intrigued. His executive producer, Tom Yellin, threw his support behind the project, one that *World News* executives bitterly fought. I would need Jennings in Southeast Asia for at least a week. Paul Friedman, who ran the news broadcast, wanted him chained to his desk on the Upper West Side. At the time, *World News* had only just catapulted into first place in the network news ratings.

I flew to Bangkok in early January, calculating that I could research and shoot the piece in six weeks. I would have Jennings for six days, assuming *World News* did not ground him in New York. He would have to touch down in Cambodia, Thailand, China, and Vietnam. It was a punishing schedule. We would split the interviews.

Pol Pot, the leader of the Khmer Rouge, responsible for torturing, bludgeoning, starving, and working to death close to 2 million Cambodians, was living in a comfortable retreat near Trat in southern Thailand, guarded by the Thai Army. His men, who could still count on the aging monster for a lecture on tactics and ideology, were engaged in a vicious guerrilla war along the Thai–Cambodian border. They helped themselves to rockets, mortars, and ammunition from warehouses on Thai soil. They used refugees from United Nations–funded border camps in Thailand—camps *under Khmer Rouge control*—as mules to ferry ammunition to the mine-infested front. There were half a million mines planted in the forbidding no-man's-land. There were no ordnance maps. Camp hospitals were full of patients with blown-off limbs in malarial delirium.

The men who brought us the Killing Fields were once again operating with impunity. One of Pol Pot's henchmen was the recognized delegate from Cambodia at the United Nations in New York, a sickening fact that hardly raised an eyebrow in Washington. Where were the war crimes trials? The position of the Bush White House was that the Khmer Rouge were "a fact of life."

In the twisted world of post-Vietnam politics, the Khmer Rouge were America's ally. They had fought the Vietnamese invasion of Cambodia. In some quarters of Washington the Vietnamese would never be forgiven for their sins. Before leaving for Southeast Asia, I walked into one think tank, a bastion of Reagan-vintage conservatism, on Capitol Hill. There I found an office laden with Khmer Rouge memorabilia, uniforms, photographs, and glossy P.R. magazines, celebrating Pol Pot's troops in both Chinese and English.

The hatred of Vietnam around the tables at the Queen Bee and Pho 75 on northern Virginia's "Ho Chi Minh Trail" across the Potomac from Washington was radiant. It burned like a phosphorous shell, fifteen years after the last helicopter lifted off the U.S. Embassy roof in Saigon.

Who stopped to consider that the Vietnamese move across the border in December 1978 had put an end to the charnel house that Cambodia had become? The Khmer Rouge who stumbled over the border into Thailand were "destroyed," Congressman Chet Atkins told us, "absolutely destroyed. And [National Security Adviser Zbigniew] Brzezinski and the Carter administration made a decision to provide encouragement to the Thais and to the Chinese in their policy of rebuilding the Khmer Rouge as a counterweight to the Vietnamese. So we were there," the congressmen said with profound regret, "from the very beginning."

I called Dick Holbrooke (later the Clinton administration negotiator for Bosnia), who was in the thick of Carter's Asia policy. Holbrooke had tried to negotiate a secret rapprochement with the Vietnamese. It leaked and failed. He was now regrouping on Wall Street and sitting by the phone in Connecticut. He was fuming.

"Leslie, you set me up."

"I didn't."

A few weeks before, Holbrooke had been sitting on my right at my dinner table in Georgetown. Mick Jagger had been sitting on my left. Jagger was in town for a concert which required him to run several miles onstage for each performance. The rock star had been exercising all day and was sipping Perrier. Jagger's passion was politics. He was a keen student of U.S. foreign policy. He had just been reading *Waltzing with a Dictator* about Washington's steamy relationship with Ferdinand Marcos of the Philippines, a work that happened to feature Mr. Holbrooke prominently in a less than flattering light. Jagger loved the book. He recalled anecdotes while Holbrooke studied his leg of lamb.

After I convinced Holbrooke that I had not put Jagger up to it, we turned to the subject at hand, the Thai–Cambodian border in the Carter years. What was Carter's national security team doing?

"We set up Task Force 80," he told me. This was ostensibly a Thai military unit to protect refugees. "Brzezinski wanted explicitly to help the Thais and Chinese on the ground," said Holbrooke. "We had many fights over this."

They fought because helping the Thais and Chinese meant helping the Khmer Rouge. Bertil Lintner, now a distinguished Asia scholar and correspondent for the *Far Eastern Economic Review*, was on the border in 1979 and 1980, working with refugees in the Khmer Rouge camp. The camp leader, Colonel Lim, was a notorious devotee of Pol Pot and battalion leader from Battambang. Lim carried a Task Force 80 walkie-talkie in his back pocket. He was extremely close with the Thai Task Force 80 liaison officer. Task Force 80 headquarters in the border town of Aranyaprathet was always full of American military advisers and intelligence men.

"Task Force 80 was instrumental in rebuilding the Khmer Rouge," Lintner told me. "Remember in 1979 how desperate the situation was along the border. I mean, thousands and thousands of Khmers were streaming across the border into Thailand. Most of them were starving. They had nothing. They were dying like flies in the camps. The whole area was littered with corpses." While aid workers like Lintner went in to feed, clothe, and revive the population, "Task Force 80 had other plans. In June 1980, we saw the first repatriation." One entire camp was dismantled and sent back across the border into Cambodia, to fight for the Khmer Rouge.

American refugee workers descended on the U.S. Embassy in Bangkok to protest. "This is horrible," Lintner remembers them saying. "They're sending these people back to Cambodia under Khmer Rouge command. The kids are going to be soldiers. The women will be porters. And the response from the American Embassy was a blunt 'So what?'"

Brzezinski had said publicly that Washington should cooperate with the Chinese on such matters as "assistance to Southeast Asian efforts to check Soviet support for Vietnamese expansion." The only effort in the works was resurrecting Pol Pot, the man who had extinguished Cambodian society and proclaimed Year Zero.

In his prime, Pol Pot's roster of those to be executed for "counterrevolutionary crimes" included civil servants, doctors, teachers, monks, indeed, anyone who could read. The most arresting footage I saw of Pol Pot's Cambodia was film of a child, perhaps three years old, toddling slowly through the abandoned streets of Phnom Penh. The entire population had been forced, in a 1975 mass exodus, to walk out of the city. People were ordered to leave quickly, bring nothing. They would all be back in a day or two. The Americans were about to bomb. Half a million tons of bombs had already been dropped in the countryside by B-52s, spilling over from Vietnam next door, so the ruse worked. The city's inhabitants poured out like blood from a hemophiliac. The child's solitude is unbearable.

In 1982, two years after Task Force 80 brought the Khmer Rouge back to life, the men who should have faced a Nuremberg trial were given a discreet cover, a coalition, with more benign guerrilla forces. These were the "Non-Communist Resistance" followers of exiles Prince Norodom Sihanouk and Lon Nol, the man who overthrew him. They were so benign, in fact, that their fighting skills were the joke of Southeast Asia. But they provided the sheep's clothing for Pol Pot.

"They really looked like rock and roll guerrillas." Lintner laughed. "They had long hair and sunglasses. Something out of a rock opera. They drove Suzuki motorbikes and didn't do much fighting." When Lintner asked their commanders why they were in partnership with the Khmer Rouge, "They smile and say, 'Well, we have to because the people who support us, they say we must cooperate with the Khmer Rouge. Otherwise, we will get no more arms and ammunition.'"

By January 1990, four months after the Vietnamese withdrawal from Cambodia, the Khmer Rouge Army and their partners of easy virtue were launching offensives that threatened to overrun the Cambodian Army. The Bush administration swore that "there was no evidence" the groups cooperated in the field. U.S. "nonlethal" support of the "noncommunists" had nothing to do with the loathsome Khmer Rouge. If you did not know that the three guerrilla groups had fought together at Sisophon, Varin, T'ma Pouk, and Svay Chek, it would be possible to believe that. No one in Washington expected us to check.

I was met in Bangkok by Satharn Pairoah, a Thai fixer for Western news organizations who had been the consummate guide (iced drinks and perfumed towelettes on all road trips) in 1988 when Andrew and I had filmed for *Frontline* in Udorn, four hours north along the Mekong. We had tracked down Tony Po, a legendary CIA man, regarded by his colleagues as the model for Marlon Brando's Captain Kurtz in *Apocalypse Now*. Po had carved out a wartime kingdom in the remote rain forests of North Laos, where the mist hung in great slabs over the triple canopy. Vertical walls of limestone karst soared over the matted jungle. Lord of all he surveyed, Po was a godlike figure to the tribes who followed him. He strung necklaces of severed enemy ears as trophies on his verandah. When the U.S. Embassy in Vientiane pressed him for a body count in his secret mountain war against the Pathet Lao, a war that raged alongside Vietnam, Po sent down a box of severed heads.

Now Po liked to drive his antique yellow Austin to the local hotel and drink Mekong whiskey overlooking the pool known as the Bay of Pigs. When he drank too much, he recited the Roxane speech from *Cyrano*.

Thailand was littered with retired American servicemen and spooks who chose to remain after the war. The Thai military had strong bonds to men like Tony Po, who trained them. Thailand had been a staging base for Vietnam. The Thai military had been active in U.S. covert operations. In January 1990, when I checked into the Oriental Hotel, tables were filled with Americans from the vast embassy compound that was still one of the largest embassies in the world.

There was a bamboo curtain between the exploding economy of Bangkok, with its Mercedes limos equipped with wet bars and cell phones, black market cassettes fresh from Hollywood, fake Vuitton bags, arms deals, heroin deals, ruby deals, and the stagnant economies of Vietnam and Cambodia. The United States still maintained strict sanctions. There was no flight to Cambodia. One had to board a Vietnam Air flight, where "first class" was an old sofa, for Ho Chi Minh City, better known as Saigon.

As Satharn and I braced ourselves for landing, I saw great clusters of bomb craters, still visible in the high grass, from American bombers that had dropped their excess load before returning to base. Walking into customs was like entering a time machine. It was 1975, or perhaps 1957. The graceful French colonial edifices of Saigon were cracked and listing. The place had a faded, sepia tone feel. It smelled of old vegetables and wet rot, and was hauntingly beautiful. There was the occasional stuttering sound of a moped and the rasping brakes of a hundred bicycles. We wrangled a car from the Vietnamese government and drove up Route 1, past the flooded paddies and market towns that had once been the province of the Vietcong.

We crossed the Mekong on a ferry of logs. The horizon was dotted with sugar palms. Pagodas and stupas marked the villages. Phnom Penh was low-built and decayed. The quiet was jarring, a city with so few cars that the jingle of a bell on a "cyclo," the bicycle cabs that cruised the dusty streets, caught your attention. We headed for the Sukalay Palace, a modest Deco walk-up pension. The Sukalay served iced coffee with condensed milk and stood strategically across the street from the only working telephone in Phnom Penh. The telephone office was a bare room with one operator making desultory dialing motions between conversations with friends. It was sometimes possible, with an hour or two of badgering, to reach Bangkok. A call to the United States was out of the question.

We heard a rumor that there was a fax machine at the post office. I arrived there to find a fax form and an attendant with a price list. With cheerful efficiency, I handed over the fax and paid. I announced with some satisfaction to a British diplomat passing through that I had conquered the communications problem and sent a fax.

"Look, I'm awfully sorry," the diplomat said, taking another gulp of my stash of gin. "I'm afraid you haven't. You see, that's my fax machine and I only lent it to the post office. Now the prime minister's nicked it."

The post office went on happily accepting fax requests for weeks. I stopped in one day to find a forlorn French agronomist asking whether they were absolutely sure a fax had not arrived for him. It was very urgent. Like a messenger in a Samuel Beckett play, I had to break the disappointing news that the machine was gone.

Satharn and I quickly established our headquarters at the lakeside

Bangkok II Restaurant, famed for its turtle eggs and cobra stew. I showered at the Sukalay with three bottles of Evian. There was an exhilarating sense of being cut off, unreachable, and under siege. Curfew was nine o'clock.

My main task was to convince the Cambodian minister of defense, General Teh Banh, to open up the west of Cambodia, which he had summarily sealed off to journalists. He argued that reporters were security risks wandering around the war zone. The Khmer Rouge guerrillas were launching attacks regularly in Kompong Speu, thirty miles from the capital. Battambang, the city closest to the front, had been burned, shelled, infiltrated. It was down the road from Pailin, now in Khmer Rouge hands, where there was a treasure trove of rubies and teak to pay for the war effort.

General Teh Banh had been refusing to see any foreigners. I was in luck, however, for he was a great admirer of Satharn's girlfriend, a Thai investigative journalist called Rungmanee Mekhasobhon, whose letter of recommendation I carried with me. The general received us at home. He was polite but firm. No one went to the west. I explained that Peter Jennings was the most important newsman in the United States. The general was not impressed. Finally, I asked him if he would join us in a trip to the front. This changed everything. Yes, we would go together. The roads were impassable but there was a plane that might be available for rent. Someone might shoot down the plane but that was the risk we would have to take.

When the camera crew arrived in Bangkok, we wasted no time getting out to the border. We checked into the Bungalows in Aranyaprathet, a collection of noodle shops, aid agencies, and dealers in stolen Cambodian antiquities. Here, our movements were watched by Khmer Rouge intelligence, Thai intelligence, and a Defense Intelligence Agency colonel whose job title here was adviser to the U.N. border relief operations.

The border was sealed off from unwanted scrutiny by a Byzantine system of permissions. We needed passes every time we moved. Yet, if we wanted to do something illegal, like slip across the Cambodian border, it all depended on our escort. I had left an assistant in Bangkok to woo the spokesmen of the Non-Communist Resistance. Carole Difalco was a lissome blonde who lived on chocolate milkshakes and was a smashing success with the Khmer Peoples' National Liberation Front. The KPNLF was famous for its corruption. The generals all had American passports and houses outside L.A., in Orange County. Their camps were sinkholes of porno festivals, grenade markets, and rackets of every description. Carole convinced them to take me to the front lines through a stretch of guerrilla-controlled territory twenty miles deep inside Cambodia touted as the "liberated zone."

I had an exceptionally seasoned crew, the same cameraman and soundman who teased me in Haiti about taking them to the "nicest places." The soundman, George Bouza, was very nearly lost in the liberated zone. My concern at the outset of traveling "inside" with the KPNLF was that their reputation for incompetence on the battlefield put us in jeopardy. I was relieved to see Thai soldiers, phantom troops who did not officially exist, fighting alongside.

We loaded up our sleeping bags, mosquito nets, army-issue repellent, army MREs (meals ready to eat), and camera gear at the Bungalows. We left Carole and the KPNLF handlers on the border and drove in a jeep through a forest of scrub. The dust was a foot thick on the road. As we bounced and pitched along the dirt track, the dust settled on our skin in a thick film, stuck to the repellent. Dust worked its way into the grooves around the camera lenses. Dust made the cassettes seize up, as did the slow-oven temperatures after dawn.

Our jeep stopped at the guerrilla base camp just inside Cambodian territory. There were wooden sheds, sleeping quarters, a crude kitchen. To move from kitchen to shack to outhouse, there were single-file paths. Step off the path, stumble, slip, and you were in the most heavily mined territory in the world. There were troops in American camouflage uniforms milling around, gaunt men with leathery skin and ammo belts smoking Thai cigarettes.

There was a general present, a jovial figure called Pann Thay, wearing shades and a dashing scarf. As we loaded our gear onto a small flatbed truck, the general offered us Hennessy brandy, supplied, he told us proudly, by the U.S. Embassy. A few days before, two mines had exploded under a truck like ours on the same dirt track. One killed, two wounded. We squeezed into the open truck, jostling with rocket-propelled grenades, Kalashnikovs, American

M-16s, M-79 rocket launchers, and recoilless mortars. (The State Department maintained that the American weapons were made in Singapore.) General Pann Thay led the way on his motorbike. We were soon enveloped in a cocoon of white dust. The soldiers with us seemed resigned to their lot. Some had been in the field ten years.

We arrived at nightfall at a second camp, with a dormitory hut lined with canvas cots. I was, needless to say, the only woman in the camp. As I climbed under my mosquito net, I could hear heavy-weapons fire in the distance. I felt vulnerable, knowing that this territory could fall to the other side in a sudden attack. It was a toss-up between a rocket landing in the camp and a mosquito, infected with cerebral malaria, dive-bombing my net. I checked the net carefully for tiny snags.

We set out an hour before dawn. I was offered the seat of honor in the cab of the truck but made my excuses and climbed into the back. A land mine under the front wheel will blow up the cabin first, I thought. In back, there is a chance of getting away with a light wound. I had a special first-aid kit with painkillers and antibiotics.

As we drove deeper into Cambodia, the forest gave way to open fields. We passed the odd farmer or peasant woman, wrapped in a sarong, balancing water cans on a bamboo pole. When they saw me, a blond woman in the back of a military transport, they dropped their loads and stared. General Pann Thay was much amused by this. "We are calling you the First Lady of Liberated Cambodia."

Passing the market town of T'ma Pouk, I saw a Khmer Rouge soldier cross the road. When the village of bamboo huts was captured by the "Non-Communists," seventy Khmer Rouge soldiers came with them. The Khmer Rouge in their Chinese green uniforms stayed behind to "maintain order." We were not allowed to stop in the village to film. "Pressure of time," we were told.

As we moved out from T'ma Pouk, the sound of field artillery grew louder. Both sides were exchanging fire. The lines were on the edge of the village of Svay Chek, which the guerrillas had just taken from the Cambodian Army, much to General Teh Banh's annoyance. The guerrillas were touting Svay Chek as their most important prize in a decade of fighting. We arrived in the village to find dozens of soldiers and two precious tanks. Civilians had been cleared out. The cameraman headed for the artillery blazing away, to get a close-up of the guns jumping and spewing smoke. After a heavy barrage of fire from our side, there was a pause. A deafening silence.

One of the tanks heaved down the road, expecting return rocket fire at any second. The driver was panicked and there were too many soldiers hanging on. George, the soundman, flipped off the back of the tank, still connected by the cable to the camera above. With the roar of the tank engine, no one could hear him scream. George was dragged through the dust, tangled in the cable. Finally, the cameraman's curses to "stop the fucking tank" were passed down the line to the driver. A shattered George was hauled on board and the tank moved out as the first rockets fell on Svay Chek.

They whistled all around us. The whistle is the most terrifying sound I have ever heard, as though the sky is ripping. The rockets were coming in fast from multiple launchers. There were dug-out shelters everywhere in the village but they were of little use. A rocket will plow right through it. You are as safe lighting a cigarette in the middle of the road as you are cowering in a trench. The noise is everywhere. There is no front and no rear with the rockets raining down. You cannot see the rocket itself until it explodes.

Our truck stalled in the center of Svay Chek. The engine coughed. The rockets thundered down. We had the footage and I was ready to leave. I did not intend to die for the Khmer Peoples' National Liberation Front. The engine convulsed. As I climbed onto the back of the truck with the whoosh of a rocket to my right, I raked my leg across the tetanus-rich metal of the flatbed and started to bleed all over the place. The truck lurched, and we trundled down the road as a soldier kindly dressed my wound.

Peter Jennings arrived in Bangkok the next evening with Tom Yellin, his executive producer for the series. After a fifteen-hour drive from the front lines, we met them at the Oriental Hotel, a paradise of crisp sheets and purple orchids sent up with the starched shirts. They had flown first-class from New York and seemed edgy. They were not entirely committed to the story. They might want to fly back the next day. Peter inspected the gash on the underside of my thigh.

"Well, you can certainly dine out on that."

They wanted to see the footage. I excused myself and called Andrew in Washington in a rage. He gave me advice. "Just tell them that you want to go home too. Right now." Downstairs, I met Jennings and Yellin in the lobby and said just that.

"No, no. We want to stay," Peter insisted.

"Really?"

"Yes."

"Fine," I said. "Let's get in the car. We're heading for the border. It's a three-hour drive. Your first interview is at midnight. We'll cross the border into Cambodia tomorrow at four A.M."

In the car, Tom Yellin handed me a care package from Andrew. Inside was an issue of *European Travel and Life* magazine with a piece about the Blackwater Valley in Ireland. The photographs by Erica Lennard were of five-year-old Olivia running along the cliff walk by the Holy Well and ten-year-old Chloe draped on a chaise longue at Castle Doddard. I had been away from home for nearly four weeks. I had to remind myself that taking on the monstrous Khmer Rouge and the covert operators who were their lifeline was worth the separation. The Khmer Rouge control of border camps, their seat at the United Nations, their acceptance by Washington were shocking. Of any story I had ever tackled, this was the most appalling injustice. There was a real chance that the Khmer Rouge would seize power in Cambodia again. I had the opportunity to stop it.

"So," said Jennings waspishly, "you have to read about your children in a magazine."

I took a deep breath and held my temper. The mood in the back of the car was glacial until we reached the Bungalows, our seedy border motel. Susan Walker was there to meet us. Her father had been one of the legendary covert operators in Laos in the Air America days. Susan was the very sober local director of Handicap International, then doing brisk business in the Cambodian camps. Refugees allegedly under U.N. protection who were ferrying ammunition for the guerrillas joined the queue for a Susan Walker prosthesis. The amputees were a staggering problem. Among the hidden camps under the control of the Khmer Rouge was one reserved for five hundred amputees. The land mines were maiming a generation. Walker made it abundantly clear that there were 300,000 refugees on the border, in camps controlled by military factions, against their will, many being forced at gunpoint back into the war. The United Nations was little more than the mess hall caterer and infirmary staff for these armies.

Jennings suddenly saw the point.

"Could the United States have done more in the past few years to inhibit the rise of the Khmer Rouge?" he asked Walker.

"The flag that flies at the United Nations is the Khmer Rouge flag," she answered with a smile. "The representatives in New York, Paris, Bangkok are Khmer Rouge. They are not members of the other parts of the coalition government."

"Seen from the ground level," Peter asked, "have the Khmer Rouge changed?"

"No."

By 2 A.M. Jennings had forgotten all about New York.

At 3:45 A.M. I stumbled out of my bungalow half-dressed to find Peter in well-pressed khakis ready for the day. He was irritatingly chipper. "You're barefoot," he observed.

"I know I'm barefoot." I roused the others, and our convoy plowed down the rutted track to the base camp. As we crossed into Cambodian territory, Peter was tense.

"How far in are we going to go?" he asked.

"If Paul Friedman knew what I was doing right now, he would kill me," I said curtly. "We'll stay close to the border."

He looked wary. "Tom says you're not afraid of anything."

We reached the camp at first light. Peter stepped off the path intent on finding some privacy to pee.

"I wouldn't do that," I cautioned. "You're stepping in a minefield." He froze, walked gingerly back to the path, and accepted the public nature of his predicament.

Just then a Suzuki came roaring up with two generals on board. Pann Thay was chauffeuring the top general of the KPNLF, General Sak Suk Sakhorn. Both were so encrusted with dust, they had thick white brows and lashes. The obliging Sak, a Californian, ordered several bowls of noodles from his cook. I had crammed the jet-lagged Jennings with facts and questions for Sak. In the interview Peter spewed out the names, places, and dates as fluently as a Cambodian scholar. He was, without question, the most talented interviewer I had ever seen. An interview is like a dance. It requires agility, grace, concentration. The stage is framed by the camera. Even in a dusty barracks, there is electricity inside that frame, the chance that something remarkable will be recorded. Peter used every pause, every hesitation in the general's voice, to probe for deception. He asked questions with cool authority. For a second, while the camera was turning, there was the illusion that Peter was the general's superior officer, entitled to some answers. General Sak admitted that wherever his troops were, the Khmer Rouge were not far behind. He confirmed there was coordination between Prince Sihanouk's forces and the Khmer Rouge. He admitted receiving covert aid from the United States.

When Jennings asked General Sak how often he reported to the Cambodian Working Group at the U.S. Embassy, a relationship the embassy was loath to admit, the general answered that he did so once every month or two, depending on the need for arms and ammunition.

"You go to the Cambodian Working Group and you tell them what weapons you want?" Peter asked casually.

"We explain what we need," Sak confirmed.

Mr. Jennings had just won my esteem.

The U.S. Embassy was in a panic. The Cambodia hands there knew we were asking awkward questions. They declined our requests for interviews with anyone in the vast walled complex, including the janitor. The excuse was they were on Washington's leash and had to obey their gag order. We must take our questions to Washington. I notified them that Jennings would be submitting written questions *by hand and in person.*

When we arrived at the main embassy gate, Peter jumped out and the camera began to roll. He knocked on the door. He waited. The marine guard stared at the star of television news loitering patiently on the sidewalk. The door opened. The embassy began hemorrhaging officials onto the sidewalk. Peter delivered the letter demanding a written response. The officials did their utmost to make it look as though they always received their important guests on the sidewalk. Wasn't this a nice surprise. It would take three months for the State Department to summon the nerve to respond.

We drove south along the border to the Khmer Rouge camps that clung like barnacles to sheer mountain cliffs dividing Thailand from Cambodia. The rock face was carved into freakish shapes by the wind. At the back of Site 8, with thousands of refugees crammed inside its perimeter, effectively prisoners of the Khmer Rouge, the peaks rose into a gaping mouth of limestone, where the wind made a wailing sound like women mourning their dead.

Site 8 was a U.N. camp, paid for by U.N. donors, with Khmer Rouge administrators and police to make sure no one escaped. Inmates were subjected to Khmer Rouge discipline, watched at all times. Children were encouraged to spy on their parents. The camp that on paper was pledged to shelter civilians from this ugly war was openly used by Khmer Rouge guerrillas for R&R. They sauntered through the crowded alleyways in uniform. They lay in the hospital, shivering and moaning, dying of cerebral malaria. Their weapons porters hobbled on crutches, dragging their stumps. U.S. Department of Agriculture rice was feeding the troops.

Under the mountain, a path, well worn by the refugees, led to one of the "satellite camps," hidden from the already perfunctory oversite of the U.N. Border Relief Operation. There were thirty to sixty thousand refugees in the satellite camps. There were no doctors, no observers. There was an outbreak of polio. Dozens of captive children died or were crippled. Some finally appeared in Site 8 one day, inflamed with fever. Most of them were already living dead.

Back in Bangkok I had tea with the Khmer Rouge. These were senior officers who frequented one of the expensive hotels in the city center. Pol Pot's lieutenants were the coldest men I have ever met. Their eyes were dead. It was as though the sight of so many corpses, so many dumping grounds littered with bones, had seared their retinas. They were wary of us. We were the enemy, threatening to upset their gravy train. We infiltrated their army, in the end, by signing up a Thai cameraman who was a Khmer Rouge fellow traveler. In his spare time, the cameraman moved arms stashed around Aranyaprathet to dumps inside Cambodia.

We caught the weekly Air France flight to Saigon and checked into the Continental Hotel. The Continental had huge airy rooms with French doors and little pink soaps. It had fallen into disrepair after the war and was only recently refurbished. My room looked across the broad avenue to the Caravelle, the headquarters for the foreign press until they boarded the choppers in 1975. I walked with Peter to the abandoned U.S. Embassy, which had been the scene of such turbulence and panic at the end, with Vietnamese whose loyalty to the Americans made them marked men, clamoring over the walls to get a ticket to Arlington.

The embassy was wide open. The paint was peeling. The drive was buckling with weeds. I imagined Henry Kissinger and General Westmoreland stepping out of their official cars, marching resolutely past the marine guards, so spit-and-polished a visitor could see his reflection in their shoes.

Saigon was impoverished now, with little in the way of nightlife. I chose an open-air restaurant along a canal, with an exceptionally attentive staff. Vietnamese officials loved this place. After we had taken our seats on a verandah overlooking the gardens, a bevy of ladies in painted silk dresses descended on Peter and Tom, adjusting their chopsticks, laying their napkins, pouring their drinks. Just as I was tucking into a bamboo shoot, thinking how marvelous the service was, Tom began shifting in his chair. He whispered to Peter. Both began to squirm. Tom suddenly announced, "We must leave." He had the prim expression of a dowager who has wandered into a strip club.

"Why?" I blurted out, missing every cue.

"Because," said Peter, exasperated by my naiveté, "this is a brothel."

"Oh, well, right." I blushed with embarrassment. "How about the roof of the Rex?"

We sped downtown. Tom announced he would retire to bed. Peter and I walked past shops selling sour plums, bottled lizards, Limoges china hawked by French colonials, to the Rex Hotel, once used by the U.S. military as its headquarters. The hotel had a handful of depressed-looking Japanese businessmen and a creaky elevator to a roof garden. There were topiary trees carved into fantastic dragons and an open-air bar that stocked bad wine and tolerable gin. They were waiting, patiently, for the world to come back to Saigon.

We drove up Route 1 past the tunnels of Cu Chi, where the Vietcong high command dug their headquarters, complete with bedrooms, dining hall, and kitchen underground. To earn cash, the Cu Chi guides had set up an AK-47 firing range beyond the punji stick trap. The Route 1 rice paddies were a shock of green, like an Irish field. The foot traffic was so heavy, we crawled along behind wooden carts, water buffalo, straw hats and black pajamas spattered with mud. At the border crossing we filled out forms asking for every detail of our baggage and currency in triplicate. I watched with interest as one bored customs official, fingers smudged from carbon paper ink, picked up a stack of the precious documents and threw them in the bin.

We were met at the Sukalay Palace by Chai Song Heng, our diminutive translator, who looked like an extra from *The Year of Living Dangerously*. We drank coffee with condensed milk, heated in the can, and listened to the BBC World Service, our only link to the outside world. There had been sporadic Khmer Rouge attacks in the countryside and rumors of an offensive against Siem Reap, home of Angkor Wat. We set out for the Red Cross hospital at Kompong Speu, where the Khmer Rouge had been sighted in the dense jungle outside the town. The wards were full of wounded, some with gunshot wounds, others with bloody limbs from mines, both in the fields and strung in the trees. The children's wing was little more than a fly-infested morgue. (When we aired the gut-wrenching footage of those children, the State Department caustically joked that I carried my own supply of flies.)

We were only twenty kilometers from Choeung Ek, where in the 1970s the Khmer Rouge exterminated seventeen thousand men, women, and children and threw their bodies into open pits. At Choeung Ek, we found bits of clothing still stuck to the bones. Skulls peered through the glass of a towering pagoda. Cambodians believed that because there had been no proper funerals for the dead, their tortured souls haunted the countryside.

Meeting Hun Sen, the Cambodian prime minister, and his cadres eroded any confidence we had that they could keep Pol Pot's men at bay. Hun Sen wanted a deal. If only Prince Sihanouk would return from exile in Beijing and renounce his partners, the Khmer Rouge. Sihanouk had the people's affection. He was the acceptable face of the guerrillas. If he switched his allegiance, the Khmer Rouge might wither and die.

Our Kampuchea Airlines charter to the front appeared at the deserted airport on Friday morning. Teh Banh, the defense minister, seemed pleased with the arrangements. The charter was an aging commercial airliner. When we boarded, we found almost every seat was taken.

"Who are all these people?" Peter demanded.

The defense minister shrugged. They all had urgent business in Battambang. We scrambled for a seat.

We flew over Tonle Sap, Cambodia's vast lake, and railway lines that had been dynamited repeatedly by the guerrillas. The roads below were washed out and overgrown. The captain circled Battambang checking for hostile fire. When we landed, the defense minister commandeered a bus and we chugged along past intricately carved pagodas and monks in saffron robes under black umbrellas. The front line was a field with a dike and gun mounts. As we walked along the dike, there was the *pop-pop-pop* of automatic-weapons fire from the tree line. We were on the outskirts of Cambodia's second-largest city.

Prince Sihanouk's royal palace in Phnom Penh was empty. The walled compound, several acres wide, was going to seed, with roosters scratching the dirt. The courtyard walls were covered with breathtaking murals from the fifteenth century. The palaces had soaring rooftops, like flames licking the stone dragons and massive carved heads with four faces, the symbol of deception, the weapon of the Khmer Rouge. An inner courtyard led to the silver pagoda covered with five thousand silver tiles. It was also called the Wat Preah Keo, the Pagoda of the Emerald Buddha.

Above the tarnished silver floor, a massive emerald Buddha towered over a second Buddha of solid gold. The room was lined with musty display cases, each with a priceless treasure fashioned from gems, rubies, and sapphires beyond the dreams of avarice. The Khmer Rouge boasted that they had not plundered the Wat Preah Keo. The government of Hun Sen, desperate for cash to buy rice and medicine, had refused to sell even one jewel. They behaved like the end of an aristocratic line, with buckets lined up end-to-end under the caving roof, hoarding the family pictures.

A Vietnamese charter arrived on Saturday to take Peter out of Cambodia en route to Beijing, to interview Prince Sihanouk. The night before, we sat on my balcony at the Sukalay Palace drinking passable French wine from the cellar of the Bunkok and reviewing questions. I wanted the prince to admit both that he harbored Khmer Rouge with him in China and that he shared weapons in the field. The next morning after the charter took off from the other- wise empty strip, Chai Song Heng returned from the central mar- ket with two dozen Cambodian roses.

"From Peter," said the tiny man.

The Sihanouk interview was devastating. The prince had the high-pitched voice of a young boy. He squealed with excitement. He was like a society gossip, incapable of keeping a secret. "Some- times," he said conspiratorially, "the CIA gave weapons to the Non-Communist forces. You know, your government and the CIA are not cooperating with each other. Your government, perhaps, ignores what the CIA might do." His other source of arms, he volunteered, was the Khmer Rouge. "They gave, from time to time, heavy weapons and ammunition to my army. We are fighting side by side."

"It is said that even in this house," Peter pressed the monarch, "you are something of a prisoner. The Khmer Rouge have repre- sentatives in this house who watch over you and who really don't let you operate freely. True? Wrong?"

The prince let out a high-pitched cackle. "Oh, no. It is very wrong. Very untrue. There is just one Khmer Rouge with me. And I never allow him to dictate anything."

The film aired in April 1990. Prince Sihanouk told Nayan Chanda of the *Far Eastern Economic Review* that after watching it, he made the decision to return to Cambodia. In Washington the film hit like a Svay Chek rocket. Congress immediately broke the em- bargo to release millions of dollars for aid to Cambodian children. Senate Majority Leader George Mitchell convened a closed-door hearing. A State Department official brought in to explain the cozy relationship with the Khmer Rouge was badly mauled. Secretary of State James Baker drove to the White House and advised President

Bush that U.S. policy had to change. Covert funding must stop. Baker prevailed.

The broadcast, which was showered with awards, changed history. In July, after Baker stormed the White House, Peter called me in Ireland. He suggested we put in a bid for the Nobel Peace Prize. It was a very fragile peace.

But another war was on the horizon. In less than a month, in August 1990, a tiny oil state on the Persian Gulf would be invaded by its neighbor. This would trigger an American war, the first major conflict since Vietnam. As the first U.S. troops poured out of C-141 troop transports and dug into the Saudi Arabian desert, I was with them.

N I N E

The Patriots

Y OU—" the immigration officer glared at me, broke into guttural Arabic, and pointed emphatically toward a row of plastic bucket seats.

"Sit."

I forfeited my place in the long line that snaked through an antiseptic corridor of the Riyadh airport in Saudi Arabia to pay for my bad behavior. I was traveling alone without a male escort. Even worse, I carried a visa with a work permit. The immigration officer looked at me as though I were a virus. Had he known that I was smuggling two bottles of Sancerre wrapped in Victoria's Secret underwear, he would have summoned the police to have me publicly whipped.

I had made an effort to get the uniform of *hejab,* Islamic dress, just right. I wore a white linen skirt which covered my ankles, a long-sleeved jacket covering my wrists, a high-collar shirt, thick stockings, and head scarf. I was ready to swelter in the 130-degree heat of an Arabian August. A breach of the dress code, a flash of ankle, and the Mutawah (the religious police) had grounds to beat me with their truncheons.

I sat, stood, argued, and sat again until the local fixer hired by ABC News arrived to release me.

I had landed in the first wave of journalists to enter the kingdom in the summer of 1990, after Saddam Hussein invaded the tiny oil enclave of Kuwait. American troops were pouring into Saudi Arabia's eastern province, just south of the Kuwaiti border. General Norman Schwarzkopf was due to arrive any moment. The Bush White House had drawn a "line in the sand," shielding Dhahran, the Saudi oil capital, from Saddam's grasp. The Iraqi leader, we were told, might turn south, rolling across the sandy wastes with Russian T-72 tanks, capturing the oceans of black crude just under the surface. National security interests were at stake.

I was in Saudi Arabia for an ABC Peter Jennings special, "The Line in the Sand," due to air in September. My assignment was to produce a military segment, assessing the state of the troops and their equipment. The Pentagon had mobilized Operation Desert Shield, soon to be Desert Storm.

Dhahran, the hub of Desert Shield, was a low-built cinder-block city of minimal charm. It was ringed with superhighways that ended abruptly in the sand. At the bottom of one off-ramp, I found a Saudi auto graveyard, a mound of late-model Mercedeses.

Thanks to an ABC colleague, Charlie Glass, I found the one decent Indian restaurant in Dhahran. All of the restaurants and hotel coffee shops had special sections for women and children located at the back of the room behind screens. I negotiated with the headwaiter to confer on me the status of "honorary man," a precedent set by Queen Elizabeth, so I could openly sit in the restaurant. Still, I had to keep watch for the government's religious storm troopers. They were particularly fond of hounding women out of cars and beating them if they dared climb behind the wheel. The Saudi government had institutionalized a particularly fanatical strain of Islam called Wahhabism, the region's most backward brand of Islamic fundamentalism.

I was billeted in Dammam, a nearby Saudi town swarming with Kuwaiti refugees. The hotel was stuffed with ill-bred Kuwaiti children roaming the halls in packs, peeling off the purple and gold wallpaper in long strips. They were attended by battered Filippina nannies who were treated as slave labor.

The Kuwaitis, who had fed so long at the trough of the welfare oil state, sat, clicking their worry beads, waiting for someone to do something. They were a generation away from herding camels. Their leader, of "royal" stock invented by the British, married a virgin every Thursday. One member of the royal family had strung up a servant at the Watergate apartments in Washington, beaten the man senseless, and left him for dead. The court documents were ignored. The great P.R. firms on K Street were spinning the press to write of the moral imperative to defend Kuwaiti human rights. No one wanted to hear that the Anti Slavery Society in London had listed at least one member of the royal family as a slaver.

As I took my seat in the pressroom of the Dhahran International, I was mildly surprised by General Schwarzkopf's first words to the assembled press: that Kuwait was the victim of "not only a mugging but a rape." Our sympathies should lie with the violated Kuwaitis, victims of Saddam (not the ravaged Thursday virgins). We were here because of moral outrage, not oil. "Not a single American," said the general, "believes he is fighting for oil."

Saudi Arabian sand had the consistency of a Southern California beach. When I arrived at the desert camp of the 4th Battalion of the 82nd Airborne, the first troops to land in Saudi Arabia, they had been shoveling it into sandbags for three weeks. The troops were hot, listless, and unnerved about a possible chemical attack. Because they were veterans of Ronald Reagan's invasion of Panama, they drew the front line. They trained their two-man thirty-one-pound Dragon antitank missiles, which they never fired, on the dunes. They prayed for clear windless days, for a sandstorm would deceive the Dragon's laser beam, locking on to the grains of sand. Their global positioning system, a handheld instrument meant to tell them their location, was melting in the heat.

"If it saves a few cents at the gas pump," said Specialist Bobby Haig from Mobile, Alabama, soaked with sweat, "it's worth being here."

"If we give our lives," said Private First Class James Woodcock from Bennington, Vermont, "it's just better that the American people are going to have that few cents difference at the gas pump."

"Doesn't that make you feel good," said General Schwarzkopf, his huge frame sprawled across his makeshift office in the Saudi Ministry of Defense, much of which was emptied out for his use, "that you've got young people out there that feel that way about their country?" The general shuffled his brushed cream suede boots. "They understand there's something worth fighting for.

That sure makes me feel good." General Schwarzkopf did not, however, personally share their spirit of sacrifice.

"If you had your choice of going to war or paying a buck and a half for a gallon of gasoline," he said brusquely, "you'd pick a buck and a half a gallon of gasoline every time. I certainly would."

The Muslim prayer interrupted his train of thought. It was piped in several times a day through the public address system.

"If they don't stop that prayer," chuckled the general, eyeing the speaker in the ceiling, "I'm going to shoot it out."

His officers had taken over the Riyadh Hyatt across the street. We found them helping themselves to the smoked salmon buffet with mushrooms in vinaigrette. They could not believe their luck. This war meant promotions, rescue from the peacetime torpor that clung like a wet field blanket to the careers of the post-Vietnam officer corps. They were chafing for Desert Shield to become Desert Storm long before most Americans could find Kuwait on a map. While the mission was still, according to their commander, 100 percent defensive—to prevent an invasion of Saudi Arabia—they were ready for action.

Their men, far across the dunes in scorpion-infested desert tent camps, dined on freeze-dried rations, MREs. We slept on the desert floor with the marines. The temperature never dropped below 90. It was dead quiet except for the scrabbling of scorpions nesting at night in the marines' boots. The only edible selection in the rations kit, featuring items like tuna casserole, was the packet of cheese and crackers. I wondered whether I should tell them about the officers' buffet.

After a few sleepless nights, the marines proclaimed the sand fly the Saudi national bird. Their only other company was ambling herds of wild camels and the odd Bedouin family, in hand-dyed clothes and delicate tattoos, traumatized by the invasion of their vast empty space.

In the microwave conditions, you could fry an egg on a tank turret. The sand was forcing Apache helicopter gunship crews to flush their engines with water. M-1 tank crews from the 24th Mechanized Division were, at the best of times, getting four gallons to the mile. Here, air filters clogged. The tank maintenance chief of the "Desert Rogues," Delta Company, 1st Battalion of the 24th, told me laconically he was "working on little problems that have been arising in the desert. The tanks don't start."

The M-1 starters had seized up.

Three of the fast sealift ships steaming to Saudi Arabia with equipment and spares had broken down. The entire 101st Division, complained Commanding General Binford Peay, "Binny" for short, had just enough ammunition for its attack helicopters to make just two missions. When we told General Schwarzkopf this on camera, he was stunned.

"Two missions?"

They were not ready to go to war.

Protective chemical gear, issued one suit per soldier, could only be worn once. Should Saddam lob two chemical agents into the Marine Corps frontline trenches, the second would hit its mark. Suiting up in the desert poised a danger of heatstroke. Temperatures inside hovered around 140 degrees. As one marine officer observed to me, "You could literally fill your boots up with sweat." The water bottle in the suit, complete with rubber straw that fit snugly in the mask, held only a gallon and a half. Having survived a chemical attack of tabun, sarin, or HD, which transformed human skin into an oozing mass of blisters, soldiers could then die of thirst.

The lunar landscape of the Saudi desert played on the imagination. The marines from Camp Pendleton had been briefed on invisible gases that would steal across the dunes from the Iraqi border and set off the signal of their M256 chemical detector kit. Their instructions were to whip on their gas masks, breathe normally, and wait while their Nuclear Biological Chemical officer, in this case CW04 Chuck Whittlesey, tested the air for "blood, blister, or nerve agents."

Chuck was from Redmond, Washington, and had risen through the ranks of Nuclear Biological Chemical officers in the Marine Corps to the senior job. He sat with me in the sand, tinted pink in the Arabian dusk, going over the cocktail of antidotes for nerve gas. The gas attacked the synapses in the brain, so we were each issued three shots of atropine to restore brain functions. Atropine was like a massive dose of speed. It produced dry mouth and skin, nervousness, agitation, and a dangerously accelerated heartbeat. To counteract the atropine jolt, we had three shots of 2-Pam Chloride,

Valium-based, to slow the system down. The next step was transfer back to sick bay to be "ventilated" with oxygen.

An attack of mustard gas, also expected, required a different approach. Chuck described the signs to me as "horrible blistering for two to six hours," like being on slow broil. The personal decontamination kit contained a "caustic solution like Clorox" to clean the mustard gas off one's suit along with hot soapy water. The gas would be tricky because a tiny glob of it on the skin in the gap between the suit sleeve and the gloves could do serious damage.

Chuck expected the gases to be delivered overland in shells fired from Russian Frog tactical artillery, by air, or even packed in land mines, all used by the Iraqis in their chemical campaign against the Kurds in Halabja during the Iran-Iraq war. He was conscious of the debilitating effect the very possibility of chemical attack was having on Lima Company, 3rd Platoon, camped around us about 140 miles south of the border. "Although they call them mass-killing weapons," Chuck said matter-of-factly, "they are mass-fear weapons. Weapons of terror."

The fear of chemicals was already draining the men.

My own fear was kept in check by my faith in deterrence. For Saddam to use chemicals was suicidal. Lieutenant General Walter Boomer, commanding general of the Marine Expeditionary Force, was based at the port of Jubail, the Cam Ranh Bay of Saudi Arabia. Boomer was a fine-boned man with a soft drawl and the cadence of John Wayne. The top marine general "in country" made it plain to us that if the Iraqi leader "went chemical," we were equipped to do the same.

"It would be a very foolish thing for him to use chemical weapons," General Boomer said on camera, "because he has to know that we have the capability to respond. I'm not going to speculate on what we would do with chemical weapons but the other side must know that we're well equipped. The consequences of him using them would be, in my opinion, disastrous for him." The light from the camouflage tent played on the general's face. "I'm saying that retaliation would bring dire consequences to his forces."

Boomer was the only general willing to suggest on the record that we had chemical weapons "in theater" either on land or at sea. "We have marines," he said soberly, "who are trained to use them."

In my experience, marines are the most straightforward of the services. When we put the question to General Schwarzkopf of whether we had chemical weapons on Saudi soil or on carriers just offshore, he replied, "I'd rather not answer that question." For decades, U.S. carriers in the region have stocked both chemical and tactical nuclear weapons.

The Air Force 1st Tactical Fighter Wing was based at the Dhahran air base. When I walked into the hangar with the ABC crew, the pilots strutted like peacocks. Yet their combat experience was still confined to a simulator. When they spoke, I thought I was in some parody from *The Right Stuff.* "I think we would all like to test our skills," Colonel John McBroom volunteered. "It's hard to describe, but it's an adventure," he said as the camera rolled. "It's something the fighter pilot has, that adventuresome spirit. He sits right on the ragged edge. He has to believe that he's better than the next person. He has to believe in himself and have that confidence. And our people have that. We'll control the skies right from the get-go. I just think that whole match, that man-machine-weapons-system match, and resolve of the American fighting man will carry the day."

Five months later, when Colonel McBroom and his boys were unleashed on Iraq, "that man-machine-weapons-system match" failed to knock out a single Iraqi Scud missile before launch. *Not one* of the lumbering, Russian-built Scuds fired at Saudi Arabia and Tel Aviv was stopped in its tracks by the U.S. Air Force.

The deadline issued by the Bush White House for Saddam Hussein to withdraw his army from Kuwait was January 15. There was confusion. Was that January 15 Washington time or Baghdad time? On the eve of the fifteenth (Washington time) ABC aired a second "Line in the Sand" broadcast. It opened with Peter Jennings walking across an enormous relief map of Saudi Arabia, Iraq, and Kuwait. It was thought that the audience, vague on details of the region, could use a geography lesson. Peter's bold strides across the map, shot by the overhead camera angle that diminished his size, grabbed the viewers' attention. Would he fall into that black shadow in Luristan? Would he trip on the Zagros Mountains?

My segment of the second special was slated the "Military Situationer." The news division was absorbing Pentagonese from the military consultants who now roamed the halls on generous retainers. Their message was sober. The Iraqi Army had three times as much artillery, twice as many tanks, sixty infantry divisions, 700,000 men. They had fought a protracted war with Iran. The men were "battle-hardened." Their engineers had laced the front with mines, napalm trenches, and walls of sand embedded with tanks. General Bernard Trainor told us we could expect "probably the most violent type of conventional clash that has ever existed in the history of warfare. It's going to be messy."

I wanted to know what the Russians thought. The Iraqis had been trained and equipped by the Russians. The Moscow bureau got an interview with Marshall Sergei Akhromeyev, the Senior Military Advisor to then President Gorbachev. He was convinced Saddam's forces, certainly his Republican Guard, would fight. "This is not the kind of army that will fall apart after the first strike," he assured us. "No. This army has been seasoned by war. It will show unyielding stubborn resistance."

(All of them were wrong. The Iraqis fled.)

My piece included footage of our troops waiting on the ground. They were edgy. A frontline marine company test-firing their $8,000 TOW missiles failed miserably. Corporal Daniel Billman was angry. "My first gunner either went over the target or had a problem with his missile. My second missile, fucking rocket motors never kicked in. So that's what you saw, the missile about fifty feet out of the tube go tumbling across the ground. So now basically if there's a real live situation, tanks have already seen my missiles fired. They know where my position is at, and since I'm dug into the ground, I can't pick up 220 pounds and run. Basically, my people and me are dead."

The night the broadcast aired, the United States had over one thousand attack aircraft and bombers ready to cripple Iraq. The pilots we interviewed were now steeped in sports metaphors. "It's kind of like the butterflies in your stomach before the big game." General Trainor sounded the darker note. "Anybody that thinks airplanes are going to go over there and have a free day of dropping bombs and shooting missiles—and hit everything they fire at—like they're playing some kind of Nintendo game is crazy. There are lots of targets that are not going to be hit unless you go after them many, many times." He was proved right.

Saddam, said the defense experts, could strike back with French Exocet missiles and Russian Scuds. The Scud missiles carried high-explosive warheads which weighed up to one ton. They could also carry nerve gas, mustard gas, and a "poor man's nuclear weapon" that held everyone in thrall called a fuel air explosive. Henry Dodds, a *Jane's Defense Weekly* pundit in London, described its horror on camera in an Oxford accent like a mouthful of Devon cream. "It's basically like a napalm charge. You're firing a blanket of petroleum air mixture over about five hundred yards. Once the blanket has spread out, it's detonated. It gives you a tremendous blast. The effect is totally devastating." Dodds addressed the effects of the chemical-tipped Scud. "It's not a clean casualty. You'll have someone coughing their lungs out. You'll have terrible blisters appearing on their skin. It's very demoralizing if you see that happening to a friend of yours."

The war began in prime time, dovetailing with *ABC World News Tonight*. Network producers had been alerted prior to the opening bombs. I was called at home by the news desk.

"The war starts in two hours."

The first footage, captured with a night-vision lens, showed the sky over Baghdad like Van Gogh's *Starry Night*. Antiaircraft fire shot through the night like meteor showers, Roman candles, Fourth of July on the Mall. My brother-in-law Patrick was under it, watching the display from Baghdad's Rasheed Hotel. Most American journalists had left the city, ordered out of Iraq by their editors. Calls poured into editorial suites from the Pentagon warning that Baghdad might be flattened and their correspondents along with it.

The Joint Chiefs of Staff wanted minimal coverage. The British and European press camped at the Rasheed (the Italians had a room stocked with pasta and wine) were astonished to see their American counterparts disappear down the road to Jordan. Peter Arnett of CNN, who stayed behind, was treated in Washington as a renegade, a loner. In fact, the Rasheed hosted a pack of journalists, including Maggie O'Kane for the *Irish Times* and Marie Colvin for the *London Sunday Times*. O'Kane was interviewed by Irish television on her impressions of the air war. "Weren't you frightened,

Maggie, when the bombs began to fall?" "Ah no," she replied in a thick brogue. "I went down to the shelter with Patrick Cockburn." The admission delighted the village of Ardmore, where the pubs filled with Patrick impersonators throwing themselves over Maggie.

The second night of the war, I sat in a bar on Capitol Hill with a claque of Senate and House staffers who specialize in military affairs. CNN droned on as part of the white noise of Washington. The barman turned up the volume when it was announced there had been a Scud attack on Tel Aviv. The effect was like someone throwing a brick through the window. There were reports that at least one warhead contained chemicals. I excused myself and found a pay phone. I dialed Tom Yellin, executive producer for the Jennings specials, at ABC in New York.

"I want to go to Tel Aviv."

"When do you want to go?"

"First flight tomorrow. I'll pick up a London crew."

In all five of Israel's wars, Tel Aviv had never come under attack. It had been a sanctuary, beyond the reach of short-range tactical weapons, well within the defenses of the Israeli Air Force. The specter of a missile bearing down on Dizengoff Street had been something from a war game, in the realm of the military theologians who plotted inside the walled compound of the Kirya, in the shadow of the Israeli Defense Forces tower that defined the city's skyline. The threat of chemicals added an element of panic. Poison gas revived memories of Auschwitz.

The Israeli leadership had promised George Bush they would not retaliate if hit. The U.S. bombers would pummel Baghdad for them. Israeli pilots over Baghdad would wreck the alliance Bush and Secretary of State James Baker had so carefully crafted with the Saudis, the Egyptians, and the Syrians. Purchasing their allegiance had not come cheap. Billions of dollars of Egypt's debt to the United States had been forgiven. Israel, too, was reaping an aid windfall, needed to resettle Russian immigrants arriving by the planeload as the Soviet Union dissolved, by agreeing to sit tight. But the tension in the Kirya and the Knesset (the Israeli parliament), now that struggling infants were forced nightly into sealed cots, was high. Generals huddled with their grandchildren hoping they would not be sick in their gas masks from fear or claustrophobia. The Israeli Air Force, accustomed to being the active partner, the one who battle-tested the American F-15s and F-16s in dogfights and bombing raids, was grounded and impotent.

I called Barry Fox, a veteran combat cameraman who had graduated to London television executive. Barry had introduced me to the Europa Hotel and the Falls Road in his native Belfast when we were both toiling for Irv Margolis at NBC. We had been friends for fifteen years. I asked him if he felt like dusting off his camera and joining me in Tel Aviv. He had covered the most terrifying battles of the 1973 war, nearly sliding out of the cargo bay of an attack helicopter in flight because the floor was awash with blood. His footage of the Yom Kippur War was so arresting that most of it was censored. He covered the War of Attrition and the 1981 invasion of Lebanon. Fox accepted instantly. He recruited his brother Peter, also a talented cameraman, to record sound.

When I arrived at Dulles Airport, it was like a tomb. The onset of war halfway around the world had caused mass cancellations. Fear of "Arab terrorists" was matched by fear of chemical attack. There was a run on gas masks in North Carolina. The British Airways flight to London might have been my private charter.

In London, I transferred to El Al. The Foxes joined me at the airport. Again the plane was almost empty. We landed at Lod Airport in Israel after nightfall on Sunday January 19. Scuds had plowed into Tel Aviv for two nights running. One had torn through the reinforced concrete of a bomb shelter in the Sephardic neighborhood of Hatikva and blown off the side of a house. There were no tour groups deplaning from New York that night, only gigantic C-5 Galaxy transport planes next to us on the strip, their cavernous holds crawling with soldiers. They were unloading Patriot missiles, hurriedly flown in with their U.S. Army crews to defend Tel Aviv. The Patriot crews built a tent city in a field along the Ayalon road and called it Hotel California. The route from Ben Gurion Airport into the city was deserted, most of Tel Aviv's residents having decamped to Jerusalem and the Red Sea port of Eilat. (Jerusalem was thought to be safe because of the Muslim shrines in the old city.)

A freezing wind whipped down Dizengoff Street, adding to the chill of darkened restaurants and storefront windows crisscrossed with masking tape to guard against bomb blast. We unloaded our mountain of silver camera cases at the Hilton on the strand at 9:00 P.M., one hour before the next Scud attack was expected. Iraqi missileers were strangely punctual.

The hotel was reserved for the press and the Israeli Defense Forces. A welcome table was set up for new arrivals to pick up gas mask kits like neat cardboard box lunches, complete with an atropine injector and dusting powder for mustard gas burns. Signs were posted everywhere: CARRY GAS MASKS AT ALL TIMES. Israeli Defense Forces teams barked instructions on how to shoot up atropine in the thigh and played a gas attack demo tape. I had always hated needles and the gas mask gave me claustrophobia.

The IDF spokesman had opened a command center in the lobby, staffed with curvaceous soldiers in tight-fitting uniforms dispatching coffee and briefings. The world's press was getting drunk in the bar. When the siren sounded, we were expected to repair to the sealed room, where all windows and doors were covered with black plastic sheeting and gaffer-taped against gas, until the all-clear sounded. The drawbacks were that the shelter had no telephone and no view. It was impossible to see the missiles. Confined to the black box, everyone's nerves were frayed. There were embarrassing scenes of latecomers locked out of the sanctuary for fear of breaking the air lock. We chose to forgo the sealed rooms. We wanted a panoramic view of the city.

The fourteenth floor of the Hilton was high enough that a camera position on the balcony covered the sweep of downtown Tel Aviv. We had the ink-black Mediterranean to our left, the massive power station and wealthy suburb of Hertzalia due north, and downtown funneling out to Arlozorof Street to the right. A battery of Patriot "antimissile missiles" was rolled into place near the power station up the coast. For Fox to shoot south toward the old town of Jaffa required a sprint across the hall. The only drawback of our elevated balcony bureau was that a direct hit on the hotel roof would send the Scud burrowing through the Sheetrock, crushing us in its path.

The ABC bureau in London had issued us plastic antichemical suits. In this kit, we looked like bag ladies dressed for a summer storm. Once the siren wailed, the sign that American satellites had spotted missiles lifting off from western Iraq, we had about four minutes to run to the elevator, ride up, tear into the room, and throw on the plastic. The worst part was waiting for the elevator. Once inside, I was sure we would be trapped. After the air raid siren stopped, so did the elevators. They were shut down.

Once upstairs, we were alone. The sealed rooms were far below us. I fumbled with the room key and all of us dove onto the balcony. The camera was already there. The roar and crack of Patriot slamming into Scud just over our heads was deafening, ear-rending, as it rolled over the rooftops. The sound waves damaged our recording equipment. It malfunctioned. A glitch, a hit, dropout and static. A shower of glittering white-hot metal plummeted down onto the city. I was transfixed by the explosion and lost, in that instant, all fear. I felt strangely calm, detached. We watched the titanic display flashing across the black sky as though it were a Pink Floyd light show. Nerve gas would reach us in seconds if it was in the warhead. We counted, "One, two, three, four . . ."

Our second night in Tel Aviv, we filmed a planeload of bewildered Russian immigrants filing into Ben Gurion. Most did not speak Hebrew or English. They were exhausted and dazed, crowded into a fluorescent-lit hall with plastic seats, where they were treated to a quick gas mask demonstration. When the syringe popped out of the box and the soldier mimicked shooting herself in the leg, the Russians looked sick. As the translator gave a graphic description of the effects of sarin gas, some of the captive audience were ready to board the next plane. This was not what they had in mind. As the week wore on, there were cases of hysteria, people injecting themselves at the sound of the siren or having symptoms of exposure to chemical agents. An Israeli cameraman was convinced he had felt the effects of nerve gas.

On the night of January 25, less than a minute after all of Israel had vanished into sealed rooms and struggled into their gas masks, the sky above Tel Aviv lit up and a Patriot missile burst into a thousand glowing shards. It was clear that the missile had self-destructed. Another Patriot streaked east across the night sky, clearing office buildings and apartment blocks by a few feet before it slammed into the city. A third missile fired at the incoming Scuds exploded in a sudden glow of red light just beside the tower of the

Kirya. A fourth shot up from the battery due north of the Hilton and then, almost immediately, doubled back along its path and crashed to earth not far from a popular restaurant called Mandy's.

I can't believe this, I thought. I'm going to be killed by an American missile.

The Patriots were misfiring, going haywire.

From the fourteenth-floor balcony, I dialed the foreign desk at ABC in New York. I shouted over the shrieking missiles, seven incoming Scuds, that the Patriots were in trouble.

"Where's Jennings?"

"He's on the air."

"Get a message to him so he can report it."

"Shouldn't you have your gas mask on?"

"The Patriots are plowing into the city. They're going to do as much damage as the Scuds. Put it on the air."

"Please put your gas mask on."

New York was seven hours behind us. Jennings reported it during an afternoon news break. At midnight Tel Aviv time, the press corps assembled in the ballroom of the Hilton for a routine briefing from the Israeli Defense Forces. After a soothing announcement that seven Scuds had been fired at the city and all seven were shot down, I noticed no one was taking issue with the briefer. It dawned on me that all but a few of them had been hunkered down in their sealed rooms. The bulk of them were also unacquainted with military hardware. I stood up last.

"Let me tell you what I've just seen," I began. He listened as I described the havoc. "What would you say the consequences are for the civilian population of Tel Aviv?"

He took a deep breath and admitted that the Patriots had "misfired." My footage of the Patriot doing a fiery hairpin turn made the news that evening. Casualties that night were one dead and several injured. We filmed in the twisted rubble of an apartment house that had been ripped in half. The walls had been peeled back like the DAS building in Bogotá, so we could see bedrooms exposed, as though they were in a dollhouse.

When I broke the story of the Patriot's failure, it was downplayed by the Israeli military. They were loath to irritate the Pentagon in the middle of the war. The scandal erupted after Saddam's defeat, in Washington hearing rooms and in Israeli Ministry of Defense internal reviews. The Patriot, never intended to be fired anywhere near a crowded city, was no longer billed as the savior of Tel Aviv.

The war overall was presented like a video game. With the Iraqi Air Force dispensed with in the first hours of the assault, pilots had plenty of time to revisit targets, five, ten times. Cockpit footage of bombing runs was a regular feature of the Schwarzkopf briefing. The general was especially proud of direct hits on bridges. I remember the spellbinding pilot's tape of an Iraqi driving across a bridge. Suddenly, the flash and shock wave of the bombs dropped behind the car dissected the bridge. The driver kept moving. "That's the luckiest man," said Schwarzkopf with brio, "in Iraq." It was brilliant theater.

Meanwhile, thousands of ragged Iraqi troops on the ground in Kuwait deserted their bunkers and their tanks. The front lines were from the start cannon fodder, units of Kurds and Shia Muslims, Saddam's disposable enemies. The Iraqi military did not want to die for Kuwait. Those who could, walked home across the frigid winter sands.

After weeks of air war and a brisk routing on the ground, the Gulf War ended on schedule. I was by then back in Washington, my gas mask packed away in the closet. I began to prepare for the long journey to Baghdad, to see what the war had done.

TEN

The Rivers of Babylon

THE IRAQI EMBASSY in Washington was locked and shuttered. The ambassador had gone to Canada. The rump staff ran a sleepy visa section under the Algerian flag and the watchful eye of countless surveillance cameras. I walked through the front gate, conscious of the cameras' whir and click. Inside, a languorous beauty sat by a silent phone. Dalfa was a reminder of the Reagan years, when the Iraqi ambassador, Nizar Hamdoon, threw the best parties in Washington. His was an invitation few refused. "The Saudi parties were the most expensive," Hamdoon told me, reminiscing one night at the Iraqi Hunting Club after the war, "but ours were the most fun."

Dalfa spent her days touching up her blood-orange manicure and watching soaps. There was no champagne to order, no Tigris fish packed in ice to fly in for the reception. The Washington lobbyists, congressmen, arms merchants, and deal makers who curried favor with Iraq had all run for cover.

The war season had ended with the June victory parade in Washington. I watched M-1 tanks and cruise missiles rumble down the Mall as squadron after squadron of bombers executed flyby maneuvers in handsome formation. The streaking airpower nearly grazed the Obelisk. A Stealth bomber screamed overhead as ANCHORS AWEIGH and GOD BLESS AMERICA floats rolled by. At veterans' picnics, tables groaned with fried chicken and biscuits. There were sweating tubs of cold Sprite and T-shirts emblazoned with B52, NO PEACE

TALKS WITH YOU, FLY BOYS, and 100 MILES FROM BAGHDAD. An Armed Forces Radio interviewer was working the crowd, asking, "How do you feel marching in this parade today? Does this make up for Vietnam?"

That night I stood on the roof of the Lincoln Memorial watching the war artfully re-created in fireworks, tracer fire, antiaircraft bursts, Patriots ramming Scuds, their cascading sparks extinguished in the dark mirror of the reflecting pool. Throughout the celebrations, no one asked or answered the obvious question. What did we do to Iraq? There was a conspicuous silence from the newly famous Pentagon briefers (one of whom I could never take seriously because of his triumph as runner-up for his French-maid costume at the 1982 Moscow Military Attachés' Transvestite Ball) who had been so fluent in front of the cameras on every numbing detail of strategy and tactics, payloads and kills. What were the consequences of dropping 88,000 tons of bombs? Eighty thousand tons' worth of ordnance were "dumb bombs," without precision guidance. Where did they fall? How did the movie end? Andrew and I kept asking the obvious questions. We convinced David Fanning at *Frontline* to give us the assignment of investigating what had happened on the ground.

As June wore into July, our visas still had not come through. In the meantime, we set out for the office of the Pentagon theoreticians, the Strangeloves of the air war. Colonel John Warden was trim, with receding silver hair and eyes the luminous blue of an ice floe. His manner was cool and composed until he stood before his blown-up satellite map of Baghdad, stuck with fifty-odd colored pins. The colonel came to life, his broad hands sweeping over the bomber targets.

He squinted with concentration. "The air campaign was classic. It combined the tried-and-true art principles of war. What we have here is the campaign Alexander the Great would have carried out and probably, in fact, was thinking about at the battle of Arbela to grab Darius and assert his power over the Persian Empire."

Military history buffs remember that after a dusty engagement in 331 B.C. (visibility was a few yards), Alexander and his shield bearers, brandishing sarissas and yelling the customary "alalalalai," pursued the Persians across the Zab River and lost him in the Kurdish mountains. Alexander threw his spear and missed, just as the U.S. Air Force missed Saddam, twenty-three centuries and a few billion dollars later. The irony was lost on Colonel Warden.

We tackled the matter of the dumb bombs.

"Of the roughly eighty-eight thousand tons of munitions, no more than seven or eight thousand were precision munitions?" Andrew asked him on camera.

"That's right. About 10 percent."

"So why did you have to drop the other eighty thousand tons?"

"Because you didn't have enough of the precision weapons." He paused and replayed. "Not so much the precision weapons, but the precision platforms to depend entirely on the precision weapons. Now, the thing to keep in mind here"—the colonel was searching for the *mot juste*—"is that the nonprecision weapons are just exactly that. Nonprecision. One almost needs to think of them like the pellets in the shotgun shell that you use when you're shooting skeet. There may be five hundred tiny pellets in one of these shells. If, when you are shooting skeet, five of those pellets hit the clay pigeon, then you see this as being a great success." He paused thoughtfully. "The other way to look at it is that 99 percent of those pellets missed their target. Which is not relevant."

Not relevant, I thought, unless you happen to be standing underneath.

In the first ten days of the bombing, the "precision platforms" had been tied up in the top secret effort to assassinate Saddam from the air. When the strategists failed to blow their elusive target to bits, an F-15E being an inefficient hit man, the colonel's simple strategy of the "inside out" war, crippling the enemy at home behind the lines, took top priority. The key was the systematic dismantling of Iraq's power grid. The colonel would demolish the electrical system, and with it the modern state.

"The elevators wouldn't work. The lights wouldn't work," the colonel said, picturing the chaos around us if his plan had been executed here on the Pentagon E-ring. "The computers, the electric typewriters, all of these things put such a burden on a society that has become accustomed to electricity and, in fact, has based everything on it. Taking that away then creates an impairment which is very difficult to grasp."

□ □ □ □

In August of 1991, visas in hand, we packed twelve-year-old Chloe and seven-year-old Olivia off to camp in California. Any misgivings they had about us were offset by the prospect of traveling West on their own. They extracted a promise that we would bring back plenty of presents. We flew to Jordan. Amman, the Jordanian capital, was overflowing with Iraqi refugees. The churches and mosques were filled with distraught families whose visa applications for the United States and Europe had been rejected. Rejection was the norm. With so many thousands of refugees, water in Amman was desperately short.

We had to travel overland to Iraq with the camera gear because sanctions had shut down the Baghdad airport. We rented jeeps from the Bisharat family next to the Intercontinental and drove to the supermarket to load up on supplies. We set out for Baghdad at dawn. The jeep ride across hundreds of miles of white-hot dunes took fourteen hours. "Scud Alley," the broad stretch of tarmac highway that cut across the floor of the Iraqi desert, was empty. I prayed we would not break down. There were no gas stations, no pay phone to call for help. The occasional searing breeze kicked up whirlwinds in the sand like Sufi dervishes. Heat waves lined the horizon with shimmering cities, tricks of light. We rattled down the highway at over a hundred miles an hour loaded with precious cargo, five weeks' worth of bottled water and foot-high stacks of Iraqi dinars from the Amman black market. The value of Iraqi money, officially three dollars to the dinar, had collapsed.

The Baghdad skyline was blacked out when we arrived at midnight. There was a power outage. The outlines of the vast city bore a strong resemblance to Los Angeles, low-built and baked. We could see there were still date palm plantations inside the city limits. The neofascist facade of the Rasheed Hotel loomed like a dark cliff against the brilliant starry night. In the shabby upstairs halls, there were half-peeled bureau logos from the departed press.

The hotel's emergency generators were switched on. The lobby that would have delighted Mussolini was lined with Mukhabarat, the Iraqi secret police. They slouched around the potted palms, chain-smoking and smoothing the creases in their designer jeans. Their boss, a raffish security chief named Jalil, seemed relieved by our appearance, a delegation from the enemy to justify his existence. All of the rooms were tapped and bugged.

Walking into the Rasheed was like entering the theater of the absurd. That first night, Andrew and I crashed a lavish wedding party in one of the banquet rooms. Onstage, the bride and groom sat motionless on heavy gilt thrones, like figurines on a cake. We surveyed the long banquet tables, set with a bottle of Johnnie Walker Black Label for every couple. Upstairs the disco beat throbbed mercilessly, the bouncers culling the crowd to make room for the children of the Baath Party elite. The only sign of privation at the Rasheed was the waiter's apologetic admission that they had no more tonic water.

By 8 A.M. the next day we were out shooting, before the light turned too white and flat for the camera under the noonday sun. Baghdad was a Potemkin city, the neat facades of the telephone tower, the government's Baath Party headquarters, and countless official buildings masking their blackened smashed innards. The main bridge that gracefully spanned the Tigris was trisected by bombs.

The broad avenues were dwarfed by freshly painted portraits of Saddam, each a different manifestation of the omnipotent leader. There was Saddam the soldier talking on the "red phone." Saddam the doctor with stethoscope, Saddam the farmer, the engineer, the sheik, his hard grin stretched across the landscape.

Every year on Saddam's birthday, artists were required to submit a portrait of their leader as a "gift." Saddam's wife would then insist they be paid. Ritual required the artists to reject the check, protesting that the birthday portraits had been painted out of love for Saddam. They could accept the First Lady's largesse only when it arrived a second time. One painter showed his singular devotion by slashing open a vein and dipping his brush into his own blood. The Saddam-in-blood series was much admired at the presidential palace.

We arrived at St. Fatima's, a stone church in a quiet, well-tended neighborhood. The Catholic community, with roots going back several centuries, worshiped here. Twice a week since the war, the grounds were trampled by hundreds of families who came for food. Catholic Relief Services was feeding 100,000 Iraqis. Many of them had been solidly middle class before their boorish Tikriti leader grabbed Kuwait and brought down the wrath of George Bush and Jim Baker. Now they were broken.

Food prices had risen 1,000 percent. Without electricity, the chicken factories ceased production. Animal feed and vaccines were no longer available. Egg production went into free fall, from nearly 2 billion a year to 2 million. A rare chicken in the market, a sad-looking bird, sold for $37. The average Iraqi salary was $450 per month.

Doug Broderick presided over the orderly distribution of bags of staples, in the colonnaded garden courtyard of the church. He was the longest-serving U.S. aid worker since the war, a skilled disaster-relief veteran transferred from the Thai-Cambodian border. Broderick inspired confidence. If a shipment of rice had to be off-loaded in Aqaba, and trucked across the desert to St. Fatima's in record time, Broderick was the man to do it. He was square-jawed and broad-chested, and talked logistics like an army general.

"Right now throughout the country, we have a classic response to a food shortage, pre-famine. You have people selling jewelry here in Baghdad. Your used-watch market is flooded with watches. I saw a mother with a ten-year-old girl selling a battered black-and-white TV. Families are pawning their carpets, their furniture, their gold, their silverware. Anything that has any kind of value. Their cameras, their videos, their radios, in order to get cash for food." Broderick thought the signs were bad. "A can of baby milk costs forty-five dollars."

I suddenly noticed that the crowds outside the two locked entrances to the church garden were bulging with women, some in Western dress, others in flowing black chadors, twisting their arms like tendrils through the wrought-iron gates. There were now hundreds of shouting supplicants waving bits of paper that entitled them to food. It was approaching 130 degrees. The women in front were being crushed against the gate, their faces squashed flat. There was a roar and the tall corrugated iron gate beyond was battered until it buckled and crashed open, the crowd rushing through like a flash flood. One woman caught her chador in the gate and was desperately trying to rip it free.

The gatekeepers raced to secure the defenses. Once inside, the rioters' raw panic that they would be turned away empty-handed subsided. The ladies straightened their skirts and examined their broken heels. The men brushed off their jackets. A line formed like a Safeway checkout. They were once again middle-class parents. Now their children would eat for another two weeks.

The United Nations had forbidden Saddam's ministers to sell oil or import spare parts until the U.N.'s conditions for destroying chemical and biological weapons stocks were met. Bush administration officials had confided, however, that sanctions would stay firmly in place until Saddam was deposed. The logic argued on the greens of the Chevy Chase Club was that things would get so desperate in the Fertile Crescent that people would rise up. Sanctions would squeeze them until rebellion was the only course. Everyone seemed satisfied that sanctions were a gentleman's weapon. Sanctions worked slowly like Chinese water torture.

But the analysts at CIA headquarters, privy to classified cable traffic, were skeptical. Sanctions showed no signs of dislodging the man who was now insisting he was a direct descendent of Nebuchadnezzar, who was rebuilding ancient Babylon with his own name inscribed on every other brick. According to the CIA's top Iraq specialists, an uprising against Saddam would be the "least likely" outcome of sanctions. Why impose them, then? The CIA men shrugged. "We don't make policy."

Iraqis told us that it was hard to rise up when you are hungry.

In the courtyard of St. Fatima's, Doug Broderick's conservative estimate was that 175,000 children would die as a result of the war. The harvest was off 30 percent. There were no pesticides, no insecticides, no certifiable seeds, no more Irish beef or California rice. With the bombed power plants operating at 25 percent of normal power, 60 percent of the people in the south were drinking contaminated water. In the town of Basra, the hotbed of opposition to Saddam, some of Colonel Warden's strategic nodes included the water treatment plant and the sewage treatment plant. The power plant was bombed thirteen times.

"The condition of the children," Broderick said dryly, "is severely declining. The diarrhea cases have increased by 400 percent. Severe malnutrition is 15 percent. There could be stunting or wasting among 40 percent of two-to-five-year-olds." The electricity

that powered the pumps that powered the machinery that chlori-
nated the water supply was knocked out. The dosing pumps, the
intake and outtake valves, were out of action. Water-borne diseases,
encouraged by the burning summer heat, were epidemic. Without
electricity, the machinery and computers at the state-of-the-art
Rustamiya sewage treatment plant outside Baghdad had seized up.
The plant that served 3 million people was now dumping 15 million gallons an hour of raw sewage into the Tigris River. Down-
stream, we watched children fill their plastic water jugs.

"I see children with an old tin can going out to puddles and
fetching water," Broderick said. "That's standing water or sewage
water. I've seen a case of a seven-year-old who was thirsty and took
kerosene to drink. When I saw him in Amara General Hospital,
they were examining him to see if he had permanent lung damage."

"How much does a bottle of water cost?" I asked.

"Nine dollars." He studied me in silence. "We are looking at a
disaster in slow motion."

The ancient port of Basra, where the Euphrates flows into the
powder-blue Persian Gulf, was a six-hour drive from Baghdad. We
now had a Ministry of Information minder, required for travel
outside Baghdad, squeezed into the car. Fawsi was an indolent man
with an unhealthy pallor. He had remarkably shiny shoes. When I
asked the drivers to stop so we could film farmers tilling dust in the
blasted landscape, Fawsi refused to step out of the car. As a secret
policeman, his duty was to shadow the cameraman, already a quarter of a mile away in the fields. Fawsi explained churlishly, "I cannot get my shoes dirty. I might have to meet an important minister."

Fawsi's extreme laziness worked to our advantage. He squealed at
our nonstop pace in the unforgiving heat. By the time we reached
the general hospital in Basra, marked by a billboard-sized portrait
of Fawsi's leader in a cool white linen suit and Panama hat, our
minder refused to leave the car. We interviewed the staff there
without our eavesdropping spy.

The staff was exhausted. The doctors rarely slept. Dr. Eman
Kammas, resident pediatrician, looked like a weary Sophia Loren.
She let us follow her into wards filled with ravaged children too
weak to do anything but stare. The air was hot and fetid. Some

withered children under six who looked like small birds were lying two to a bed. Some would die that day. Mothers in black *hejab* fanned away the flies. Dr. Kammas explained she was seeing forty to fifty cases of severe malnutrition each week. She had epidemics of typhoid, cholera, and hepatitis and was faced with the reappearance of rabies and polio, last seen in 1957. The power was out and the hospital generator was broken. The vaccines that required refrigeration had spoiled. The incubators were shut down.

Basra was the most heavily bombed city in the war. It was close to the Kuwait border and had done a roaring prewar trade as the Las Vegas of Iraq. White-robed Kuwaiti patrons could cruise the glitzy nightclubs to drink in sequin-and-gauze-draped hips and free-flowing Scotch. Here were the fleshpots of Babylon. The old town that the explorer Gertrude Bell had loved so much when she was posted here as adviser to the British colonial administration was still partially intact, the graceful latticework balconies suspended over the souk. Just down the street, the Al Hakimiah neighborhood, which had the flavor of fifties Palm Springs, was heaped with rubble. Forty-eight houses had been showered with dumb bombs. Following the path of the craters, the strategic target had been the local Pepsi-Cola bottling plant. I thought of Colonel Warden's patient explanation of shooting skeet.

We found a cluster bomb canister, with unmistakable American Air Force markings, on the sidewalk. The retired couple whose house was just the other side of a cactus garden were frightened to touch it. Down the street, we stumbled on a funeral tent pitched by a family holding a traditional vigil for a relative. Among the mourners, we found a marine engineer, Ali Rida, who had survived the thunderous 1 A.M. bombing. He assured us that everyone in Al Hakimiah understood it was all an unfortunate mistake. Eighteen of his neighbors were killed. In the wake of the tragedy, Rida and his family were still puzzled by the air force decision to target Pepsi.

Driving along the Shatt-al-Arab waterway, we passed the weird memorials to the shattering war with Iran, eight years of carnage, where men died on the stupefying scale of World War I. Dozens of colossal stone soldiers stood on the bank, arms outstretched, pointing to the far shore. Iran, the enemy, was a short swim away. The sweep of statues reminded Basreens whom they should hate. For the locals, the accusing fingers could just as easily point to Baghdad.

Basra was a Shia Muslim town, more akin to the ayatollahs' Iran than Saddam's Sunni capital. The Shia in the south listened to Iranian radio and used Iran as a sanctuary for their desultory guerrilla raids. But when they rose up in revolt against the Iraqi Republican Guard, neither Iran nor George Bush, who urged them brazenly to rebel on CNN, lifted a finger. The March uprising was crushed. The streets were littered with debris from both the uprising and the bombing.

We filmed a crowd of Basra children splashing in a foot of sewage water from cracked pipes.

Iraq's power plants were all state-of-the-art models imported from Japan, Germany, and Italy. In the days when Iraqi oil bought anything and anyone, the engineers flew in regularly from Europe to tweak the dials and ensure everything was in order. Now the Al Hartha plant that served southern Iraq was a wreck. Its towering funnel had a giant hole like a bull's-eye from an oversized cannon. The heart of the plant looked like it had been attacked by angry dinosaurs. Gargantuan heaps of twisted metal were the product of thirteen bombing runs. The first raid had put the plant out of action. The dozen subsequent raids ensured the plant would never function again.

In the *Frontline* hour, we ran the cockpit tape from the first F-15 to bomb Al Hartha, a raid flown the second night of the war. It was the first time pictures from the air and the ground were matched. The pilots exchange pleasantries through heavy breathing in their oxygen masks as the target, like a giant Erector set, moves into range. You can hear the pilot's "bombs away" when a brace of dumb bombs goes wide, falling short of the stacks. Colonel Steve Pingel misses the target. "Shit."

The tape was never shown by General Schwarzkopf. Only direct hits were aired on the war show. We evaded the censors and broadcast the first unedited glimpse of the war, thanks to Colonel Pingel donating his own tape. Pingel was anxious to know what he had hit. The explosion dug up the Al Hartha bomb shelter. "The thing about dumb bombs," Colonel Pingel said with regret, "is they don't always go where you want them to."

In Amara, a good-sized city south of Baghdad, we checked the general hospital's children's ward. There was a typhoid epidemic. Dr. Amman Beiruti, a European-trained obstetrician, was at his wits' end. Two thousand cases a day were turning up at the health clinics in the surrounding province. "It's a catastrophe. Once the electricity stopped, the water pump stopped, homes were deprived of pure water, the processing of sewage stopped. You can imagine, the whole environment was polluted. That's why we are getting infectious diseases like typhoid. I mean, electricity is not only light—not only light."

I thought of Colonel Warden's assessment that the effects of his campaign to disable the electricity grid would be "difficult to grasp." Watching children die of typhoid allows you to grasp it instantly.

Outside the window of the typhoid ward, there was a bridge that had been bombed twelve times in February and finally cut in two. The bridge was two hundred feet from the hospital. The glass in the entire six-floor hospital building, including the room where we now stood, was blown out. "February was a very cold month," Dr. Beiruti remembered. "We had a big problem keeping babies warm, no electricity, no glass, it was horrible. I'll tell you something. Because of the bombing, a lot of ladies got premature contractions, fifteen premature babies in February. Six of them died because we couldn't warm them." By August, eleven thousand children were dead from war-related causes, mostly from infectious diseases. "Not one Iraqi baby," said Dr. Beiruti dolefully, "invaded Kuwait."

The Baghdad–Basra road was hazardous after dark. Highway robbers manned roadblocks and plundered the passing trade. A bus had turned up in Basra loaded with men stripped to their underwear. As the light faded, our drivers floored the gas. I tormented Fawsi, our feckless Ministry of Information minder, by ordering the drivers to stop. We needed to film the red sun over the floodplain, a passing herd of goats, useless power lines stretching to the horizon. Fawsi wriggled and squawked. He was terrified of being waylaid and shot.

The moment we reached Baghdad he quit. New minders only took the job because the alternative, punishment for insubordination, was too terrible to contemplate. The lower ranks knew that

Saddam once invited his cabinet members to voice their own opinions. One foolishly obliged. Saddam ordered him into the next room for a swift execution.

We made foray after foray into the blast-furnace heat of the countryside, down to the holy city of Karbala, where Shia militants had hung Saddam's local representatives by the towering rafters of the great mosque. After the bodies were cut down, Saddam's men retaliated by bulldozing the entire neighborhood. The mosque itself, one of the holiest sites in Shia Islam, was preserved, indeed regilded, to avoid irritating the ayatollahs in Iran, who regarded Karbala and neighboring An Najaf as their Jerusalem.

We drove north across the scorpion-rich landscape to the oil province that bordered Iraqi Kurdistan. In Kirkuk we found army veterans. One was a carpenter who had been drafted and sent to Kuwait. A shrapnel wound in his knee the second week in February had turned gangrenous and the leg was amputated. He gave up carpentry to try his luck at jewelry. His military compensation was 100 dinars per month, enough to buy two bags of flour.

Beyond Kirkuk was the no-man's-land between Saddam's Iraq and the protected territory of Kurdistan. American A-10 spotter aircraft roared over the jagged cliffs with feet to spare and dove into the valleys watching for signs of Saddam's tanks. The Baghdad administration refused to let us travel across the plain into the Kurdish mountains, where the spring saw thousands of Kurds flee in desperation from Zakho and Arbil and Sulaimaniya. Whole families walked up the steep slopes of frozen mud where Saddam's troops would not follow.

Like the Shia uprising in the south, the Kurdish rebellion was silenced with helicopter gunships. Rockets slammed into the cities. George Bush had promised the Kurds that if the Iraqi military took to the air, they would be shot down. The promise was broken. The Kurds evacuated en masse, in a blind panic. Supplies that might have sustained them on the freezing hillsides were left behind.

When they began to die on camera, Washington consented to offer aid. MREs, the army's inedible rations, were dropped in heavy crates. There was plenty of ham to go around. No one stopped to think that Kurds would rather starve than eat ham. Six months later, the U.S. Army rations turned up for sale in the Baghdad market. When we dined with Iraqi Christians, they served the ham in a simple but nourishing casserole.

To get to Kurdistan, we were forced to make an arduous circle thousands of miles long, driving back across the desert floor to Jordan. The staff of the Ministry of Information were beside themselves with joy at our departure. They had made a halfhearted effort to charge us an exorbitant "television crew departure tax" in exchange for an exit visa. I flatly refused. Why, they wanted to know, was I being so difficult? Everyone else had paid. I explained patiently that we were not in the business of paying foreign governments. We would be compromised. They would be compromised. I launched into a spirited defense of journalistic integrity that lasted for over an hour. Andrew waited patiently. The Iraqis surrendered and stamped our papers.

From Jordan we flew to Ankara, Turkey, changing planes for Diyarbakir, the capital of Turkish Kurdistan, where a guerrilla war was in full swing. (It landed you in jail in Turkey to simply say the words "Turkish Kurdistan.") The Turkish government was fighting a faction of Kurds called the PKK, whose leader looked like Joseph Stalin. The Turkish military was blowing up Kurdish villages. They did not care for journalists. We tried and failed to keep a low profile. In Diyarbakir, we stayed in the medieval Caravansary, where the rooms around the courtyard resembled fourteenth-century stone bread ovens. We escaped asphyxiation by lingering over dinner in the open air. Suddenly, a huge troop of officials swept into the Caravansary courtyard, led by the new "supergovernor" of the region. As Andrew and I tried to blend in with the Turkish salads, the governor, flanked by men, ordered us to join him.

His aides competed for the privilege of translating. None of them was much good. In an expansive mood, the governor announced he was introducing something translated as "human law" to the war-torn region. We looked puzzled. "Human rights?" we offered as the words they were searching for. "No, no, no," came the emphatic reply. "Not human rights." Everyone laughed heartily. "Law and order."

We were polite. We stressed that we were just in transit. If the governor disliked us, we would never get our papers to pass through his territory to the Iraqi border. The next morning I sent off our Kurdish guide to collect the stamped and signed documents. Everything was in order. We drove through ancient hilltop villages under Turkish military occupation, where we were frequently stopped.

"Your papers, please." The soldier would then study the stamped permit for a very long time. I suspected some of them could not read.

Ilker Calabras, the guide, kept staring at me. As we reached the rugged frontier where thousands of Iraqi Kurds had walked out of the mountains after their failed uprising, he blurted out the story of an English couple he had escorted to the border not long before. They had been mysteriously killed. It was presumed the man had been robbed and murdered and the woman eaten by wild animals. "You look just like them." Ilker blinked impassively. "They were alive when I left."

At the Turkish border post there were demands for huge sums in "exit fees." Ilker was ordered out of the car by a fearsome-looking customs official and hauled off for questioning. We were clearly in trouble. I thought of *Midnight Express,* the horror of Turkish jails. All of us began to chain-smoke. Ilker appeared after what seemed like hours, his face deceptively blank so as to betray nothing. He climbed into the van.

"Let's go. Quickly."

"How did you get out of there?"

"I promised him a tea set."

We wound up into the mountains, passing huge oil tankers loaded up with black market Iraqi oil. Here there was no government, no passport controls, no visas. We called it Free Kurdistan. Checkpoints were manned by "Peshmurga," Kurdish fighters who looked like something out of an etching of Lord Byron in the Orient. Wrapped in soft wool pantaloons cinched with cummerbunds, the fighters were draped with necklaces of amber, silver, and machine-gun bullets. They stood poised on mountain crags fingering the stocks of their rocket-propelled grenades and Kalashnikovs. The name Peshmurga meant "those who court death." Without a second's hesitation, they would slit the throats of a neighboring clan who crossed them.

Our exuberant Kurdish driver hailed them with Kurdish salutes and rebel songs banned in Turkey. In the sheer canyons below, there were rushing waterfalls and fields of sunflowers. Tent encampments littered the rocky ground, full of women in indigo-dyed dresses carrying water tins. The air was fresh under the snowy mountain passes of the Zagros that led to Iran.

We arrived in Zakho, the oil smugglers' boomtown that bordered Turkey and Iraq, armed with letters of introduction. The letters were slightly crumpled and smudged from being hidden at the bottom of my purse in Baghdad. They were typed in Kurdish by the overseas representatives of the Kurdish military factions, with humble Washington offices on Gallows Road. In Zakho, the heavily stamped documents opened all doors. We were billeted in a dilapidated village house with a hopeful sign—PUBLIC RELATIONS OFFICE—freshly painted on the doorway.

This was the local headquarters of the Kurdish Democratic Party, the group taken the most seriously in Washington. The KDP letter was addressed to Massoud Barzani, the KDP chief and leader of the Barzan clan, whose father had died in an American hospital after an unhappy alliance with the CIA. Between 1972 and 1975, the CIA had enthusiastically embraced and just as enthusiastically discarded the KDP at the whim of the Shah of Iran. When the shah made a deal with Baghdad, the Nixon administration ditched the Kurds. The one constant in Washington's Kurdish policy was the fact that they were expendable. A senior U.S. diplomat expressed the sentiment perfectly when he said, "We have bigger fish to fry. The Kurds are not very big fish."

The letter to the rival faction was addressed to Jalal Talabani, leader of the PUK, the Patriotic Union of Kurdistan. Talabani's best friend in Washington was Peter Galbraith, a Senate foreign relations staffer who often sat at my dinner table and would later become ambassador to Croatia. Peter was the Kurds' champion in Washington. When the Bush White House failed to stop Saddam rocketing Kurdistan with his gunships, Peter complained to the National Security Council. He got a cold rebuff. "Our policy is to get rid of Saddam," he was told, "not his regime."

We filmed in the Zakho refugee camp, where five hundred Kurdish families who had been driven into the mountains by Saddam remained homeless. After the huge outpouring of sympathy for the Kurds in the spring, they were left with makeshift tents that would soon be flooded by the September rains. The United Nations had promised to ship emergency roofing. Nothing had arrived. The local U.N. representative had a comfortable office in Zakho and an air-conditioned Range Rover. At dusk, our Belfast cameraman, Peter Fox, happened to be outside the U.N. office filming street life. Fox watched as a thin exhausted man climbed the hill. The man approached, explained that he was a defector from the Iraqi Army and had just walked for miles across the no-man's-land that divided the Kurdish enclave from Iraq proper. He was famished and needed rest. Peter escorted the defector to the U.N. office. They knocked. The curtain opened slightly as the U.N. representative peeked out. The curtain fell. Peter knocked again and explained the man's dire circumstances through a crack in the door. The U.N. response was clipped.

"Go away," said the representative sourly.

Fox was livid. He reminded the U.N. bureaucrat of his humanitarian responsibilities. The man slammed the door and locked it. The Iraqi wandered off dejected.

We were alerted by the "Public Relations Office" that their leader, Massoud Barzani, was due at Rawandiz, miles to the east, the following evening. If we caught up with him, we could have an interview. We set out early down a tortuous dirt track that cut through a spectacular river valley. There was an unnatural primeval emptiness about the place, like a Bierstadt landscape. On closer inspection, every hillside was dotted with piles of stones. We could see old village walls and foundations of houses. Saddam Hussein had reduced nearly four thousand Kurdish villages to rubble. When we reached the ruins of Barzan, the KDP leader's ancestral home, we stopped to film. We wandered through the deserted wreckage getting just the right shot through what was left of a window or a crumbling doorway. The Kurds had neglected to tell us that Barzan was a minefield. (We found out months later from the mine clearers hired to dig them out.)

Saddam's troops had sown mines around the villages so no one would be tempted to rebuild. It was my third brush with land mines, after Central America and Cambodia, a weapon I was coming to despise. The mountain passes through the Zagros were also filigreed with mines during the Iran-Iraq war. No commander had the presence of mind to make a map.

Driving through the cities, Dohuk, Salahuddin, Arbil, I kept running into posters with a photograph of the missing Englishwoman, Ilker's former charge. She was blond and athletic-looking. I pictured her wasted, freezing, perhaps wounded in the minefields. Andrew and I both thought there was something decidedly creepy about the way Ilker kept raising the subject. Was he an accomplice? Or just a guide with a morbid fixation? On a lonely stretch of road where we stopped to drink water, Ilker gestured to the serrated mountain range as inviting as a shark's jaw. "That is where she disappeared."

"That's enough, Ilker," I rounded on him, "I've heard enough."

After twelve hours of punishing travel on the washed-out roads, our driver flush with Kurdish nationalism careening through rivers, we reached Rawandiz. At nightfall, we found Massoud Barzani in a billowy tent receiving feudal lords. They sat respectfully in rows fingering their worry beads until it was their turn to kiss Barzani and express their support. We made a date to interview the Kurdish leader in the morning and joined the medieval gathering for a banquet.

Sitting crossed-legged on the floor, we ate from huge common platters with our fingers. I was the only woman present, and thus an object of curiosity. My dinner partner, an aging vassal of Barzani's, studied me closely. "I am thinking," he volunteered in a purr, "of taking another wife."

Distracted by this proposition, I reached out with my left hand to grab a morsel of fragrant Kurdish rice. I realized with horror that I was committing a breach of etiquette. The left hand is unclean. I dropped the rice. "You must meet my husband," I said brightly.

Our accommodation was the floor of an Assyrian village house occupied by the U.N. zone warden. Carlos had delicate bones and a sickly complexion. He was a Peruvian aristocrat who owned a large hacienda in the Andes, surrounded by the Sendero Luminoso, who enjoyed a reputation as the world's most bloodthirsty guerrillas. In the Peruvian jungle, Carlos lived in splendid isolation, occasionally venturing out to buy books on the conquistadors. He collected sixteenth-century artifacts from the days of Francisco Pizarro. The plight of 100,000 Kurdish refugees in his zone who were about to face a raw winter was of passing interest to him.

Carlos was in Kurdistan by a bizarre twist of fate. Having flown to Geneva to discuss agricultural problems with the United Nations, he was recruited on the spot by the U.N. Commission on Refugees and shipped out to Kurdistan. It seemed so unusual, I couldn't help fantasizing that he was the liaison between the Sendero guerrillas and the rough PKK Kurds. The American chargé d'affaires at the U.S. Embassy in Ankara had told us in strictest confidence that the two groups, seven thousand miles apart, were locked in an alliance of terror. Now my imagination was running away with me, wondering at his strange circumstances. Our host poured himself a tumbler of rough Turkish vodka.

Hoshyar Zubari, the KDP spokesman, rolled up with a short-wave radio. Hoshyar was round and jovial. He sprang from a well-connected family of Kurdish brigands. He announced there had been a coup in Russia. I studied his face lit by a hurricane lamp. "This is a joke." He switched on the BBC news from Moscow. No one was certain who was in charge. The Kurds thought Saddam might take advantage of the chaos. Our host from the shadows said, "Hoshyar, you should put your Peshmurga on alert."

The spokesman vanished into the darkness. We spent a fitful night in the village house and woke up early to film in the Diyana gun market. Machine guns, artillery, rockets, grenades—arms that flowed in from Iraq, Iran, and Turkey—were on sale. The market was packed with Peshmurga fighters, bristling with weapons, examining English holsters, Soviet ammunition. The tent market was also stocked with Sony VCRs, cassette players, and computers, contraband on the smugglers' railway between Iraq and Iran. Sanctions had depleted so much Iraqi capital that merchants were unloading goods abroad at fire-sale prices. The Kurds, also squeezed by sanctions, took a cut. The two commodities on sale in huge quantities in Kurdistan were guns and cigarettes.

Food and shelter were scarce. At the Diyana Clinic, Dr. Salam Mohammed Sultan was ministering to seventy thousand patients, all of them homeless. He was one of eight Kurdish doctors in a region with 500,000 refugees. In a month, he said, it would be too cold to sleep outside. "They have no place to go." Roughly five hundred patients were camped daily in his front garden. The severe shortage of milk was causing malnutrition. The price of a can of baby milk in the market was fifteen to twenty Iraqi dinars, a tenth of the average civil servant's salary. In any case, there were no salaries being paid. Dr. Sultan told us the U.N. High Commission on Refugees office, run by Carlos, was not providing food to the mothers with hollow cheeks and pale-haired children who haunted his waiting room. There had been only one food distribution in Diyana in five months.

"What about shelter? Is anyone from the United States providing shelter?" I asked.

"No," Dr. Sultan shrugged. "Not here."

The leader of the Kurdish Democratic Party received us at his commodious headquarters, teeming with fighters clicking worry beads. Barzani took a jaded view of Washington's policy. He singled out Henry Kissinger as the man who sacrificed the Kurds in 1975. Not much, in his view, had changed. The latest calamity, the lack of food, shelter, and electricity, had forced him into talks with Saddam Hussein, the man who had razed his family village for the sixteenth time. The Kurds living in Iraq had been saddled with twelve months of U.N. sanctions just like Saddam.

"What would you do," he asked me intently, "if you were in my position?"

General Hamid Afandi, a seasoned Kurdish military campaigner, invited us into the mountains to film his Peshmurga training. We drove until the road disappeared near the Iranian border. From there, we walked up steep slopes to catch up with the general. In his seventies he bounded up the switchbacks like a mountain goat. Afandi's men were wild-looking fighters, draped with thousands of rounds of ammunition. We marched up to a mountain meadow on the border and the fighting began. Through the mortar and rocket smoke, we watched the advancing Kurds clutch bushes to their chests and crouch down, the branches obscuring their faces. It was the moving forest, the trick that confounded Macbeth. Volley after volley of live fire was unleashed, the wounded lifted into stretchers, and with beaming smiles, removed from the field. The battle ended with an exuberant victory dance with a few hundred rounds fired into the air. The Kurds loved war.

We were sure some of the Peshmurgas had been drafted by Saddam before the Gulf War and shipped to the front in Kuwait. We found one survivor among Afandi's men. Sahal Majid was a Kurdish conscript with a mechanized unit in the Iraqi Army.

"Soldiers tried to desert. Especially the Kurdish soldiers. Anyone found trying to escape was executed," Majid said. "Some who managed to escape were killed by Allied bombing." In his mechanized unit of eleven men, he was the only survivor. "We withdrew the night before the ground attack. We were in Al-Ahmadi, 150 kilometers deep inside Kuwait, stationed between the shore and the city. The attacks came from the air and sea. The Iraqi forces retreated in disarray before receiving orders and were attacked while withdrawing." He added quietly, "Morale was low." The front line was a graveyard for Saddam's enemies.

The road from Diyana to Kalakeen was walled with sheer rock faces and waterfalls. We were heading to the headquarters of Barzani's rival, Jalal Talabani. This was a strategic pass controlled for centuries by a family of feudal lords called Surchi. The Surchis grew rich off the spoils of traders passing beneath the towering rocks commanded by their gunners and lookouts. In this century the empire had expanded to include the largest construction company in Iraq as well as businesses in Morocco and London. We had met two members of this formidable clan at the outset of our trip at a little Middle Eastern café behind the Mayfair Hilton in London. Jawar Surchi had enough clout to leave his Range Rover parked in front of the Hilton. The only other people who could do that were probably Conrad Hilton and the queen.

Jawar's Uncle Omar was a Kurdish feudal lord of the old school. Rakishly good-looking in his advanced years, Uncle Omar insisted on feeding me little tidbits from the Arabic salads by hand. The Surchis had survived Saddam's regime by making endless compromises. They were collaborators. Just before the Kurdish uprising, they changed sides and joined forces with Barzani, over the pass to the north, and Jalal Talabani, whose stronghold, Sulaimaniya, was down the road to the south. They now formed a solid block against Saddam, though the Surchis were receiving seductive appeals from Baghdad to defect. Saddam's regular correspondence with the family stressed that the outside powers could not be trusted. They broke their word given the chance. Coming back into the fold would mean the return of vast assets that had been confiscated. Jawar was wary. "Saddam," he said with a scowl, "wants to kill us. It's a trap."

As we approached the village of Kalakeen, I fished the letter of introduction from Jawar and Uncle Omar out of my purse. It was addressed to Jawar's father, Hussein, the patriarch of the family. Kalakeen was whitewashed and prosperous. The Surchi compound was sixties Bel Air. The distinguishing feature of this lavish villa was the presence of approximately 150 heavily armed men in the courtyard. They were seated in a circle in what appeared to be an outdoor council. There were heated exchanges in Kurdish. Hussein al-Surchi, with the bearing of a Supreme Court judge, was in the place of honor, flanked by lesser members of the family and his nephew Zaid. The atmosphere was charged.

There was nothing to do but march in and present our credentials. The letter was read, reread, and discussed. Cardamom tea appeared with bowls of pistachios.

It emerged that we had interrupted a council of war. They seemed to regard our arrival as auspicious. The plans to do battle that night for control of a nearby mountain were hastily scratched. We would all attend a wedding party instead.

The first order of business was to drive to Sulaimaniya, a charming hill town across an arid plain, to inform Jalal Talabani's men that the war was called off. Andrew and I were ushered into a pickup with a dozen fighters, armed with grenade launchers, rocket-propelled grenades, and a machine gun trained out the back. With so many well-armed bodyguards, we were suddenly transported back to Colombia, in the mean streets of Cali. Our companion, Shalaw Askari, was an aide-de-camp to Talabani. Shalaw was a dashing figure in his headdress and waistcoat, laden with daggers and bullets. "Hi," said the extravagantly handsome Peshmurga. "Where you guys from?"

It was Shalaw's job to call off the battalions of the village clans. We stopped at several compounds and waited while Shalaw spread the news that the war had been postponed. Safeties off, we roared back into Kalakeen. Caked with dust, I raced into the manse to throw on a dress suitable for a wedding. Hundreds of people were waiting in the village for our entourage. The women wore sequins and silk in electric colors. The bride and groom paid homage to the Surchis. The Kurdish Frank Sinatra, flown in from Germany for the occasion, wove both the feudal lords and us into his lyrics. I was dragged onto the dance floor that covered the town square for energetic Kurdish folk dancing. Fortunately, Hussein Surchi had banned celebratory gunfire from wedding parties because of recent casualties. I was flanked by the patriarch and another feudal lord who fixed his gaze on me in the middle of the festivities and said, "I am thinking of taking another wife."

"Really," I said flirtatiously. "How many do you have?"

"Three."

"You must meet my husband."

We retired to the Surchi villa at two in the morning. A long table was spread in the garden, laden with Johnnie Walker Black Label. The court magician took a seat at the head of the table and performed conjuring tricks until the first course was served at four. He pulled chiffon scarves out of his ear. Zaid, the patriarch's nephew, was getting sloshed and lamenting his fate. "I don't want to be a feudal lord. Everyone coming to me with their problems. Every day. Problems, problems, problems. I am thinking of buying an apartment in Stockholm," he said. "Away from all this."

Before the lamb and goat courses arrived at 5 A.M., I made my excuses and retired, leaving Andrew to carouse until daylight. I fell into our soft double bed on the roof. The sun woke us before eight. Both Andrew and I had crushing hangovers. I sat up in the open air like a piece of badly mending porcelain.

"Let's go home."

Frontline broadcast "The War We Left Behind" in the fall. Hundreds of viewers called to send checks to Doug Broderick at St. Fatima's. Catholic Relief Services called us to say the Pope had urgently requested a tape. There was a Vatican screening. Pope John Paul came out publicly against sanctions as inhumane.

The Kurds called whenever their delegations descended on Washington. They rarely got an audience at the State Department or the White House. The "not very big fish" turned up dejected at our door. One night we had seven feudal lords, including the patriarch Hussein Surchi. By 1996, he, too, was a casualty. In the heat of the summer, Massoud Barzani invaded the village of Kalakeen and massacred forty members of the Surchi family. The massacre led to a civil war between the Kurdish factions, with Talabani turning to Iran for arms and Barzani calling on the services of Saddam Hussein. Zaid escaped to Iran. Uncle Omar went into hiding.

ELEVEN

The Thousand and One Nights

A T THE FOUR SEASONS in New York, I was studying the composition on my plate. A wisp of endive and the odd shrimp gave it a spare, minimalist look. Pellegrino was bubbling in my glass. The decor was postindustrial. The headwaiter arranged his diners like actors on a stage. Patrons did not eat at the Four Seasons, they made deals. This was Tina Brown's canteen. The editor of *Vanity Fair* had already turned a moribund magazine into an instant success and was busy conquering literary New York. This shy, intense woman sitting across from me in her boxy suit had an unerring eye for a story.

Tina invented The Formula. A splash of Hollywood, some stylish art, crime in high places, and one or two first-rate stories on Washington or foreign affairs gave everyone something to read. Her genius was that everyone, every starlet, every congressman, every hairdresser and White House staffer *had* to read it. She understood that politics was sexy. She also threw the sort of parties where you could walk slowly down a marble staircase carrying a blue cocktail. *Vanity Fair* was an event.

It was January 1992, four months since we woke up on the Surchis' roof. Tina wanted Andrew and me to write a piece about the thin upper crust in Baghdad, the Saddams and their friends. Who were these Tikritis? What had happened to them since the war? This was one of the world's most impenetrable stories. The Saddams were reclusive and violent. No Western journalist had ever come close to Saddam's sons, famous for shooting on sight anyone who displeased them. They were dangerous. I was sure we could crack their circle. I suspected they were like the Colombian drug lords, isolated, longing for distractions, killing time watching *The Godfather*.

We packed our bags and headed back to Amman. The next morning we were once again at the Bisharat office, hoping to find a driver willing to make the trip to Baghdad. Nasser, who accepted the job, was married to Saddam's sister's hairdresser. It was a start.

Nasser managed to run out of gas three times in the Jordanian desert. The weather was frigid. There were snowdrifts in the sand. At midnight, halfway across the Iraqi desert, the car died. There was no heat, and given the arctic temperatures, we were bound to freeze by morning. I thought of the Donner party, the ill-fated California pioneers who ate human flesh to survive the Sierra Nevada winter.

Nasser lifted the hood, stared blankly at the engine, jiggled a few pipes, and opened a bag of pistachios. There were no other cars on the road, no highway patrol. Our only hope was the very occasional eighteen-wheeler that made the run at over a hundred miles per hour. They could not even see us.

I walked out into the middle of the highway and waited. If the headlights picked up a blonde standing in the truck lane, the driver would have to investigate this apparition. Maybe. A half an hour went by. No one came. The only sound was the ice wind blasting across the desert floor and the snap of Nasser's Rutba nuts. At last there were headlights. I held my ground with the huge truck bearing down on me until I was blinded by the light. The truck roared by. I stood shivering in the dark, wondering whether this *Vanity Fair* assignment had been the right choice.

Two miles up the road, we heard the roar drop to an idle as the driver slowly came to a halt. He backed up the rig and jumped down from the cab. The Good Samaritan had a bad limp. He surveyed the car, marveled at its passengers, and fished towing ropes out of his cargo hold. The dead car was hooked up to the eighteen-wheeler by a shaky umbilical cord and towed in the dead of night for over a hundred miles.

When we reached a sleepy town called Ramadi, it was pitch-black. The towing ropes broke on a jerry-built bridge over the Euphrates. We knotted the ropes again and pushed. They snapped. A third time we managed to push the car over the rickety span. The real bridge had been bombed. The truck driver towed us to his house. We must, he insisted, spend the night. This was the most generous man I had ever met. We politely declined and woke up the local taxi driver, who, for vast sums, drove us to Baghdad. The city was enshrouded in the Terap, an eerie yellow fog. Nasser was in a state of nervous exhaustion. In spite of his palace connections, Nasser announced he had made up his mind to buy a fake passport in the morning for $2,000 and join his brother in Sweden.

On a Monday night, we were snowed in. It was the worst winter in recent memory. Our plan to venture out to Moudif, famous for its Masgouf fish pulled from the Tigris, was abandoned in favor of a lazy evening at the Rasheed. We wandered down to the National Restaurant, an expensive little bistro done in Casbah gold leaf and black lacquer. Mr. Abdullah was strumming his santir in the corner. The tables were full. Suddenly, it was as though an electric shock ran through the room.

A phalanx of men carrying Uzis poured through the doors. They parted to allow a powerful-looking man wearing a designer jacket and trim beard to lead the pack. We recognized Uday Saddam Hussein, the Iraqi president's eldest son. In his pocket, he carried a golden gun. It took less than three minutes for every table at the National to be cleared. Families, businessmen, government ministers vanished. Full glasses of wine, steaming coffee, a special of the day, were left untouched. It was the sort of scene that puzzles archaeologists.

Two of the bodyguards headed straight for the kitchen to taste the "Excellencies'" food. Uday, with eight close friends, sang a number from what he called "The Days of a Thousand and One Nights." The twenty-eight-year-old son of Saddam Hussein nursed his own decanter of cognac and beat rhythm with a Havana cigar. This was the dutiful son who bludgeoned his father's valet to death for acting as a go-between with Saddam's mistress (the ex-wife of the chairman of Iraqi Airways). An angry Saddam threatened to kill his eldest son and was dissuaded only by King Hussein of Jordan, who flew in to mediate the family crisis. First Family relations were now smooth.

One of Uday's dinner companions appeared at our table. Andrew and I were seated with two other journalists. The four of us represented the entire Baghdad press corps. The gentleman kissed my hand and offered to introduce me to "Their Excellencies," Uday and his brother, Qusay. "Here there is a lion," said the Saddam family friend with a leer. "There you see the two cubs." I spotted Qusay, dressed out of a J. Crew catalog. He had the watered-down features of the face in a thousand and one portraits around town.

The last time Uday fancied a woman in a restaurant, Baghdadis whispered, he shot her army officer husband on the spot. Andrew was looking pale. On the other hand, Uday never talked to journalists, ever. This would be a coup. The fact that the brothers had walked into the National at all was providence. If I did not accept this invitation, I would never forgive myself. I got up from our table and was soon wedged into an intimate corner, with Uday studying me from behind his cigar.

He had long feathery eyelashes that seemed to weigh him down when he blinked. There was something very feline about Uday. I was pressed against the wall on one side and Uday's twenty-five-year-old brother on the other, who had clammy hands and an awkward laugh. Qusay was nervous. He tried to charm me with facts about Mesopotamian culture, explaining to me the meaning of the thousand and one nights, all the while glancing furtively across the table for his brother's approval.

"So you're the baby of the family," I said to Qusay.

"Not such a baby now." His big brother, Uday, laughed. "He runs all the security services."

Qusay's secret police, the Mukhabarat, excited the same frisson in Baghdad as the Duvaliers' Tontons Macoute had in Port-au-Prince. Every waiter, every man in a short leather jacket and a vacant look, could be Mukhabarat. In the past nine months of the Hujoum al-Mudhad, or "the Counterattack," as the rebuilding of Baghdad was known, the Mukhabarat had tightened on the city like a vise. Even among those who were reaping the immense profits of reconstruction, with a contract to rebuild a bridge or a government office block or a tasteful three-story mansion for a deputy minister, the small at-home dinner party had become very popular. "We can't talk in restaurants," remarked one beneficiary of the Counterattack to us. "People get arrested for making a joke."

Their Excellencies, the cubs, were above all of this. Uday and Qusay, who as children confided to playmates that they were allowed to witness torture sessions in preparation for the tasks ahead, had immunity. Uday flaunted his immunity every morning when his newspaper, *Babel*, hit the stands. "Iraq's only independent daily," as its editor proudly described it, *Babel* had a circulation of seventy thousand. It was the talk of Baghdad because its columns were rife with uninhibited attacks on the government (the father of the proprietor excluded).

Babel's editor in chief, Abbas Jenaby, was Uday's best friend, confidant, and secretary. Jenaby had the privilege of sitting next to His Excellency across the table. He chain-smoked and sipped Johnnie Walker Black Label, the Iraqi national drink. Uday poured another cognac from his personal bottle. This was insurance, I thought, that he would not be poisoned. The conversation turned, as it often did in Baghdad, to the widely advertised covert operations being mounted by the Bush White House to "get" Saddam and his family. The cubs laughed at the notion, proclaimed by Pentagon briefer Pete Williams, that there were "cracks in the inner circle," cracks to be exploited by a well-financed replay of the Kurdish and Shiite revolts that failed so miserably after Desert Storm.

"Look," said Uday, fixing me with his unnaturally large brown eyes, "this business about splitting us is nonsense." He pointed his cigar down the table littered with Scotch. "I have two Shiites here. I have a Kurd who works for me." Jenaby, the editor, nodded in tandem.

To buttress Uday's claims of national unity, Jenaby whipped out a tiny passport photo. "This man," he said gravely, "is a Kurd. He was burned to death by the Kurds. The Kurds are begging for Saddam." The editor drained his whisky. "They are praying to God that Saddam will come." The cubs beamed. There were no splits at this table. Uday took a dim view of dissent.

Johnny, the Sudanese waiter, was dashing nervously around the table, lighting cigarettes and sweeping off offending crumbs, careful not to meet anyone's eye. His demeanor reminded me of the cabdriver outside the compound of the Cali cartel's chief of production. As some fragrant snuff was offered around the table, a junior officer from one of the security services swaggered into the restaurant, registered the identity of the customers, and bolted from the room.

I was sitting with a very dangerous man. "Speak civilly to blondes," I told myself. If I behave normally, so will he. Then he will not smell the fear. I was aggressive, teasing, I listened with rapt attention. Uday began telling me about the intellectual career he had wanted so badly. His dream, he said shyly, was to be a nuclear physicist. In 1979 and 1980, before the Israeli Air Force knocked out the Osirak reactor, Uday told me, he traveled to the States to prep for an American university.

"I did my SATs, everything. I did very well," he puffed. "Passed with high marks." But he was forced to abandon the pursuit. "You see, I wanted to do nuclear studies. At the time, there was a problem with Iraqis' doing that." He studied his cognac. "I wanted to go to MIT."

The instant Uday thinks he has confided too much, I thought, he can march me out of here at gunpoint and no one can stop him.

Now, with the United Nations inspection teams rifling through the top secret documents in the wreckage of Iraq's nuclear installations, Uday's dream of building the bomb was on hold. Still, there were consolations. With no prospect of nuclear tests in the desert, Uday had more time for tending the plants in his extensive greenhouses behind the tennis court and driving his black Porsche.

No one at this table was suffering the effects of eighteen months of economic sanctions. Two Armenians, one with an enormous gut who was boisterously drunk, the other very thin and even more drunk, were the beneficiaries of the economic boom that had enriched those with connections to Their Excellencies. The thin one was the family jeweler. He preyed on the postwar travails of middle-class Iraqis, pawning their gold for dinars to buy the astronomically expensive food.

His well-fed colleague one place down was Saddam's tailor and court philosopher. The tailor passed a beefy hand over his pomaded silver hair and began grilling me loudly, "Do you know Howard

Hughes? Well, you know who he is. You know the Armenian who worked with him? Owns all the casinos?"

"No," I admitted.

Uday, across the table, was amused by this exchange.

"How come I know more about America than you do?" asked the court tailor. "Because I'm from Sacramento. I'm from the Mafia. If you ever need any help, the Mafia can help you. I'll fix it."

He recalled happy days in Las Vegas. "What is the name of this guy, you know, with the rings and the big heart? Liberace. Oh, he was such a good man."

The Armenian turned to Saddam's eldest. "Do you know Liberace, Las Vegas?"

"No," said Uday with a lazy stare. "Only Engelbert Humperdinck."

Uday had tolerated enough competition from the Armenian. He wanted my attention back and brought up the salacious gossip that had reached the Middle East about then candidate Bill Clinton's girlfriends. Uday was disgusted that private trysts would have any bearing on the national debate. "This woman Flowers," he said disparagingly, sympathizing with the candidate. "Really, this has no place in politics."

Uday's entourage vigorously agreed. Everyone at this table was testimony to the fact that money was flooding into the pockets of the ruling family's courtiers and associates, promoting the kind of loyalty that kept the regime in power. As one wild-boar-hunting companion of Uday's put it after ordering a bottle of champagne sent to the other table, "Business is very, very good." He poured Andrew a glass. "It's a great time for buying and selling."

From behind a cloud of smoke at the head of the table, Saddam's heir assured me there was an upside to an economy devastated by war and sanctions. "With this situation there's a lot of trade to be done," he said, adding modestly, "So I am doing some trade." He paused as Mr. Abdullah, who was careful not to look at his patron, picked out another melody.

Uday closed his eyes. He opened them and sat very still, watching me. His gaze ran down my neck.

"This is a Kurdish song," he observed. "Very beautiful." He drained his glass of Rémy Martin XO Special and burst into song.

It was time to excuse myself. Either I left now or I would pay dearly for ignoring the warnings.

When I returned to my table, Uday's pimp clutched my arm. "You're a tiger."

So long as we stayed inside Baghdad city limits, we could move around without a government minder. Free of spies and cameras, people felt more at ease talking.

"There are the rich who smuggle, the rich who take bribes, and the rich who steal," said one prominent Iraqi over an afternoon arrack the next day, in what he hoped was the privacy of his garden. The "new billionaires," as he called them, had seized the business opportunities afforded by sanctions and Iraq's porous border with Jordan, Syria, Turkey, and Iran. These were Uday's boys. He allowed them to operate and they in turn swore allegiance. With food prices, in some cases, twenty to sixty times what they were before the invasion of Kuwait, and with the need for spare parts so acute, the profits were almost limitless. Anyone with access to an import route, including contact with the insurgent Kurds in the north, was smuggling.

Tariq Aziz, the canny foreign minister who faced Secretary of State James Baker across the table in Geneva in the final days before the bombing of Baghdad, was sanguine about the explosion of profiteering. Deputy prime minister and in charge of what was left of Iraq's relations with the outside world, he ranked number six in the ruling Baath Party hierarchy. This kept him near the center of power and comfortably settled in a vast suite of offices. The cavernous room, the plush carpets, the sprawling acres of walled grounds—all spoke of a solid conviction that the regime would stand. The only sign that something had rattled the status quo in the preceding year and a half was the profusion of small pyramids— the tops of bunkers—throughout the grounds, and the skeletons of bombed-out buildings beyond the gates.

"It's not the government that sells Scotch whisky and fine clothes," explained Aziz, as he relit a pipeful of expensive tobacco. "It's the merchants. They are smuggling it. If they smuggle it through Turkey, we cannot stop them. At least the rich people can buy things. The upper class can buy whatever they wish. The lower class, they are not starving." The government food distribution system now managed to supply people with an exiguous thirteen hundred calories a day. If the government shut down the trading, Aziz reasoned, "then there would be a mess like the Soviet Union." In short, the new billionaires were a phenomenon that any American should appreciate. "This," said Aziz, obviously amused, "is the result of the free market."

How long the massive welfare system could continue without oil revenue to pay for it was a question Aziz chose to answer with uncharacteristic brevity. "State secret."

Aziz looked at both of us with deep interest.

"May I ask you something?"

"Of course."

"You're married?"

"That's right."

"What's it like working together?"

We pieced together the answers to the delicate question of the Saddam regime's cash flow over the next several weeks. "They are printing money around the clock," observed one Iraqi flourishing in the boom. "The soldiers guard the mint day and night." Iraqi officials were also turning up around the Middle East with gold ingots to sell; bribes paid by Western companies for Iraqi construction contracts in the prewar days had left a lot of dollars sitting in Swiss accounts; the government was quietly selling off majority stakes in state-owned enterprises (payment in dollars only); and loot from Kuwait was still on hand, for which there was a good market in Iran. The traffic flowed through Kurdistan.

Although there were more direct routes farther south, the bribes extracted there by the local Iraqi Army commanders were considered outrageously high: "Fifty percent, who can make a profit on that?" merchants lamented. The Iranians paid in dollars. Smugglers agreed that everyone and everything in Iraq was for sale. A lot of people from the elder cub on down were getting rich.

This fortunate group could lavish dinars on what Ali Hassan al-Majid, the prudish defense minister (famed for gasing Kurdish villagers at Halabja), had recently called denigrating nocturnal activities. He was chastising one of the new rich, who was moved to ecstasy by a Baghdad belly dancer and hurled a blank check at her feet.

We went in search of denigrating nocturnal activities at the Embasy (*sic*) nightclub, just down the street from the forlorn-looking American Embassy, then staffed by four Polish diplomats. Patrons slouched over Black Label watched as five blondes poured into satin sheaths danced with one enormously fat man. He grinned expansively at his multiple partner, his tiny feet steering the train of well-fed hookers.

We adjourned to Anduls, described to me by the barker at the door as a "family nightclub." The floor show, lit by strobe lights, was a blur of red crepe. As the band struck up a deafening Yemeni pop tune, a young mother in three-inch *peau de soie* heels escorted her daughter to the stage. Together, the pair moved gracefully around the dance floor, the little girl tapping her Mary Janes. The bill for one beer and one Pepsi came to 120 dinars, three weeks' wages for a junior bureaucrat. "Business," the manager said, flashing a radiant smile at us, "is excellent."

One way to earn the price of an evening at Anduls, besides smuggling, was to be part of the construction boom fueled by the Counterattack on the wreckage left by Allied bombs. Saad al-Zubaidi, prematurely gray and brimming with brisk technocratic energy, helped plan Iraq's comeback from what an apocalyptic U.N. report of the time called a preindustrial state. Zubaidi's job was to find solutions without importing parts and expertise. "We reinvented the suspension bridge," he said defiantly.

As the house Zubaidi built for himself on a palm-lined street in the upscale district of Mansour attests, the rewards for the heroes of reconstruction were considerable. Even dump-truck owners were getting 1,000 dinars a day (roughly five times the average monthly wage).

Rooting in his drink cabinet for a bottle of Glenfiddich (saying Black Label was not good enough), Zubaidi talked of the pride he felt that Iraqis were rebuilding on their own. "All the oil exporting had a similar disease. They were totally dependent on foreigners. It was easier to send a telex to Japan when you needed something." It delighted Zubaidi that foreign companies, who so readily turned over blueprints to the air staffs of the United States and Britain for targeting, were losing multimillion-dollar contracts to rebuild. Sanctions cut both ways.

The Baathists had become the party of business. With the New Deal for contractors, Saddam had gained some fast friends.

Keeping the civil service happy was another priority. "A lot of the ministers are building big houses now," said one observer on the receiving end. "The government gives them a plot of land, and they get a very cheap price on all the building materials. These are people, in some cases, who are just coming up in the world. They don't understand a Jacuzzi or a sauna. It has to be explained to them that a pool is a good idea. It makes them better than their neighbors."

Nor was the army being neglected. Gold "Mother of Battle" medals, bestowed by the fistful, came with cash. Some of them came with cars. Alluding to the hopeful speculation in Washington about a possible coup from inside the ranks of the military, Aziz smiled. "When we speak about the army, they are all our own men. For every officer there is a relative, a brother, a cousin, a brother-in-law, in the Ministry of Interior, the Ministry of Information, the Ministry of Communications. So how is this man going to organize a coup? Against his own people?" It was worth remembering that the Baathists considered the entire family guilty for the act of a traitor. The family bloodbath was an effective deterrent.

Aziz was dismissive of opposition leaders abroad. "Who are these people, these figures who are being paid by the CIA? Thirty million of the CIA budget, which is paid by the American taxpayer in this period of recession, would be spent on whom? They don't have a power base in this country. Mr. Bush is complicating his own situation. I am 100 percent sure this scheme is going to fail."

These were lean days in Baghdad for the men who forged the U.S.-Iraq relationship. At a quiet dinner at the Iraqi Hunting Club, the air was thick with nostalgia for Washington and the alliance. Nizar Hamdoon, a deputy foreign minister, made his mark as Iraqi ambassador in the Reagan years. "The Potomac," he said wistfully, "reminds me of the Tigris." As ambassador, he moved freely in the halls of power, persuading the Reagan men to funnel intelligence through him to Baghdad. Up-to-the-minute satellite photos of Iraq's battlefront with Iran, wide-ranging plans for arms supplies, not to mention massive trade deals, passed through his hands. Hamdoon had mastered a pitch on the dangers of the Iranian threat that prompted the U.S. assistance to Iraq. He mused now about whether it might work a second time around.

As a beautifully browned two-by-three-foot Tigris fish was laid on the table, Sa'doon Zubaydi, Saddam's official translator, thought sadly of "April." The American ambassador, April Glaspie, whose diplomatic career was the first casualty of the Gulf War, was a favorite of Zubaydi's. "Poor April," he murmured. "They made her scapegoat." It was disconcerting hearing Zubaydi reminisce in an affected English accent, laboriously acquired during his Shakespeare studies in Birmingham, England. ("I know this will absolutely shock you, but to me Birmingham is *such* a lovely city.") It was Zubaydi's voice that made the moment so chilling when Saddam asked British hostage "little Stuart" whether he was getting his milk and "cornflakes too." Tapping his lip neatly with his damask napkin, Zubaydi said with pride, "You know, I coined a word during the crisis. Absolutely everybody used it . . . 'guestages.' "

Ambassador Hamdoon cleared his throat and turned the conversation to the American electoral campaign. He thought Bush might need another foreign adventure to pull up his numbers. Down the table, Zubaydi was struck with a foreign policy inspiration. "Qaddafi," exclaimed the Shakespearean scholar. "Qaddafi could be an out for Bush. A replacement for Saddam Hussein." The table agreed that bombing Tripoli would be preferable to bombing, say, the Hunting Club.

Such wisdom from pro-American diplomats was going to waste. All agreed that in early 1990, there were "such high hopes for Bush." There was an awkward silence. "America," lamented Zubaydi, "has lost a *very* good friend in the Middle East."

The highest-rated program on Iraqi television was *Portfolio*, a day-by-day account of what happened during the bombing. Created and anchored by a former correspondent for Kuwaiti television who modeled his style on that of Alistair Cooke, *Portfolio* riveted Baghdadis, whose memories of the bombing were a confusion of blackouts, block parties, and deafening explosions. Even those who freely satirized "Himself" in conversation sat rapt in front of the set. As they listened to details of the 88,000 tons dropped, they repeated in amazement the statistics for one day's load: "Four kilos of ordnance for each Iraqi." It was common currency that the war was aimed at them—not at the army of occupation in Kuwait, not at the regime, but at *them.*

With the images flickering on the screen, there was also a wave of war nostalgia. Uday's friend the wild-boar hunter recalled happy days at his country house. "We had a great time, playing cards by candlelight, drinking, watching the cruise missiles going overhead."

Andrew and I were invited to a war-anniversary dinner party that reunited three families who floated from house to house during the bombing.

"I drank myself through the war," announced one guest. His wife, a midwife, recalled delivering babies in the dark, "no candles even, just feeling for the head." In the private hospital where she worked, things had improved. Tucking into a plateful of lasagna and dumplings, the fare of a well-connected group, she sighed, "The war was great for losing weight."

"The kiddies think we won the war," says one Iraqi matron who does not hide her disdain for Saddam. "They're indoctrinated at school. 'He' has become very popular again. He stood up to thirty-one countries and they withdrew." Perhaps because casualties in Kuwait were low, the war was fading from memory, replaced by the standoff, the U.S. versus Iraq. "Not many soldiers died in the war. Maybe fewer than 25,000. All the boys we know who were there walked home. They deserted."

The memory of war death in Baghdad, however, was very stark. The anniversary of the bombing of the Amariya shelter, when two direct Allied hits incinerated upwards of three hundred women and children, was a macabre event. We arrived for the ceremony, produced by the cinema department of the Ministry of Information, with streams of mourners in black chadors. Outside the shelter, in VIP seats, the families of the dead were asked to sit and be viewed. They sat, hour after hour.

Inside, the blackened walls and the ugly bomb crater with its skirt of twisted metal were lit by tall, medieval candles. Their smoke turned, as the day wore on, into an almost impenetrable gloom. In a side chamber, a chanting children's choir lined the walk to a grim altar, where a priest was saying mass. The prescribed tour route was banked by wreaths for the dead, still in crisp plastic wrapping. There was an eddy in the crowd as the minister of information, unkindly known as Rent-a-Thug, walked briskly through the scene, flanked by heavily armed guards. He had a dissipated face, with eyebrows that looked painted on. Suddenly, a woman began to scream hysterically. She was mad with grief. Her son was burned to death in this awful place. The crowd surged around her. There was real anger, tapped artfully by the cinema department of the Ministry of Information to revive the hate.

Uday, Saddam's son and heir, was not among those present at the Amariya spectacle. At the National Restaurant, a world away, he puffed languidly on his Havana and said to me, "You must go to the little people. They will tell you that since the war they are anti-American. They will tell you that." He may have been right. But the little people, amid their troubles, were also whispering the name Uday. It seemed to me the excesses at his table might one day draw the angry crowd from Amariya over to the National.

Before we left Baghdad, a sign was posted at the Ministry of Information saying that all journalists who were in Iraq for more than ten days were required to have an AIDS test. The four of us in the country conferred. Andrew and I said we would never submit to an Iraqi syringe. The wire service reporter agreed. A young CNN producer, in the country on his own, thought he should abide by the rules.

"Don't," I said. "They won't force you until they want to expel you."

The AIDS-test variety of intimidation was unsettling. I was glad to get out. We arrived home after twenty-four hours of driving and flying with pounded silver bracelets and belly-dancing costumes for the girls.

Tina loved the piece. In Baghdad, the Saddam family was apoplectic with rage. Copies smuggled into the country were passed around like a forbidden samizdat. Nizar Hamdoon, the worldly diplomat who was still representing Iraq at the United Nations, asked to meet us for a drink at the Stanhope bar, his favorite haunt across from the Metropolitan Museum on Fifth Avenue. In the intimate wood-paneled room, Nizar broke the bad news.

"You're blacklisted."

"We can't go back?" I asked.

"Well, you might get a visa to go back," Nizar said with a faint smile. "But it's very unlikely you'll come out again. I would advise you to stay away from Iraq. Uday will kill you."

In December 1996, I assumed that at least that threat was behind me when a gunman seeking revenge for the death of his uncle ambushed Uday in the manicured Mansour district of Baghdad. The hit man fired a machine-gun burst through Uday's car window at point-blank range. Intelligence reports said the lion's cub was left paralyzed with permanent brain damage. In fact, the reports were wrong. Uday left his hospital bed in June 1977 on crutches, having survived the effects of eight high-velocity bullets with, presumably, his grudge against me intact.

In the meantime, there was another crisis unfolding to the south in Africa, in a country where no one wanted to go.

The Music of Mogadishu

"S OMALIA." Nurse Johnson, inoculations specialist at Georgetown Hospital, studied the latest international health bulletins. "Water, undrinkable. Food, unfit for human consumption. Especially you with that stomach."

I was six months pregnant.

Our usual consultation the week before any expedition to load up on gamma globulin shots, typhoid shots, tetanus shots, and polio boosters had a certain edge this time. It was October 1992. The newspapers were calling Somalia the most dangerous country in the world. A catastrophic famine had transformed whole towns into charnel houses. I had just picked up my ticket to Africa at the ABC News bureau on DeSales Street.

"Given the malaria problem, you've got a choice." Johnson trained her clinical gaze on me. "Take the pills and take the risk. Don't take the pills, get malaria, and . . ."

"I'll take the pills."

"For the cerebral malaria, you need the treated mosquito nets. String it up over your sleeping bag without fail. You can pick those up in Nairobi. Under no circumstances use chemical mosquito repellent. Not in your condition. You've got to pick up the natural stuff when you go through London. Oh and by the way," she said, turning back to her paperwork, "can you send me a postcard?"

"There's no mail service. I doubt they make postcards anymore."

"Well, good luck."

My reasons for mounting this ABC News expedition in the heat of the East African dry season were journalistically sound, though a Red Cross famine relief worker called it "a new low in prenatal care." Tom Yellin, who was the executive producer of *Peter Jennings Reporting*, was launching a weekly series called *Day One* and had signed me up to produce three foreign stories. I was appalled that the coverage of the Somalia famine, while unleashing a short burst of aid and sympathy, was little more than a montage of wizened children and crazed gunmen. The cause of the disaster, the fact that it was man-made, and the reasons why the country had collapsed into anarchy had been largely ignored. The U.S. military sound bite of choice was "it's just like *Mad Max*," a glib comparison with the film about a post-apocalyptic world that was brutal and insane.

The world's response to the disintegration of Somalia had come six months too late. There had been warnings in the early spring that conditions were deteriorating, drinking wells had been poisoned, fields ravaged, by the legions of the old dictator Siad Barre (propped up in turn by the Soviets and the Americans), as they fled the country for exile in Nigeria in the midst of the Gulf War. The United Nations behaved badly. As the iron grip of the old regime loosened, defeated in a bloody civil war, the U.N. office shut down. Once the horror of children who could wear a wedding ring above the elbow was recorded on videotape, the agencies flocked back. But the common perception reinforced by the cameras that charged in with them was that Africa is, by nature, plagued by famine. Children there are condemned, in the grand scheme of things, to starve.

The first wave of journalists had done their "stand-ups," shouted their copy down the satellite phones, and left. The violence had escalated to the point where others were reluctant to replace them. One ABC correspondent ordered to Mogadishu flatly refused. "I can't stand the death," he announced hysterically. It seemed the right moment to step into the breach, while the "pack" was gone. It was two months before President Bush would order U.S. forces to land on the beach.

Tom Yellin was game. He had hired a correspondent from National Public Radio, John Hockenberry, who was equally keen to go. I found him unpacking boxes in the ABC offices on New York's

Upper West Side. John had given up NPR for the bright lights of the network. I had just flown back from Colombia, covering Pablo Escobar for *Vanity Fair*. In the annals of war coverage, John and I made a bizarre couple heading off to the front. I was pregnant and John was in a wheelchair, crippled by a car crash he miraculously survived sixteen years before.

Our party became increasingly colorful as I signed up Carlos Mavroleon, one of the first journalists to capture images of the dying country. He was English, a Somali speaker (as well as Arabic, Farsi, and Pashto), and a Muslim convert. By reputation, he dressed like a Somali and had encyclopedic knowledge of Somali clans. He was a modern T. E. Lawrence and I gambled that he could keep us alive. My itinerary was very ambitious. I wanted to travel the length and breadth of the country, crossing numerous clan lines. I knew enough about Somalia from my days in East Africa to see the wisdom of recruiting a first-class guide.

I dispatched Carlos from London to Mogadishu to handpick our militiamen, the private army who would staff our "technicals," jeeps mounted with machine guns and grenade launchers. (The word "technical" came from an ill-defined line item in relief agency budgets, heavily armed men slipped in as "technical" assistance.) We would rendezvous the following week. At the London bureau, I was fitted with a steel-plated flak jacket, size extra-large. It was crushingly heavy and hot, barely accommodating my stomach, already known affectionately as Charlie. (I knew the baby was a boy.)

Fortunately, I was in peak condition and my doctors had plied me with iron and vitamins. If Andrew was worried, he never let it show. It was the Scottish boarding school training.

There were no scheduled flights into Somalia. U.S. Air Force C-130 transports were making emergency food drops, touching down and unloading rice with engines running. The crews were based in Mombasa, an old Arab traders' port on the Kenya coast. The U.S. military was loath to sit on the ground in Somalia for more than five minutes for fear of a burst of machine-gun fire or a rocket-propelled grenade plowing through the fuselage.

We checked and rechecked the baggage. Priceless food and water, camping equipment, and medical kits left less room for camera gear. The cameraman, Alex Zakrzewski, was a master at stripping down his camera, lenses, cables, tapes, to the barest minimum. We would do without lights.

My last obstacle was boarding the military plane without invoking the raft of Pentagon regulations about a pregnant woman being transported, let alone dropped, in a free-fire zone. When a U.S. Air Force general inquired solicitously about my condition in Mombasa, I fired back, "You really know how to hurt a girl."

Our departure time was well before the equatorial dawn. We strapped ourselves into jump seats that lined the cavernous open hold stacked with palates of rice. By the time the plane lumbered over what appeared to be the deserted airstrip outside Baidoa, the air force crew was nervous. In the cockpit, the pilots surveyed the dust-colored plain below, broken by scrub and thorn trees. The crew chief descended into the open belly of the plane and shouted over the engines that we would not be allowed off the aircraft.

Trouble was expected. A reconnaissance team would have to "check the perimeter" before anyone could deplane. The crew chief and his mates were not anxious to do the job. I realized that none of them had ever faced an "enemy" of any kind. They were terrified.

I am not going back now, I thought. I have moved mountains to get here.

> What makes the Hottentots so hot?
> Courage.

Odd how things come to mind at times like this. I suddenly saw the Cowardly Lion on his way to Oz. Having flown seven thousand miles, I was not ready to cut and run.

"I'll go first," I volunteered over the engine roar. "I'll check the perimeter."

To my astonishment the crew chief gratefully accepted. This would be Charlie's first act of reckless valor.

Pouring with sweat, and hardly a match for guerrilla fighters looking to commandeer a valuable cargo of rice, I clambered over the palates and leapt off the back of the plane. Waves of heat rolled over the desolate landscape. No one fired a shot. Two jeeps appeared across the tarmac, fitted with machine-gun mounts and equipped with enough rocket-propelled grenades, grenade launchers, and Uzis to carry on a small war. The fighters were thin and sleek with sweat, chewing huge wads of *qat*, a narcotic leaf that dulls hunger but sets the nerves on edge. (Shoot-outs were far more common in Somalia after the midday delivery of *qat*.) They wore glistening ammo belts and Easy Rider shades. One, with his head wrapped like an Arab trader, was not Somali. But under a thick black beard and skin burned brown, it was difficult to tell what he was.

"You must be Leslie," he said with an appealing command of the situation.

"And you must be Carlos."

The fierce-looking band was our welcoming party. They had driven from Mogadishu, several hours of bad road to the east. The chances of ambush by a hostile militia were better than even. Out on the burning tarmac, there was little time for introductions. The crew of the C-130 kept the engines running as they disgorged our team and a dozen metal cases of camera gear, eyeing our disreputable-looking escorts with suspicion. Another jeep tore onto the runway with CARE stamped on the side. CARE was one of a dozen or so aid agencies with representatives scattered around the country. Their business was strictly humanitarian. We expected the warm greeting of a fellow foreigner in a dangerous place. Instead, two officious Europeans jumped out yelling orders.

"You must leave immediately. No journalists are allowed in this zone. Aid workers are being evacuated."

There was heavy fighting just down the road between the forces of General Mohammed Farah Aideed, a clan leader from Mogadishu who had been instrumental in toppling the former dictator in the long and torturous civil war, and General Morgan, the former dictator's son-in-law, a veteran of military intelligence training in the United States who sported a beard like Fidel Castro's. We were ordered to reboard the military transport at once and head back to Kenya. It was a trying day.

"We are staying," I said politely. We did, after all, have a lot of guns on our side. Carlos unfurled a superb map on the ground and pinpointed the locations of the units now fighting.

"We'll do our best to avoid interfering," he offered tactfully. The CARE men repeated the orders and talked at length into their radios. It was unclear who was on the other end. As diplomatically as possible, we reminded the gentlemen that Somalia had no government, that neither CARE nor the United Nations (which they invoked) had any authority beyond their immediate operations. As the country was in a state of total anarchy, we were, whether they liked it or not, free to do as we pleased. They made churlish noises about how they could not be held responsible if we were dead by morning. They themselves were expecting to evacuate the region at any moment. A charter was on standby to get them out. We would not be welcome on board. Like the Mad Hatter and the White Rabbit, they roared off in a huff.

A great green behemoth, the C-130 thundered down the runway and our little party was finally left in peace. With the exception of a few weaverbirds, it was dead quiet. At that moment, when the lifeline to civilization is removed, when there is no telephone, no hotel, no restaurant, no police station, no amenities, and no rules, you feel vulnerable and pleasantly light-headed, like a glider when the tow plane has released the cable and left you at the mercy of the next updraft of air.

Our first order of business was to gather information quickly, information that could prevent a disastrous misstep, a wrong turn, a run-in with a hostile patrol, a dangerous slight. Things were changing rapidly. A decision had to be made on what to do in the next hour, not the next day or week. In the back of the jeep, we reviewed the pattern of fighting, the structure of makeshift authority in the town. We stopped to pay our respects to an "official" representing the faction currently in charge of the streets just outside the airport gate. He peered at our passports from every angle, inspecting our vital statistics upside down. This "formality" ended with demands for a fee.

Our canned and dried food and bottled water were packed under tarps. There was an ample supply of army-issue mosquito repellent, the kind that ate the lettering off pens. The fumes from five-gallon containers of fuel wafted through the jeeps where everyone was nonchalantly lighting up. The heavy flak jackets, with their steel plates designed to stop a bullet from an AK-47, turned out to be useless. Somali militiamen delighted in using them for target practice, to see whether they were as good as advertised. I propped mine against the door of the jeep, invisible from the outside, giving me the comforting illusion that I was traveling in an armored car.

The town of Baidoa was a decayed relic of the Italian colony of Somalia. The low stucco buildings were washed with once brilliant Mediterranean colors, turquoise, ochre, aquamarine, burnt reds, coral, and citrine yellow. The African sun had beaten them into pastels, now pocked with shell fire, machine-gun bursts, from battles that had raged throughout 1991 and 1992 and won nothing. The ecstasy that swept the country when the dictator fled in January 1991 faded as the edifice he built, financed first by the Soviet Union and then, in a cold war swap of alliances, by the United States, fell into ruin. The country's coffers were left empty. Foreign finance dried up. The shiny high-tech factories, the World Bank projects, the fruits of International Monetary Fund loans, were now blackened shells, spooky monuments to the end of progress. Miles of telephone wires were stripped, the poles left like grave markers.

Everyone fled with the dictator. The American ambassador and his Russian counterpart left on the same plane. The diplomats, the oilmen, the businessmen, the communications men, the travel agents, the U.N.—all packed their bags and shut down modern Somalia.

Somalis themselves had emigrated in droves ever since the civil war began in earnest in 1988, when the dictator took to bombing his own cities from planes that fueled up at the local airport and dropped their cluster bombs on the crowded marketplace, the school, the hairdresser. Norine Mariano, a Somali woman of breathtaking beauty draped in yellow silk, ran a Somali aid group in Hargeisa. She remembered mercenary pilots being ordered to "bomb or shoot anything that moves." Block after block of her town was flattened. We walked through the ruins, crowded with squatter families in tents made of patched cloth. "It was not a secret. The world knew it," she told us with a sad smile. "Siad Barre," the dictator, "was taking people from the embassies in Mogadishu to show them the lesson he had taught his people. The American ambassador, the Russian ambassador, the Arab League, the African ambassadors, they all came, saw everything, watched it, were escorted by tanks through the streets."

Professional Somalis with means, the doctors, lawyers, and accountants, moved their families abroad. Somalis educated in Europe and at Harvard and Yale, Somalis under suspicion for antigovernment sympathies, vanished into refugee camps across the borders. In the crowded camps we saw along the Kenya coast, there were Somalis who arrived in a dozen waves of upheaval. The country was hemorrhaging. Teenage militiamen, mounting the guns on their souped-up jeeps in Baidoa, grew up with war. Their fathers died in the civil war. "The gun was their friend," said Norine. "It was their toy, their father, their uncle. That is what they were taught."

Some of the militiamen who prowled the streets were children. We had one on the roof of our jeep, whose job, assigned by his uncle the driver, was to man a grenade launcher that weighed nearly as much as the boy. He hugged his weapon like a sibling, and could dismantle or reload it in seconds. His frayed T-shirt had BOSS printed in large letters across his chest. He was a beautiful boy, sweet-natured and loyal. His ambition was to die fighting. "When I grow up," he said with radiant pride, "I'll go in between the bullets."

Before setting out to film, we had to establish a base. The Italian colonial architects built compounds, houses with modest courtyards planted with shade trees and sheltered with high walls with gates that locked after dark. Now they were locked at all hours of the day. Our best bet was to prevail on one of the few remaining aid groups to lend us a bare floor where we could roll out sleeping bags, string nets, stow gear. Our jeeps roared up to one set of locked gates after another. We banged on the gates, which opened fast and closed immediately after the jeeps were inside. The aid workers appeared drained and jumpy. They refused to take us in, even though we required nothing but a floor. One small room for all of us. The reasons were vague. Some said they might be evacuated. Others thought our presence might bring trouble. They lived in constant fear of being invaded, robbed, rocketed.

Our situation was beginning to look desperate. I thought of Manger Square in Bethlehem, where the basement attraction under the church was the tour guide's heavy breathing, simulating the stable animals keeping Mary warm at night. Our last stop was the

Red Cross compound, run by a Frenchman who looked as though he had spent too long in the bush. He responded to our entreaties with a glassy stare. He was about to send us into the street when I played my only card. I offered him a bottle of excellent Sancerre I had carried several thousand miles. He accepted without hesitation. We struck a bargain, a six-by-twelve floor for six dollars a head. For the wine, a rare luxury, he threw in one camp cot. I had spent my capital on the first day in Somalia.

I offered the cot to Hockenberry.

"No, no," he said, addressing my stomach. "That's for Chuck."

At midday in Africa, it was impossible to film. All shapes were bleached and flattened by the sun. Activity stopped. The dirt roads were populated with lethargic dogs, all with short fur and large pointed ears, known generically as common African garden dogs. In Baidoa, there were very few dogs. Most were dead from starvation. We waited until the late afternoon shadows stretched across the town, bringing out its occupants in sharp relief, intensifying the color of the diaphanous veils worn by Somali women. At the best of times, the Somalis are an extravagantly handsome people, nomadic camel herders, their lean bodies sculpted by the harsh conditions of the landscape. Now after months of hunger, they were elongated even more, like a Modigliani portrait or the highest-paid Lagerfeld models. It was strange to see such striking beauty in the midst of the horror.

Flatbed trucks made their rounds picking up the dead. They were stacked with what looked like mummies, bodies carefully wrapped in shrouds, tied with sisal that cinched in the folds around the emaciated forms. There were tiny shrouds, the size of rag dolls. We found the place where the dead were prepared for the trucks. They were washed with great care. Women poured buckets of water on the skin stretched over bones. They caressed the face, swabbed the arms, and gently massaged the feet. They took time purifying each corpse, fetched more buckets, until the dead glistened in the sun.

What was left of the hospital compound had been commandeered by the International Medical Corps, a Los Angeles aid group. They specialized in SWAT teams of surgeons and nurses, required to work around the clock in appalling conditions. They were tough, no-nonsense people, the kind you find in inner-city emergency wards. In Baidoa, they had no surgeon. In shabby rooms with shortages of everything a doctor needs—anesthesia, cotton swabs, water, electricity—a surgeon's aide removes the bullets. As we entered his operating room, nothing stopped. Raymond Pollack had his hand inside a victim's foot cleaning out the wound. He was young and jaded, talking nonstop in a stream-of-consciousness southern drawl. His last assignment was just like this one, D.C. General in Washington's ghetto.

"The two predominant rounds here are 5.56 and 7.62." Raymond's voice echoed in the cement chamber that smelled like a butcher shop. "Uh, I'm sure somebody has done studies and determined they equally blow apart bodies. I know a lot about guns. A missile injury is a missile injury whether it's in Washington, D.C., or Somalia. There's jerks with guns there who will kill you for tennis shoes just like they'll kill you for shoes or a shirt or a bag of rice here, you know. As far as I'm concerned, there's rabid dogs all over the world. The only problem here is"—Raymond peered inside the foot—"everybody is a rabid dog."

Raymond was on call for every gunshot wound in Baidoa. The wards were full of them. He did the job at immense personal risk. Gunmen who daily brought in their wounded comrades threatened to kill him if he did not drop everything to stitch them up.

"Everybody that wanted a nickel has dumped weapons into this place. It's a money thing, you know. It's like everything else. If they weren't getting paid for the weapons, they wouldn't have brought them here. And, you know, we can thank just about everybody for that." He washed his hands to get ready for a chest wound. His Somali assistant prepared the patient. "Okay. Tell him it's going to hurt. If he can take a deep breath, okay, he's got several fractured ribs here."

Before U.S. troops were dispatched to Somalia two months later, no one in the Bush White House asked Raymond's opinion of what would happen to the troops deployed in the name of saving Somalia. He saw the future with great clarity, from the vantage point of this room awash in blood. "Whatever troops they send here, if they think they're gonna really control the situation, other than making a token gesture, somebody's gonna get killed, okay? Period."

That night there was a tropical rainstorm. We showered by simply standing in the courtyard. Afterward, the air smelled like a bag of fresh topsoil. It was absolutely still between the sporadic gunfire, which might have been a turf war for control of a town block or an argument that turned ugly. The town was loosely under the control of militiamen loyal to General Aideed. At first light we set out in the direction of the fighting the CARE men were so exercised about, the disputed countryside to the southeast. In this man-made famine, the closer one got to fighting, the more likely one was to find the worst starvation, in areas cut off from aid deliveries. Perversely, the weather was ideal for planting, if villagers only had the seeds or the energy to till the fallow fields.

The landscape stretched to the horizon like a camel-hair blanket. Gnarled trees, baobabs and acacia, spread their branches like giant umbrellas to offer shade to passing caravans. A hundred camels appeared out of nowhere, a neat line of ambling giants making their way to the market in Mogadishu via a chain of alluvial riverbeds. A dozen herders and their families walked alongside, whistling and shouting camel chants, ancient lilting phrases punctuated by the snap of sticks against camel hide. The camels wore wooden bells around their necks. The sound of the bell was deep and melodious. The procession moved slowly, with great concentration, to keep the camels in line. It was jarring that these nomads were unaffected by the disaster that surrounded them. They depended as they always had on their herds for milk, meat, and barter.

The famine that ravaged Somali families who lived as farmers and traders, the war that decimated the lives of Westernized city dwellers, left these ancient people unscathed. The almost post-nuclear conditions that dragged Somalia back to the dark ages, the rise and fall of civilization, meant nothing to the nomads. The car factories, the Hilton hotels, the oil refineries, the fighter planes, the Italian restaurants, the discos, were in ruins. What did it matter? They never needed them. They never watched a television or made a phone call to Rome.

The road was empty except for the occasional troop trucks, bristling with weapons and fighters who shouted uproariously as they passed. None threatened to molest, rob, or detain us. For the first of many times, our little convoy came to a halt. Our Somali escorts jumped out and pulled shovels from the back of the jeeps. They explained apologetically they must stop for a burial. By the side of the road were a skull and a pile of bones, picked clean by vultures. Attached to the bones were shreds of clothing. The men carefully wrapped the bones in the tattered cloth and buried them with a Muslim prayer.

"It is bad luck," said a sober militiaman, "to leave the dead unattended." There were skulls all along the route and we stopped each time one was spotted.

We reached a village with throngs of people in the market. Shoving and pushing, the sea of humanity was displaced regularly by an automatic weapon fired in the air. The people looked bedraggled; the food in the baskets set along the road was meager and selling at exorbitant prices. Just outside the village, we found what we were looking for: huge vats of Unimix porridge, famine food, stirred with enormous wooden spoons. Hundreds of women and children sat on the ground surrounding the vats, with bowls of every description in their laps. They were stick figures, with hardly enough energy to lift the bowl. Many walked for days to reach this place. Children with bones like small birds were expiring. Anyone who approached the vats out of turn was beaten with a switch.

There were few aid workers in this region, only those from the most intrepid groups. The Irish were here. They ignored the dire warnings from the United Nations that they must pack up and leave. They were prepared to be ambushed or shot so that some of these desperate people could live another week. The Somalis held them in high regard.

In Third World villages, it is difficult to carry a camera, to get a decent shot. Hordes of children are constantly bumping it, wrecking the picture with constant jiggles. They leap in front of it and wave. They peer into the lens from a foot away. Here, no one moved. No one paid any attention to the man wading through the ranks of little bodies. They were deadened, inured. They were conserving every ounce of energy to lift their bowls. Alex, the cameraman, went through the paces, a wide shot here, a pan there, a close-up. What was he thinking? His mother nearly starved to death as a child, hiding under the floorboards in a Warsaw Ghetto attic. One day, she could no longer stand the slow death. She walked through the Warsaw Ghetto gate hoping to be shot. She walked with her eyes closed waiting for the bullet. It never came. Why didn't they shoot the waif who dared walk through the gate?

By the Unimix vats, women approached to admire my stomach. Their bodies were so weak, no one could carry a baby. Their youngest were dying like the sand flies that clustered around their mouths. We left knowing that very few of the hundreds in that camp would survive.

Somali roads were full of potholes, deep trenches, craters. Villagers with initiative had started a freelance business, filling the holes. Travelers threw them a few bills, worth pennies, for their efforts. To remind the passing trade to pay, the pothole fillers did a dance. They waved a cloth in the air, twirling and spinning like Isadora Duncan. In the twilight, they looked otherworldly, like dervishes or djinns. On the road to Mogadishu, there were dozens of them, working frenetically to keep the road open.

Turning off the main east-west road, we headed for what was once a prosperous agricultural center and trading post, a town we knew had not had assistance. The town was scarred by fighting. The trees were scorched black. Buildings collapsed two years before by precision bombing had not been repaired. There was rubble everywhere. When the townspeople saw us, they approached like zombies, like *Night of the Living Dead*. It was a sickening feeling to invade their privacy without anything to offer, no gruel, no medicine. It was impossible to explain that we were there to inform the world about what was going on. The concept of mass communication, the power of the media, was utterly lost in translation. As far as they were concerned, we were strangers who had arrived empty-handed, without purpose. As they in turn could not extend the requisite hospitality, they were impotent, wretched. It was a scene out of Dante's Inferno:

> Virgil said to me,
> "What are you staring at? Why let your vision
> Linger there down among the disconsolate
> And mutilated shades? You found no reason

To delay like this at any other pit.
Consider, if counting them is what you plan:
This valley extends along a circular route." (XXIX)

On the approach to the capital, we saw a vast factory complex, smokestacks, warehouses, factory floors, truck parks. It had been looted top to bottom for scrap, which was then sold to Sicilian mobsters. Mafia companies had also been dumping toxic waste off the coast. We explored the complex, just after the sun dipped below the horizon. In the gloom, the black stacks against the red sky had an apocalyptic look. Sheltering in the warren of factory allies, a woman was lying on the ground, coughing. She was dying of tuberculosis, and sounded with each cough as though her lungs would be expelled. There was a child of three sitting watching her. The little girl was absolutely still, her hand touching the convulsed body. She waited patiently for her mother to get up.

In the good days, the American Embassy in Mogadishu was famous for its golf course and Thai restaurant. The vast compound with its high defensive walls and massive gates with guard posts encased in bulletproof glass was built on prime real estate. The view of the Indian Ocean port, with its glittering whitewashed houses and elegant mosques, was unsurpassed, particularly from the terrace of the ambassador's residence. The bay looked like a flawless Pailin sapphire. The water was so tempting it was easy to forget that Mogadishu harbor was infested with sharks.

The last residents to have cocktails on the terrace were the Bishops. Ambassador John Bishop was a career diplomat and Africanist, whose previous posting had been Liberia. Because his tenure there coincided with the collapse of the Liberian government, Somalis were delighted with his appearance in Mogadishu. They were sure his presence would ensure the downfall of the Siad Barre regime. Consequently, they nicknamed him "the gravedigger." (Somalis are all amateur poets; they invent names and verses for everything.)

The Bishops spent only four months in this house, before the helicopters landed in the compound and carried the Americans away to ships offshore, in an evacuation reminiscent of the last days of Saigon. The ambassador gave me his home movie of the embassy staff crouched on the roof, dodging fire from the surrounding streets, sending urgent messages by radio, saying farewell to the Somali staff, who were welcome to all the cash left in the safe. He loved this posting. "How pretty the city was. How lively the Somalis were, and how much zest for life. If you know the city of Monrovia," the sleepy, malaria-drenched capital of the old Americo-Liberian enclave in West Africa, "you can appreciate that coming to Mogadishu was a relief."

His mission, as he understood it, was "to see that Somalia stayed with us in the run-up to Desert Storm," the war in the Gulf. "We knew that there was a good chance we would not serve a normal tour. That the country could dissolve into the same kind of violence that we had left in Liberia. There were three little armies in the field challenging the government. There was criminal violence in the city as underpaid members of the military and police were hijacking cars. The criminal violence with political overtones became very substantial in late December [1990]. I went around to talk to President Siad Barre just to see for myself whether he had any game plan for dealing with the problem that seemed to be unmanageable. If he had one, he didn't share it with me."

I pictured Bishop, lean and pallid, like one of the traders Conrad was always running into upriver, walking up the gleaming white steps of the presidential palace, past the exotic tropical birds caged in the lush gardens, up one of the two gracefully curved staircases to the city's other great terrace. They talked while the heavy chandeliers made a haunting sound in the breeze coming off the bay, the sound you hear when you lick your finger and rub it lightly around the rim of a crystal goblet.

The embassy, so closely identified with the dictator, came under siege. "Somali soldiers and gangsters and thugs came to the gate of the compound, trying to make their way in. We were telegraphing back and forth to the State Department. They told us that there was a helicopter carrier on the way and that C-130s were near."

On the final morning in early January 1991, sixty U.S. marines and navy SEALs climbed over the compound walls at dawn. The embassy was overflowing with diplomatic refugees. "We had to send people out to rescue them. We rented a Somali officer who at our behest and in our pay went and led the Soviets from their mission to our mission. The Soviet ambassador and I played tennis regularly. He left with his tennis racket."

Our first stop in Mogadishu was the ambassador's terrace, now carpeted with broken glass. The airy modern house with its dramatic picture window was stripped, ransacked. There was a copy of *Out of Africa* on the floor, next to a calling card of a long-departed embassy attaché. The city at sunset still had a magical quality from this vantage, a setting for Babar and Celeste on one of their seaside jaunts. There was a steady rumble of big guns and the rat-a-tat-tat of Kalashnikovs.

Tahir Salad Hassan, a militiaman with the Aideed forces that controlled the embassy grounds (Aideed had not yet gained the villainous stature he acquired with the arrival of U.S. troops), sat with us listening to the salvos, *whomp-whomp. Thwack.* He read the guns like Morse code, deciphering the action. The battle lines were ever changing, complicated by the fact that the military command structures of the two main rival clans were in total disarray. One controlled North Mogadishu, one controlled the south where we were sitting. In reality, every four blocks was the territory of a different militia.

"Boom. Boom." Tahir laughed quietly. "This is the outcry. A kind of outcry. There are people who say, 'Do you know the music of Mogadishu? The bullets. Boom. Boom. Boom.'"

Weapons poured into Somalia because the country was strategic. It was vital. I remember a time in the seventies and eighties when the phrase "Horn of Africa" captured people's attention. Senators devoted hearings to it. The Council on Foreign Relations debated it. The Pentagon declared it a matter of national security. Somalia was just across the water from the Arabian Peninsula. The port of Berbera was an inch on the map away from Aden in Yemen. Just behind Yemen was Saudi Arabia, the oil fields.

Somalia was wait-listed for cold war action, an understudy in the great drama who never got the call. General Al Haig explained the cold war logic for propping up a dictator who made the Duvaliers look restrained: "Berbera as a port was an item of contest between the superpowers. The United States did not particularly want the base itself. But it did not want the Soviet Union to have it. These wars became tit-for-tat operations. And it's been my conviction that tit for tat has the practical consequence of telling the other side you're not serious. And that all they have to do is match your new level of tit," he laughed, "for a tougher level of tat."

The cold war junkyard we found at Berbera was full of mementos from both the Soviet and American occupations. It had been nearly two years since the hurried American departure. The base was a ghost town, the offices beneath the empty control tower strewn with top secret documents. File cabinets were bulging with water-logged reports, memos, maps, and confidential lists. Rusting Russian tanks and wings of old aircraft were disintegrating outside. On the surrounding hillsides, riddled with mines, antiaircraft missiles were still pointing at the skies. No one could remember how to operate them.

In the name of this strategic asset, never used in conflict by either side, the old dictator was given free reign. His job was to keep order. Ensure stability. Once the famine began to rage, congressmen felt guilty. Howard Wolpe, a Democrat who served on the Africa subcommittee, thought Congress was a party to the crime. "We have been complicit. His regime was totally corrupt. It was repressive. I fault our own government for continuing to provide the kind of armaments we were providing. It was wholly inexcusable." The United States sent $700 million to the dictator, $250 million in military hardware and spare parts.

"In the end," said the congressman, "the arms were used to put down popular rebellions. Large numbers of people were slaughtered. The country was falling apart."

I sought out another longtime Somalia watcher, Ken Hackett, who was running East African operations for Catholic Relief Services. Hackett's people were, like the Irish, some of the most intrepid in the field. "We propped up Siad Barre for so long. He was a Marcos. He was an Idi Amin. He served our interest for a while. Then we didn't need him any longer. He was a difficult guy to manage. We let him go. We have Diego Garcia sitting right out there off the Straits of Hormuz. We don't need Berbera. We did Desert Storm without Somalia. We dropped the ball."

Wandering at dusk through the U.S. Embassy grounds, trashed, looted, smeared with graffiti, I imagined people rushing to make their appointments. I thought of overworked officials sitting down to urgent meetings, executive assistants telling callers, "The ambassador has stepped away from his desk." There, in a bare room that smelled like a urinal, the military attaché once pored over troop deployments. Down the hall, the CIA station chief thought up code names for his sources. Upstairs, beneath the twisted fallen girders, the embassy's most efficient secretary ordered canapés for the reception. In the spacious office with the gaping shell hole, the deputy chief of mission brooded about his career. Outside, the marine guard cursed the fine Somali dust on his shoes.

Driving through the streets of Mogadishu, I felt the tension, palpable as a rusty knife. Gunmen mounting checkpoints, hundreds of fluid roadblocks, eyed us like cuts of meat. Carlos, in charge of our "technicals," and I plotted who would be just the right guide to usher us through each blasted neighborhood. The guides rode shotgun. They haggled, negotiated, pulled rank on the ragged, *qat*-soaked gunmen in the street. There was endless trouble. Every time we stopped to shoot, Alex deftly pulled out the camera. He moved like a tai chi master, smoothly maneuvering into position. For the first ten seconds everything was calm. Then the gunmen appeared.

They popped up from behind a wall, with so many shell holes it looked like latticework. They tore around the corner in jeeps, hanging off the gun mounts. A conversation, an explanation, an assurance of the highest authorization, turned into a bitter shouting match. A bazooka was trained on us. Machine guns swung around in our direction.

Nothing concentrates the mind like the barrel of a gun pointed at your chest. In that instant, an internal alarm goes off. You feel the imminent danger like a spasm. The air is electrically charged, and built-in sensors say, Get out. Get out now. There is a fluidity as everyone leaps in and slams the doors. We pull out fast. Move, move, move. When it is over, we drive and breathe for a while. My stomach muscles are still tight. After a minute of silence, the guide apologizes, assuring us that yesterday, that street was under control.

The man who claimed to be in command of these neighborhoods greeted us in a spacious villa, draped with purple bougainvillea. Jacaranda trees shaded the host of bodyguards lounging inside the thick garden walls. The U.N. compound was just down the street. The general was a small dapper man with smooth, almost polished skin and perfectly manicured hands. His name was Mohammed Farah but everyone called him by his nom de guerre, Aideed.

The room where he received us was bare. The general sat carefully, as though not to wrinkle his tropical suit. Everything was quiet. There were no phones ringing, no aides rushing in and out, just the occasional thud of a mortar round somewhere in the city. Aideed spoke in hushed tones using arcane phrases, elevated language, the sort of expressions that cast a torpor, designed to make a listener forget the realities outside. It is invariably used by heads of state who are capable of ordering a massacre before settling down to the soup.

"We have a new program for security and order, a plan to overcome all difficulties," he assured us. "I've been against the bandits. In our program, we plan to arrest them." What he needed was a good supply of uniforms. The U.N. had failed to attend to this matter. The general was disappointed with America. "America says that Somalia is no longer a strategic interest." (When American troops finally arrived, Aideed looked on benevolently as U.S. soldiers were dismembered in the street.)

"I have this vision," he told us, "a vision to see Somalia free. Where fundamental rights, civil rights, and human rights will be respected. This is my personal vision."

There was a plan, a program, for every contingency. Outside the walls, no one had heard the plan. Within a few hours there was a ferocious gun battle right outside his gate. The gunmen fired their RPGs, the long weapon that nestles on the shoulder with a shell like a Russian onion dome, with relish. They liked the hefty kick and the satisfying puff of smoke. The sound crackles, whines, thumps. The general was safely out of harm's way, closeted with his vision.

The International Medical Corps gave us beds in their walled compound around the corner from the general. At night bullets ricocheted between the buildings outside my window. The mosquitoes carrying cerebral malaria were voracious. The occupants of the compound rushed in for quick meals at their communal table and disappeared back to the operating theater. Sam Toussie, the head surgeon, assured us the compound was safe. There was only one shell hole in his office wall. One of the doctors blew in to gather help for treating fresh casualties. Militiamen guarding the U.N. compound had opened fire on an unarmed crowd outside the gates. There was at least one dead and several wounded. The doctors had been told to keep it quiet. They knew the embarrassing facts because they were sewing up the wounded.

Carlos and I had ventured over to the U.N. compound several times. The scores of bureaucrats bustling through the hallways were hunkered down. They hated the city beyond the gates. They regarded us with suspicion because we had come from outside. Outside was full of barbarians. The U.N. was paying its staff per diems of $250 a day above and beyond their salaries. If they could keep their heads down, it was a gold mine posting. The busiest office in the building was the U.N. airline office. A crowd spilled out into the hall, waiting to get their names on the manifest for "rest and recuperation" flights to Nairobi, Djibouti, or Addis. R&R was foremost on their minds. They chatted to one another about food, not rice deliveries or the children who were too far gone to swallow porridge, but their own three square meals a day. They thought the U.N. dinner menu was a disgrace.

What did they all do here? There was plenty of paperwork. Above all, they were waiting. Troops were due to arrive to protect them. A contingent of 3,500 had been approved. Five hundred Pakistani soldiers were at the airport, but they had not left their bunkers. Equipment was on order.

The United Nations loves acronyms. This was UNOSOM, as opposed to UNTAC and UNPROFOR. UNOSOM was headed by an Algerian diplomat called Mohammed Sahnoun. He had been hired six months before and was on the verge of being fired. He was too outspoken, too critical of U.N. lethargy. The U.N. bridled when he raised a fuss about a U.N. charter with clear U.N. markings that was caught carrying cash and weapons to one of the warlords, Ali Mahdi, a former hotelier who was now boss of North Mogadishu. A World Food Program plane making covert arms deliveries broke every rule of neutrality. The U.N. buried the investigation. Resolution 733 of January 23, 1992, that embargoed deliveries of weapons was ignored.

The U.N. food delivery effort, the justification for the presence of a fat staff, was a shambles. Between October 12 and December 3, 1992, the World Food Program was meant to deliver 100,000 metric tons of food supplies. They managed less than a fifth of that, or 18,990 metric tons. Of the food that arrived, between 10 and 80 percent of each shipment was looted.

Then there was the unfortunate incident of a cool $3.9 million in cash lifted from the U.N. compound safe. Who could scale the battlements of this place to get it? "It had to be an inside job," says Ken Hackett, now executive director of Catholic Relief. "Blame the management. Cash was being carried around in paper bags. There was a lot of hanky-panky. They were in it for the money, in for a short term, huge per diems. They're not there to help the people. Not for any great humanitarian reason. The U.N. starched shirts had to have everything taken care of. The whole system stinks."

The U.N. "system" had infected everyone in Somalia. More and more bags of cash were paid out to the U.N.'s "technicals." Inflation was spiraling. By October 1992, the price of a jeep with arms and men was $300 per day. U.N. labor relations were notoriously poor. The technical "contractors" fleeced them out of growing malice. The "system" was crippling for the private aid groups. "Everyone's armed to the teeth," Hackett said, feeling a terrible burden of responsibility. "We, in order to do our best to bring our great human concern to people and stop them from starving, are financing it."

Our transportation in and out of Mogadishu had to be carefully planned in advance. The U.N. office in Nairobi had reserved seats for us on one of their flights to Hargeisa in the north, where we were due to film a demining operation. The north of Somalia is sown with millions of land mines, antitank mines, antipersonnel mines, Italian, Russian, American, and Pakistani models with names like "Toe Poppers." They were planted in the days when the dictator was losing control and getting desperate. The mines were now being removed, one by one, with sticks probing the earth. There were frequent casualties. The operation would take fifty years.

Faxes flew back and forth between Nairobi and New York to ensure that we were on the flight manifest. Getting stuck in Mogadishu was an unnerving proposition. The gunmen around town knew us too well.

Everything was settled. Our instructions were to check in at the UNOSOM compound. The bureaucrat at the airline office said as far as he was concerned, we had no claim, no priority. The faxes, the satellite phone calls meant nothing to him. Besides, the man from Geneva standing behind us in line had some vacation coming. The system had broken down and the consequences for us were a nightmare. Carlos and I made the rounds of everyone in town who might have access to a plane. Médecins sans Frontières, the French aid group, had heard that a French Air Force plane was due to land at Baidoa, over 200 miles back down a treacherous road. They pulled strings with their friends in the air force to get us on board. The transport was scheduled to make a pit stop at Hargeisa. We were on the manifest. I clutched the piece of paper.

I was worried because I had been losing weight. At six months pregnant, I should have been gaining steadily. My appetite for the safe, tinned food I had packed in my suitcase had diminished to nothing. It tasted vile. I kept my concerns to myself. Right now, I was responsible for getting the team out of the capital, where we had become far too visible as a target. We packed and sped to Baidoa.

Our arrival at Baidoa airport was perfectly timed, leaving just minutes to spare. We knew that the gunmen who had claimed this strip as their turf were particularly vicious. We listened for the approaching military transport. Nothing appeared. There was one light aircraft on the strip, far too small to take us anywhere. Before taking off, the pilot passed along the news that the French Air Force transport was held up in Djibouti with engine trouble.

The gunmen appeared. The self-proclaimed airport militia walked slowly around our jeeps, peering in the windows. Our militiamen were tense, fingering their weapons, damp with sweat from the blistering midday sun. The two militias were sniffing around one another. This was bad. Both sides were apt to forget we were in the middle. There was a conversation, then an argument. Both sides massed and began to shove. There were two dozen men pushing each other, moving in a human whirlpool with their safeties off. Twenty yards to the side, a gunman from the hostile militia slowly set up his bazooka. He was aiming it with precision at our jeep. Someone yelled, "Oh God. He's gonna blow up the fucking jeep. Stop this. He's gonna blow us up."

I jumped out and forced my way into the knot of gunmen, shouting. I had about ten seconds to diffuse this. I calculated that my stomach would finally pay off. A pregnant woman would shock them, put them off balance.

"Stop this now, do you hear me? Stop. Get that bazooka out of here. Tell your man to back off right now. There are people in that jeep."

The men grew quiet. I did not stop talking until one of them ordered the bazooka's owner to move away. My condition, mixed with a stern voice, must have reminded them of their mothers. Who knows? I was trembling. Luckily, they did not smell the fear. Everyone started to shuffle, disburse. We drove off with nowhere to go, to the far end of the empty airstrip. We had no plane, no lodging, and an angry hostile militia at the airport gates.

Carlos and Alex wandered off to stretch. They headed down the deserted center lane of tarmac, where we first landed on the C-130. There was no sound but a dry wind whipping across the field.

"Hey."

They heard a voice call to them from under a bush.

"Hi."

Hiding there, under camouflage of tumbleweeds, were two American special forces men. There were not meant to be any American military on the ground in Somalia. These were "black" forces, Pentagonese for covert. Carlos explained our dicey predicament. The men in the bushes immediately called in a C-130, something they were not authorized to do. They would be reprimanded for blowing cover. On our behalf, they took the risk. When Carlos came back to report this miracle, my estimation of the American military rocketed upward.

Back on the Kenya coast, in a Mombasa hotel with crisp sheets, phone lines, and native dancers where the American military was billeted, I called the commanding general to extend our thanks. I asked him to pass along details of our rescue to the superiors of these phantom troops, who did not officially exist. I could not give their names because we were never properly introduced.

The story aired on *Nightline* roughly a month after we flew out of Somalia. The film had been designed for the premiere of *Day One*, but this was the night U.S. forces landed on the beach. No one wanted to wait. Ted Koppel was with the first wave. Everything was washed into the *Nightline* special like a weir. Sitting in the control room in New York, I was told half the thirty-minute piece would be cut "for time." An hour before, Peter Jennings had promoted it on the air as "extraordinary." I was warned by the ABC rank and file that this was the kiss of death. "If Peter loves it, Ted hates it." *World News* and *Nightline* were like North and South Mogadishu.

The troop landing on the shores of Mogadishu was called Operation Restore Hope. It was an event, a vehicle for anchors, special correspondents, pundits. It was theater. The directors in that control room were masterful. The floor-to-ceiling bank of screens each displayed a freeze-frame of tape fed from different cities, other countries. "Okay, give me Washington on one. What am I looking at?" barked the director. "I want the White House. Give me the Pentagon on two, please. Okay, what's happening, guys? I'm losing Mogadishu. Where the hell is Ted?" Koppel appeared on a Mogadishu rooftop, straightening his collar, patting down his hair. He had just arrived with the U.S. troops and hadn't a clue what was going on. Who cared? He was there. He could be briefed. He had wire copy. The story was, after all, the troops.

The Bush White House spin was bathed in good intentions. It was the post–cold war mission of mercy. "Give me studio on four. What am I looking at? Will somebody tell me who that guy is?" Names of experts, none of whom had set foot in Somalia, were typed into the computer. "Give me backgrounder on five. Cue it up, please." My story, a piece that challenged the wisdom of dispatching an eighteen-year-old boy down a Mogadishu street because he would have to fight a legacy that was too big for him, that would crush him, appeared on the screen. It was packaged between teases, bumpers, ads for Tylenol, Ben-Gay, and a jeep parked on the edge of the Grand Canyon. "Okay." The *Nightline* director paused. "What am I looking at? Is that a skull?" For the first time, he really wanted to know.

THIRTEEN

The Great Game

CHARLIE WAS BORN in Washington on Super Bowl Sunday, 1993. He arrived after the sorbet and blackberries at the end of a long leisurely lunch party. I had vanished into the kitchen numerous times for some energetic Lamaze "huff huff" breathing, watched with amusement by eight-year-old Olivia. I huffed. I paced. The longer I stayed on my feet, the better the chances my labor would be brief.

Our guests were unaware of the drama taking place in the kitchen. I returned with salmon kedgeree, a salad with edible flowers, some Cashel Blue cheese from county Tipperary. Between contractions, everything was normal. Down both sides of the long narrow British naval refectory table, people were locked in conversation about the Clinton administration's first days in power, a dazzling display of indecision on everything from administration appointments to the fate of Haitians washed up on the beach. For several days, observed Christopher Hitchens, the White House did not even answer the phone. We had just weathered an outbreak of Hollywood on the Potomac when the entire Santa Monica A-list showed up for inauguration week to graze at VIP-ticket-holders-with-special-stickers-only buffets. The only bright spot was writer Walter Mosley turning up at my table with a copy of *White Butterfly*. His inscription to me read, "larger than life in more ways than one." My stomach was one.

As the guests said their good-byes, I grabbed Andrew. "I think we'll go too."

"Where?" asked Christopher.

"The hospital. I think we ought to go right now."

I had waited until the last possible second. We arrived at Columbia Women's at 4:40 P.M. Charlie appeared at 5:08. He was a nine-pound two-ounce towhead. The obstetrician dashed in to do the episiotomy. We dragged the pediatrician away from his Super Bowl party to count fingers and toes, and the hospital sprang us at 10:30 P.M. Word of the speedy birth flashed up the eastern seaboard. Ever since Charlie's gestation in Somalia made the Talk of the Town, he had a following. Everyone agreed that the little boy with the mop of flaxen hair had rhythm.

He was christened in a hand-me-down white lace robe worn in 1850 by Lord Kitchener, who went on to distinguish himself leading the British forces at the battle of Omdurman in the Sudan. For British colonial history buffs this was a big moment. The 1898 victory meant the sinister empire founded by the Mahdi, a Dongolese called Mohammed Ahmed ibn Seyyid Abdullah, was smashed. The Mahdi had carved out his Islamic state with a view to swallowing Egypt. He and his Mahdist claque were feared and despised ever since they hacked up General Gordon in Khartoum. The Mahdi regarded himself as the imam of God. His spiritual descendants were just putting the finishing touches on a bomb that nearly collapsed the twin towers of New York's World Trade Center.

The February bombing came as a terrible shock. The monuments of glass and steel in lower Manhattan were light-years away from the alleyways strung with laundry in Asyut in Upper Egypt, where the mosques were so crowded, the faithful rolled out their prayer rugs in the dusty streets. The clerics preached holy war with the West through the scratchy loudspeakers. They wanted to throw a veil over Egypt. Some in their movement advocated pulling down the pyramids and blowing up the sphinx. Plans were fomented on religious package tours to Khartoum.

The most militant in their ranks were arrested, expelled from Egypt, Algeria, Saudi Arabia, Kuwait. Their refuge was remote and mountainous, inhospitable to infidels, another fundamentalist empire built, oddly enough, with $3 billion from the CIA. The bombers and their brethren were *jihadis*, holy warriors, trained in the long fourteen-year war in Afghanistan that was the Soviet Union's Vietnam. They were not, however, Afghanis fighting to expel the Soviet occupation. They did not even speak Pashto or Dari. They were Arabs, militant fundamentalists, who for years wore the rough wool caps of the mujahedin fighters (known as "the gallant mujahedin" in Washington circles), and now trained their sights on the United States. Intelligence men had a word to describe their Frankensteins coming back to haunt them. It was called blowback.

By June 1993, I was on my way to the Afghan border. This was my second expedition for *ABC Day One*. At that moment, Afghanistan was without question the most dangerous place on earth. If things went terribly wrong, there would be no medevac to haul us out.

Since the Soviet withdrawal from Kabul in 1989, Afghanistan had disintegrated into a battleground for a dozen armies ripping apart the spoils of their victory. The government the Soviets had installed folded in 1992, leaving four factions in a titanic battle to capture the prize, the capital city. Three of the four armies had been built and financed by the U.S. government. They had stockpiles of CIA-supplied weapons, mountains of lethal firepower shipped through neighboring Pakistan in the eighties. They peddled the most virulent strains of Islamic fundamentalism.

In their midst, religious radicals from Egypt and the Gulf trained in secret camps. Family members of the fiery blind Sheik Omar Abdel Rahman announced two of his sons were there. Mohammed Shawki Islambouli, the wanted brother of one of the assassins of President Anwar Sadat of Egypt, was a resident at the Samarkhiel Guesthouse in Jalalabad. At the camps, they learned to fire mortars, rockets, and how to construct bombs. In the aftermath of the most expensive covert operation in history, Afghanistan had become a terrorist boot camp.

I managed to reassemble the Somalia team, with the exception of Alex Zakrzewski, who was shooting in India. Alison Craiglow, a stalwart associate producer, joined up. I needed a combat cameraman and called Nick Ludlow in London. His father, Ken, had been a senior NBC cameraman when I was just twenty-four. Nick had spent part of his youth in Beirut. He was steeled to the conditions we were about to face. I warned him that in the Afghan capital, seven hundred people had been killed in the preceding six days. There were, according to the Red Cross, three thousand wounded. Three-quarters of a million people had fled in the previous year. He accepted the job on the spot.

Tom Yellin, who ran *Day One*, lobbied for the project in the ABC News executive suites. I had stressed that we would be shooting in the Pakistani border town of Peshawar, the former headquarters of the CIA's secret war. I told Tom we might venture across the lawless border of Afghanistan, but had been vague about my plan to lead our caravan across the length of the blasted, mine-strewn, bandit-controlled terrain looking for a man known as the Black Turban.

Gulbuddin Hekmatyar had collared more CIA money and arms than any other "resistance leader" during the Soviet war. He was now harboring Arab terrorists wanted in several countries. He had an arsenal of American-supplied Stinger missiles, shoulder-fired missiles that brought down airliners. One of his close friends was blind Sheik Rahman, spiritual mentor of the World Trade Center bombers.

"Gulbuddin," said a senior U.S. official who had been deeply involved in the U.S.–Afghan operation, "was a very dangerous, very nasty piece of work. We all knew that."

Those who got in his way were beheaded or shot.

Carlos was indispensable on this treacherous mission. He spoke both Pashto, the language of the eastern region of Afghanistan, and Dari, spoken in Kabul. He had fought with the mujahedin. Everywhere in Afghanistan strangers called him by his freedom-fighter nom de guerre. He dressed in the costume of an Afghan fighter.

The key to our survival was securing armed escorts from a neutral faction. There was only one. It was led by Abdul Haq, one of the great mujahedin commanders. Abdul's forces had conducted guerrilla operations against the Russians in and around the ancient capital. There were hit-and-run raids, sabotage missions, infiltration behind the lines. They were up against MIG fighters, T-72 tanks, heat-seeking missiles, and the cruelest weaponry a superpower could devise. Abdul had been the Kabul commander. He was wounded a dozen times. One foot was blown off by a land mine. He has a bushy beard, lively eyes, and gray hair at age thirty-five.

He was now living in a shaded compound in one of the British colonial neighborhoods of Peshawar. His family owned ruby mines in Afghanistan. Since the Soviet war, the method of extraction had been dynamite and grenades. The former commander's brother was governor of Nangarhar Province. His headquarters in Jalalabad was the old king's winter palace. Abdul gave us the men we needed for protection and extended his family's hospitality in Jalalabad.

The commander served tea on his terrace screened from the beating sun by deep pink bougainvillea. He was hesitant to speak frankly. "I have never said these things. I'm going to get into trouble with the CIA." He had argued passionately with the men in charge of the secret war at the CIA, the State Department, and the Pentagon, over their taste for the most radical, most anti-American religious fanatics. "We would tell them, what the hell is going on? You're creating a monster in this country." Men like the Black Turban were not brilliant fighters. They squirreled away weapons to use after the war. They destroyed the old tribal system in a country where family, not religion, was the guiding force. They were hired because they were zealots. The faulty logic was that they would therefore hit the Russians hardest.

The fundamentalist radicals got the lion's share of the billions' worth of arms, food, and support, even though "the fundamentalist role was not decisive," said Selig Harrison of the Carnegie Endowment, who has forgotten more about Afghanistan than most pundits ever knew. "These people weren't essential. After giving them the bulk of the weapons and the money, the results are tragic and predictable." As Harrison and Haq both understood all too well, the religious zealots "amounted to nothing before the war. The war distorted everything. We came in and the Saudis came in to support factions that still don't represent the mainstream." It was as though militant Christian fundamentalists were handed billions in arms and cash to take over the United States.

Now the country had spun out of control. "You don't need a visa, you don't need a passport, all you have to do is go there and you can find Stingers, Blowpipes, tanks, rocket-propelled grenades, mortars, everything. You can get training. Afghanistan is a unique country." He laughed bitterly. "You have both terrorism and heroin. Afghanistan is just one big poppy field."

Haq had run into the Arab mujahedin, imported from the Middle East, hundreds of times when he was in the field. The commander of Kabul was not impressed. In his view, they were there to do the logistical work, transport, supplies, routine support that CIA personnel could not do openly without blowing the extent of their involvement. Although CIA Director William Casey was visiting their training camps, the fiction was maintained that assistance and direction were coming from Pakistan, not the United States. Abdul Haq was plagued by CIA officers who wanted to micromanage his military campaigns. Still they bought weapons from the Peoples' Liberation Army in China to camouflage their role, and to supply foot soldiers, cleared out the mosques in Cairo and Mecca.

Our base in Peshawar was Dean's Hotel. Dean's consisted of a dark, cheerless lobby and a block of shabby bungalows. At least three intelligence agencies were tapping the telephones. Pakistani ISI listened directly on the line. I was in touch with active members of the radical Egyptian Islamic Group based in Peshawar and the followers of a key recruiter for the CIA's secret war, Sheik Abdullah Azzam. I knew little about "the Fighting Sheik" Azzam when I arrived in Pakistan except that he had taught Islamic law at the university in Jordan and had mobilized fighters among religious zealots in the United States. After years of serving as the link between recruiting offices around the world (in places like Atlantic Avenue in Brooklyn) and the mujahedin leadership, Azzam and his son were blown to bits by a car bomb in 1989, the year the Soviet troops quit the war. One of his volunteer guerrillas, Mahmud Abohalima, was accused of bombing the World Trade Center.

I wrangled an introduction to the sheik's widow. Dressed head to toe in a flowing chador, I was admitted to her chambers. The house was a commodious but spare concrete villa, one of hundreds built in housing developments financed by the Saudis. I entered a room with no furniture. Heavily veiled women sat against the walls on pillows. The widow of the martyred sheik was speaking with fervor about Islam. The others deferred to her. She said with great pride that her husband had indeed recruited fighters in the United States. He had offices in twenty-eight states. She had traveled with him on his American tours. Faded newspaper clippings were produced which called the dashing sheik "the Prince of the Arab Mujahedin." His close friends, like Gulbuddin Hekmatyar, the Americans' resistance leader of choice, vowed revenge for his murder. His widow had cherished his photographs. One showed Sheik Azzam seated between Hekmatyar and the other beneficiary of the bulk of the CIA's largesse, Abdur Rafool Sayyaf, leader of Ittehad Inquilab Islami. Azzam had recruited thousands of their fighters.

Tapes of Sheik Azzam preaching were still popular in the mosques. The widow had a stack of tapes and a large television set with a VCR. She played me the sheik's memorial tape. It was very bloody, macabre, dwelling on the carnage left by the car bomb. She took on a beatific smile and explained that the martyred sheik had ascended to the highest level of heaven. His blood smelled like perfume. It was a miracle. The ladies in veils nodded and murmured. One of them spoke broken English. It turned out she was an American convert from Florida who had been sequestered here for three years. She spoke in glowing terms of this place and their regular migrations to the Sudan for spiritual refreshment. She and a French member of the sect made a valiant effort to recruit me.

The sheik's widow confided that her husband had made it known before his death that he would take the holy war back to Jordan, Saudi Arabia, Egypt, even the United States. He was hugely charismatic with a worldwide following. She thought the CIA had the best motive to cut short his career. She hastened to add that was only her opinion.

The American Club in Peshawar had a proprietor gone to seed. He was fat and sweated profusely. He claimed to have once been a presidential speechwriter. His menu featured beer and nachos along with peanut butter sandwiches. The former presidential speechwriter hopped from table to table, collecting scraps of information. He was irritatingly curious about our movements. Before setting off for the border, we collected supplies in the warren of the Peshawar market, full of loot from Afghanistan. I bought lapis and silver bracelets, and a midnight-blue silk burka, a shroud with an embroidered screen for the eyes, for the journey. It was possible to hide completely under a burka.

We were granted an interview with a formidable Egyptian *jihadi*,

Abu Hamza, who had the same massive features painted on the ancient sarcophagi in the Cairo museum. He was also called Mustafa. In fact, he had several names. He sat in the courtyard of a Peshawar house swatting flies, spitting with rage. Why was the U.S. government strong-arming Pakistan to expel him and his friends when they had done so much for the cause? "You called us heroes. Now we are terrorists."

Abu Hamza had been making the *hadj*, the pilgrimage to Mecca, in 1986 when he was called up to fight in the holy war. "People were pushed," he said. "We were told 'you have to join, leave school, leave your family, join your brothers in the *jihad.*'" The Saudis, he said, "were convinced by the Americans that if they allowed people to go to the *jihad*, this would be the vent. The Afghan *jihad* was meant to divert people from problems in their own countries," to let off steam, "like a pressure-cooker vent. If you keep it sealed up, it will blow up in your face. The Afghan *jihad* was the vent." Abu Hamza estimated that ten thousand Arab mujahedin had received training and had fought in the *jihad*. Now he was concentrating on the holy war in Egypt to topple President Mubarak.

We collected our militiamen, courtesy of Abdul Haq, and set out through the wild tribal area of northwest Pakistan, where guns and opium are the staples of the market stalls and the road winds slowly up through the sheer cliffs of limestone and shale that flank the Khyber Pass. Persian, Greek, Seljuk, Tatar, Mongol, and Durani conquerors passed this way. From the Shandi Bagiar the road climbs to the Shagai plateau. Here was the fort of Ali Masjid commanding the heights. The road zigzags to the river and down along the Loargi Shinwari plateau. At its narrowest point, the Khyber is fifteen feet wide between the two-thousand-foot cliffs of Rhotas hill. The ruins of British forts crown the peaks. In one spot, all of the British regiments carved their names in the rock face. This whole stretch of Pakistan was now closed to foreigners. There was an advisory circulated by the American consulate that U.S. nationals were forbidden to travel here.

The timeless village of Landi Kotal, famous for its cutthroats, overlooked the plains of Afghanistan. Around us were modern fortresses, the retreats of some of Pakistan's best-known heroin and hashish traffickers. We then descended to the gateway to Afghanistan at Tourkam, literally a small stone gate with crenellated castle turrets. Hordes of Afghanis in mustard and sapphire silk burkas, in handsome wool caps and tunics, milled back and forth across the border on foot. They looked like the chorus on opening night at the Met.

We attached ourselves to three militiamen loyal to Abdul Haq's brother, who ushered us into the pickup truck and drove us, with a store-bought police siren blaring across the scorched plain, to Jalalabad. Our first stop was the old king's winter palace, threadbare and forlorn. We arrived as the governor's guests, but like a dinner in an Agatha Christie novel, the host never appeared. We were ushered into a splendid dining room with forty-foot ceilings and seated at the long polished table. The walls were intricately painted. Several courses arrived. We were then instructed to retire to the hotel as its only guests. That night, we were eaten alive by bedbugs.

At 5 A.M., after the morning call to prayer, our mujahedin with their Kalashnikovs crowded into the backs of two jeeps. I wore a long white eyelet veil, careful to cover my ankles and wrists. The heavy silk burkas were like a furnace in the June heat. We drove west, past teeming refugee camps, into the floodplain of the Kabul River. The refugees had fled the fierce fighting in Kabul, where we hoped to be by nightfall. To reach the Black Turban, we had to travel through the worst neighborhoods in Afghanistan.

Yoked oxen plowed the fields along the Kabul River. Primordial caves dotted the rock face beyond. The wet green landscape gave way to dry stony soil. There was wreckage everywhere, tanks, jeeps, armored personnel carriers, refuse from Soviet convoys ambushed, rocketed, set ablaze. I was struck by the glittering rock on the hillsides. On closer inspection it was a carpet of bullets, shells, shell casings, millions and millions of them. We could not step far off the road to pee. This stretch of road all the way to the capital was sown with mines.

We approached our first ad hoc checkpoint. Anyone with a rocket-propelled grenade could set up a checkpoint. The grizzled, gaunt-looking men with green eyes were often bandits rather than mujahedin. Our escorts were polite but firm, making a point of showing off the small arsenal we carried with us. The road, which seemed at times to hang suspended above the rushing river, had chunks missing. When the terrain flattened out, there were eerie mud-walled villages in ruins, looking as though someone had kicked a sand castle. The villages that were inhabited were famous for their energetic looters. Bandits, brigands, starved soldiers from hostile factions, the journey was full of unpleasant possibilities. There were times when no one spoke. Abdul's mujahedin deftly negotiated their way through all of this.

The steep climb to the Kabul plain left the passengers looking straight down thousands of feet of sheer vertical rock. There was an intense feeling of vertigo, as though we were rappelling in the jeep. The beauty of the river gorge was so staggering, it was worth the risk just to see it. Above, the Kabul plain was in the hands of the Rabani faction that controlled large parts of the city. The mountains that ringed the city were in other hands. The night before, rockets killed sixty-four civilians. The rockets were fired from the camp of Gulbuddin Hekmatyar, the Black Turban. His stated aim was to turn Afghanistan into a "true" Islamic state. Rockets whistling and crashing into the neighborhoods were meant to do the trick. Before paying a call on Hekmatyar, we would have to spend a night in the neighborhood he was targeting.

The city was lined with shade trees and high walls flecked with bullet holes. We could hear the rumble of big guns, like a late afternoon thunderstorm. We passed smooth Mongol faces, Tajik and Uzbek faces rimmed with black ringlets, and the long aquiline Pashtun faces with eyes like cool jade. Everyone carried a weapon. Carlos directed the drivers to what had once been the colonial German Club. The compound was shut. We shouted over the wall. The old caretaker who seemed to have inherited the place opened the gates and directed us to charming old summer cottages, past the empty swimming pool and cracked tennis court. Weeds had grown up through the rusted slides and swings of the children's playground. The swing needed oil. The baby pool was dry. The rooms were immaculate, as though we had booked in weeks before. Our Afghan host was so thrilled to see us, he made plans to cook an Afghan banquet the following night. Heavy shells pounded the city. A Mongolian shopkeeper appeared to hustle some business. His brother lived in Moscow. The shopkeeper had excellent caviar. The price was absurdly low. We ordered several tins for dinner. The city was pitch-black, which made the stars look like strings of Christmas lights. Tracer fire probed the blackness. There were no human sounds in the city, no cars, TVs, radios, nightclubs, ball games. The dogs barked at the rockets.

The next morning we sent word through the front lines that we wanted to see the Black Turban. In the meantime, I wanted to film in the Karta Sea hospital. To get there, we drove through a no-man's-land, a gash in the city center. Mile followed mile of ruins, every foot rocketed, shelled, bombed, burned. The latest weaponry from the hoarded CIA stocks, the abandoned Soviet arsenal, turned this exquisitely beautiful city, with ancient houses perched precariously on the cliffs, into the ashes at the bottom of a fireplace after a long night.

We had to cross a green line, a free-fire zone, in front of the zoo. The elephants, the zebras, the bears, the lions, the giraffes, had all been eaten. Rockets were crashing into this district at the rate of one per minute. The air shuddered. In the children's ward of the hospital, the ceiling was embedded with shrapnel from a near-direct hit the night before. In the beds, the little victims, without an arm or a foot, or with crude stitches running the entire length of a stomach, ignored the screams of the incoming rockets in the streets all around us. They were fascinated by us. They giggled when I instinctively ducked. They were proud of a poster pinned on the wall, though they could not read it. WHAT DO YOU WANT TO BE WHEN YOU GROW UP? it asked. ALIVE!

I was embarrassed to show fear in the face of such bravery. Everyone in the room was already crippled by this war. Would these children make it? It was doubtful. Their families, poor Shia, were blocked by militiamen from leaving the neighborhood. They were turned back at the two exit roads. They were used as a human shield. The pounding of ordnance was ceaseless. Soon the district would be rubble. On a slow day of fighting, the Red Cross informed us, there were at least 100 dead, with 20 to 30 percent unreported. As things livened up, as they did at that moment, the toll was 150 dead. We tore back across the no-man's-land, mindful of snipers, and just made it out by noon, when the escape route was sealed off by heavy fighting in the streets.

Touring the city's wreckage, I thought of Berlin, of Dresden, of the Roman ruins. Those unable to leave Kabul seemed resigned to the madness. At dusk, I sat on the filthy floor of a hotel room, now open air thanks to a rocket, in the abandoned Intercontinental Hotel. The halls were black, the doors twisted off their hinges, the windows blown out. The ghostly structure sat high above the city, in an area of fierce fighting. I watched houses exploded by heavy weapons, followed by deafening deep bass booms and columns of smoke. I wondered, in that instant, is this the twenty-first century? A blackened Intercontinental Hotel with a superb view of mindless demolition? From our third-floor rocketed suite, we raced to the darkened stairwell. Under my white veil, I wore a flak jacket with steel plates. Here, the jacket was practical. It might stop flying shrapnel. The stairwell opened out into the gloom of the darkened lobby, empty of guests, rattling with every *whomp-whomp*. As my eyes adjusted, I saw that in this God-forsaken place, a small man was standing silently behind the reception desk. He had no registration forms, no phone, no computer, no credit card machine, no keys, no messages. He was just standing in the dark, waiting. We raced past him, leapt into our cars, and drove at top speed down the hill. We passed a taxi with a wounded boy in back, hemorrhaging blood from the back of his head.

During the curfew that night between 10:00 P.M. and 4:00 A.M., not even the cats were out. The deep thundering booms had penetrated my skin. The sound was vibrating in my stomach. Just then I had a terrible longing to see four-month-old Charlie. Why did I come here?

Tracer fire lit up the sky over the mountains, followed by the thud of mortars. Sitting on the stone steps in the compound of the German Club, we could see strange flashes in the sky and then rolling thunder—real thunder and lightning competing with the man-made display going full tilt below. We were watching an apocalyptic *son et lumière*, a flash of fork lightning, then tracers, then rockets. It was like an angry argument between God and man. The terrifying spectacle went on for hours, until heavy rains, a sign of mercy for Muslims, forced the gunners and rocketeers inside. The freak storm was so intense, an entire neighborhood slid down the mountainside, burying whole families, who had survived eighteen years of war, under an avalanche of mud.

In the morning the air was fresh. We drove through the frontline checkpoints of the Rabani faction, the Dostum faction, and the Hekmatyar faction. The alliances, as they were then, were not important. Everyone changed sides to suit their convenience. In that way it was an *Alice in Wonderland* war. The man we were looking for had his camp in a fertile valley to the south, within rocket range directly over the ridge. The road was clogged with hundreds of donkey carts, camels, wild-looking men festooned with weapons, and women hidden beneath the blinding color of their silk burkas.

The fighters milling around the camp were hard-bitten. Some were obviously not Afghanis. They spoke Arabic and watched us with suspicion. We walked through an archway into a compound where the Black Turban was waiting for us. He was dressed in black from head to toe. His head was wrapped in black. His eyes were black. We all settled down in the garden around the camera. His skin was very pale with a faint blush in his cheeks. I had been advised by the BBC's Afghan stringer that the eight beheaded bodies just found at the border were executed on his orders. (Two years later, the BBC stringer himself was executed by Gulbuddin's followers after an acrimonious interview.)

Gulbuddin was very strict about modesty. I saw that my wristbone was uncovered and quickly rectified the problem. He was calm, deliberate, and spoke in a soft voice that sounded like rustling leaves. He was, he said, a man of peace. He had not fired any rockets the night before. The memory of old American friends, backers of the mujahedin like Congressman Charlie Wilson of Texas, brought a smile to his lips. "He was a good friend." The Black Turban remembered when he was invited to the White House by Ronald Reagan. Gulbuddin refused. The reason he was America's favorite resistance fighter, he said, was that he was the *only* resistance fighter.

As for the Arab mujahedin, some of whom were suspects in the New York bombing, "it was not possible to stop them. All the borders were open. Maybe some bad people were included. We don't want to train anyone here in Afghanistan against any government. The governments themselves were encouraging the people. Why are they accusing our mujahedin today? We were heroes, freedom fighters." Gulbuddin warmed to his theme. "Now the freedom fighters have turned into fanatics. It shows that the Americans are not good friends. There has been no change in us. How was it we were freedom fighters, heroes of history, and today we are fanatics? Very strange."

We asked who was responsible for the Egyptian cabdriver with a green card, who came to Afghanistan to fight, joined the ranks of mujahedin, was trained to make bombs, went back to Jersey City, rented a truck, filled it with explosives, and blew up the World Trade Center. "Who was responsible for that?"

The Black Turban smiled. "The one who provided him with a green card."

Before leaving Kabul, we stopped in at the American Embassy. It was a spacious compound with an imposing modern building and an acre or two of gardens. The gardens were dead. The building was locked and shuttered. We shouted for anyone who might be a groundskeeper. Three or four startled-looking local staff appeared. They thought, just perhaps, one of us was the new ambassador. Word had it in Kabul that the day the American ambassador returned, the fighting would cease. We were sorry to disappoint them.

They explained that the ambassador and his men had left, taking the key. They were locked out. Every day, they came to work and sat in the dying flower beds. One eagerly showed us a lean-to bomb shelter they had constructed against the constant rocketing. Gulbuddin, said the retainers, had fired on the embassy many times. The abandoned staff were at a loss for useful work. They had begun collecting all the spent shells and shell casings, the projectiles and bullets, that landed in the embassy grounds. They set them out neatly around the bare flagpole. It was a little museum.

If we happened to see anyone at the State Department in Washington, would we be so kind as to let them know the loyal staff had not fled? They were grateful for the small remittance that came every now and then from the embassy in New Delhi. Perhaps, if they had a bit more money, their sad little bomb shelter might become something any American could be proud of.

□ □ □ □

The film aired in July. We broke the story that thousands of radical Arab fundamentalists had been recruited and trained in the CIA's secret war. We had stopped in to see Benazir Bhutto, then between terms as Pakistan's prime minister, in Karachi. "I don't think the CIA had any idea," she told us with disarming frankness, "that these people would come back to bite the hand that fed them."

In Afghanistan, the United States had treated a cold with malaria, a phrase once used to describe U.S. Army intelligence, when the ashes of World War II had yet to cool, hiring Nazis (like Klaus Barbie) to wage the cold war against the Soviets. Here, billions of dollars had created an insurgency to fight the Russians that was far more dangerous in the long run than the Soviet occupation. The covert operation of the century had bred a militant force that was now infecting Bosnia and would soon plant bombs in Riyadh. I would follow them to Upper Egypt and the Arabian desert. Their holy war was far from over.

Meanwhile, my thoughts had turned to another forbidden country, run by Washington's most dedicated enemies. It was time to pay a call on the ayatollahs.

FOURTEEN

Lunch with the Ayatollahs

"YOU'RE AN OUTLAW," said *Vanity Fair*'s new editor, Graydon Carter, opening a bottle of chilled white wine in his Madison Avenue office. "You can't be a mother of three."

Tina Brown's successor was the former editor of *Spy* and, along with Morley Safer and Peter Jennings, a member of New York's Canadian mafia. He was an Anglophile, a romantic, and a devotee of Flashman, the libertine hero of George MacDonald Fraser's novels. (My late cat was called Flashman.) In Afghanistan, I imagined an updated version of *Flashman in the Great Game.* He would have stolen the Black Turban's wife, escaped from Kabul dressed in a burka, and then been decorated by Queen Vicky for heroic statesmanship.

Graydon liked to say that Andrew and I went places he preferred to read about.

He and Tina now controlled rival duchies at *Vanity Fair* and *The New Yorker.* Each took a booth almost daily at the Royalton, across 44th Street from the old Algonquin roundtable in midtown Manhattan.

As a *Vanity Fair* husband-and-wife team, Andrew and I had already been dispatched by both of them to Iraq, Colombia, and the equally hazardous "Little Colombia" in Queens. Our correspondence from Pablo Escobar was tucked away in a drawer. We had penetrated the world of China's Red Princes. Now Andrew persuaded Graydon to send us to Iran to do a story on the men who had issued death threats against the writer Salman Rushdie.

Our reception there was chilly.

"I am sorry," the airport immigration officer said curtly, after prolonged inspection of my passport. "Your visa has expired."

It was 4 A.M., Tehran time. I realized with horror that in this time zone we were four hours past the visa stamp deadline for entering Iran. I explained that in Washington, it was still the day before.

"It is too late. You will sit here, please." It was January 1994. We had just dropped off Charlie with the McCarthy family in Ardmore, our Irish village. As our fellow passengers, a disreputable-looking group who boarded in Paris, shuffled off into the neon-lit airport, Andrew and I settled into the orange plastic bucket seats. This time, I was swaddled in a black Armani veil, my *hejab*. Our holding pen looking like a squash court. A man in a white tunic and wild beard occasionally checked on our progress. We resigned ourselves to the fact that the Iranians were likely to boot us out on the next jumbo jet.

I felt a stab of sympathy for Bud McFarlane, White House emissary to the ayatollahs, in the days when the Reagan administration wanted to keep its arms deals here swept under the Shiraz. When McFarlane arrived at Tehran International, with his fake Irish passport, his pallet of Hawk missile parts, six Blackhawk .357 Magnums in presentation boxes, and chocolate cake shaped like a key from a kosher bakery in Tel Aviv, was he also forced to sit in these plastic seats?

Three hours passed. An officious bearded member of the Revolutionary Guards sorted through a large stack of very important papers. This did not look promising.

At that moment, Iran topped the White House list of "outlaw states." Secretary of State Warren Christopher had just publicly slapped the ayatollahs for their "egregious behavior." CIA Director Jim Woolsey accused them of making shopping trips for equipment to build a nuclear weapon. Not least, they had yet to lift the five-year-old *fatwa* against Salman Rushdie, the death sentence handed down by the late Ayatollah Khomeini. The father of the Iranian revolution had enjoined zealous Muslims to execute Rushdie on the grounds that his novel *The Satanic Verses* defamed the Prophet Mohammed. The Clinton administration's top terrorism official had just declared Rushdie part and parcel of U.S. policy. "It is an extremely clear manifestation of Iranian government use of terrorism as an overt and explicit instrument of policy." We were in Iran to see the men who wanted Rushdie dead.

The revolutionary guard behind the stack of papers announced that our visas were canceled.

"You will wait, please."

This was a nightmare.

We had just seen Rushdie in a London hotel on Park Lane. The condemned writer had dressed casually, the tweed jacket matching the salt-and-pepper beard, thin black-rimmed glasses framing his heavy-lidded eyes. He sipped Indian tea. He remembered that after his death sentence was announced on Valentine's Day in 1989, "A pattern got set. Khomeini died and the pattern stuck. What would really be death would be to allow myself to get institutionalized as a prisoner." Behind the Japanese tourists and the tea trolleys, two Special Branch bodyguards watched every move. Two more stood sentry at the door. One waited in the maroon Sierra in the forecourt.

"The only reason I ever agreed to go into this sort of invisible world was because we thought it wouldn't take long. The thing was so crazy it would be fixed." He left his cucumber sandwiches on the plate.

Rushdie knew little about his jailers in Tehran. Andrew and I thought we could assume the unique position of shuttling between both sides. We wanted to answer the question that was on everyone's lips in London and New York. "Do they really want to kill him?"

Now, stuck in our plastic airport seats persona non grata, we would never be able to answer the question.

Another revolutionary guard with an unkempt beard appeared. We knew that somewhere beyond the fluorescent lights was daylight.

"You will come this way, please." The guard ordered us to follow. We trudged into the lobby.

"You can go."

Excuse me?

"You can go now."

Our bags were waiting. Without explanation, we were turned loose into the Tehran morning traffic. Bleary-eyed, I checked to see that no blond wisps of hair were escaping from my veil. There was a chill wind whipping down off the Elburz Mountains dusted with snow.

For most of my career Iran had been the enemy, the pariah, the terrorists' lair. During the White House contra operation, Iran was the secret partner, the administration's shocking dirty laundry. To finally be in Tehran was like looking at the past fifteen years from the other side of a mirror. Here, people still called the United States "the Great Satan," a catchphrase from the revolution in 1979. I wondered whether I was, at this moment, the only American in Iran.

The city's architecture was strikingly ugly, a monument to the cement mixer. The energetic mayor had made a desperate attempt to beautify it with fountains. I imagined the late shah sitting on his Peacock Throne, extolling the virtues of "the new," the modern, all things Western. Mile after mile of drab, water-stained low-rises stretched before us. Now they were canvases for portraits of Ayatollah Khomeini. In his honor, the town was decked with strings of colored lights. It was the eve of the fifteenth anniversary of the day in 1979 when the ayatollah flew back to Tehran from exile in Paris and commandeered the revolution. On Charimkhan Boulevard, there was a massive painting of the American flag. In place of stars were neat rows of skulls. The stripes were smoke trails of falling bombs.

DOWN WITH U.S.A. it read.

There was no American ambassador in residence. We inspected the crumbling embassy of the Great Satan, now given over to cadets drilling for the Revolutionary Guards. Someone had painted flowers on the walls. The Nest of Spies office on the embassy grounds was selling the multivolume set of the shredded top secret documents, pieced together over several years by Iranian students, that was America's legacy. The enduring historical significance of the Revolutionary Guards taking fifty-two American hostages in the heat of the rebellion, was that it gave us *Nightline*. It gave us Ted Koppel.

Our destination was down the street, the embassy of the Lesser Satan, the massive fortress belonging to the British that covered a city block. We found the Lesser Satan himself inspecting the fresh bullet holes in his private bathroom.

"God," the British chargé d'affaires said dolefully, "I could have been sitting there. Contemplating."

The shattered glass and scarred ceiling from a full magazine burst of AK-47 gunfire were little reminders that the government protecting Rushdie had offended the faithful. The assault on the chargé's loo was one of three attacks on the British Embassy in January alone. "On the fifth we had a petrol bomb. On the thirteenth, two more bombs." Geoffrey James, the senior diplomat here, ordered tea with resignation. "We found a note on the street promising more attacks."

The trim young James, in his rambling office with a skeleton staff of fourteen, did not have a clue who was responsible or whom in the Iranian government to turn to. "I have very little access to these people." He flipped casually through the CIA's secret directory of Iranian officials. "[President] Rafsanjani doesn't have the clout to rein these people in." James was hoping we might have better luck. There were no invitations for revolutionary festivities on his mantelpiece. The ayatollahs never called. He roamed his dreary fortress waiting for the next bomb.

We left the chargé and sped up to North Tehran to call on the cousin of friends in New York. North Tehran was the old stomping ground of the shah's courtiers, the upper class, and foreign delegations. It was free of the pollution that settled over the old city like the sludge in Turkish coffee. Before the revolution there were more Hermès scarves and Chanel bags per square inch in North Tehran than anywhere else on earth. (Now adornments were discouraged. Visitors were required to declare lipstick and compacts on the customs form.)

Over strong sweet coffee, we told our friends' relative that Rushdie thought there was a chance the *fatwa* might be dropped. She shook her head in disbelief.

"There isn't anyone in a position to reverse the *fatwa*," she said emphatically. "Khomeini was so powerful. So charismatic. He could get 500,000 people out on a Friday. He was powerful enough to change things. Music was banned. Then he saw that people were depressed. So, he said, 'Okay, you can listen to music.' Chess was banned for a thousand years. He said, 'Chess is okay.' None of this lot could do that. Whatever Khomeini said, we're stuck with," added the North Tehran matron. "Thank God he said music and caviar were okay before he died."

Since his death there had been endless squabbling in the clergy to fill his shoes. His successor, Ayatollah Khamenei, was a pale imitation. "Nobody likes him. He sits in a big theater, on a platform, above everyone else." If there was an election, she thought, he might get 10 percent of the vote. Khomeini's son, the next generation, was a three-hundred-pound opium addict.

We had arrived in Tehran with another introduction (thanks to a senior U.N. official), to a man in the stratosphere of the Iranian political scene. He was an ayatollah, as far removed from the old bastion of the shah as you could get. He had served for eleven years as Khomeini's aide-de-camp. Ayatollah Doi'e had run Khomeini's home and office, looking after his family and his finances. Because the late Khomeini was now practically deified here, the Ayatollah Doi'e's proximity to Khomeini put him in an enviable position in the pantheon of ayatollahs.

We drove to his downtown address, a large, bustling publishing house. When Khomeini divided up the spoils of Iran, he gave his closest friends huge businesses. Doi'e got this publishing empire, including one of Tehran's biggest daily papers. He ran it while at the same time serving as the speaker of the clergy movement for seven years.

We asked the front desk to announce our arrival. We were ushered up. The ayatollah, it turned out, had already been briefed about us. He had received word that we were coming from the U.N. in New York. In his sixties, the Ayatollah Doi'e looked spare and distinguished. He wore long flowing robes. As we talked, he frequently picked up the phone, at times, two lines at once. The ayatollah held two seats in the Majlis (parliament), one in the so-called hard-liner camp, the other in the moderate camp. No one else had that distinction. He also wore the coveted gold star of this regime. He had been on the plane bringing Khomeini back from exile in Paris when millions thronged the streets to receive him. Everyone who was anyone in the Iranian regime had kissed the ground that day at the airport with the imam. The adjutant general of the father of the revolution invited us to lunch.

In his private dining room, the ayatollah passed the duck with pomegranate sauce and pronounced on Salman Rushdie. "We pray for his death soon," he said, beaming. "May he die soon to bring comfort to everybody."

Ayatollah Doi'e's prayer for death was received with approbation around the table. "He deserves it," kicked in Rajai Khorosani, chairman of the Foreign Affairs Committee of the Majlis and ambassador to the United Nations in the Reagan years. At the end of the table, heaped with Persian delicacies, the cool, detached Iranian vice-president, Sayyid Mohajirani, sipped a Zamzam cola. "He's already dead."

Now we could safely report that at the upper reaches of the regime, everyone wanted Salman Rushdie to die. But would they order his assassination? Everyone hedged. As the duck was cleared away and replaced with sweet rice and tender chicken kebabs, all insisted to us that the publication of Rushdie's *Satanic Verses* was part of a deliberate Western plot. "That's how we see it," declared the energetic chairman of the Foreign Affairs Committee. "We think it was a sort of orchestrated, well-planned program to embarrass the revolution." This would come as a great surprise to Rushdie.

After lunch, Vice-President Mohajirani wanted to meet again. He asked us to join him in his office inside the presidential compound, a city block cordoned off by massive concrete barriers arranged like an assault course. No one could penetrate the defenses in a van full of explosives. The vice-president was the in-house Rushdie scholar. We were trying to get straight whether they really regarded *The Satanic Verses* as a threat and whether the *fatwa*, the death sentence, was still real. The vice-president's book *A Critique on the Machinations of "The Satanic Verses"* got rave reviews in Tehran. "It went through six editions," he said proudly. The author of this blistering attack was the boy wonder of Iranian politics. At age twenty-five, he was in parliament. Twelve years later, he was director of parliament. Now he was President Rafsanjani's right-hand man.

In a room cluttered with hundreds of books in several languages, including a sizable collection of Persian poetry, the vice-president began to discuss Rushdie. "He has an extraordinary vocabulary. His work is both in the school of magical realism, following on García Márquez, and stream of consciousness, after Faulkner and Joyce. I see a lot of similarity with *A Hundred Years of Solitude.*" The vice-president thought the writer drew on Godard for inspiration, and saw his characters as comparable to the heroes and anti-heroes of Faulkner and Camus. He stopped short of placing Rushdie alongside Joyce. "I prefer Joyce more than any other writer," he explained with reverence. "I can compare him only with Dostoevsky."

The vice-president had little trouble understanding why writers rallied to Rushdie's cause. "They believe Rushdie should be able to write anything because he is living in a free society. Like Harold Pinter, for example. Or Susan Sontag." Pinter, one of Rushdie's most ardent supporters, was a great favorite of the vice-president's. "They believe in liberty, so they defend Rushdie. But," he said, withdrawing cautiously into his role as top Iranian official, "their concept of liberty is different from our concept of liberty."

It was Rushdie's revival of the story of the Prophet Mohammed's false revelation (known as The Satanic Verses) and Mohammed's assurance to polytheists that their gods were not forbidden by the faith that rankled the revolutionary regime's literary critic. Rushdie's liberal use of the Satanic Verses episode was, according to his critic, "tantamount to seasoning a delicious food with glass flakes."

"There have been many books against Islam—Dante, for example," said the vice-president. "But Rushdie wrote this book in a very important and sensitive period." Khomeini, he explained, "was sick. His condition was very bad. There wasn't much time for discussion."

"Khomeini was very depressed after the [Iran–Iraq] war," remembered a Tehran journalist sipping a fruity homemade wine. In early 1989, it seemed that the ayatollah was condemning people to death left and right. At the same time Rushdie felt his wrath, an Iranian woman got the death sentence for confessing to Tehran radio that her idol was a Japanese soap opera star. The interviewer was conducting random woman-in-the-street interviews.

"Who's your ideal woman?" he asked.

"Ossen," said the woman. In the soap opera, Ossen was dirt-poor. She survived on turnips. She dragged herself out of poverty to run a chain of Japanese supermarkets. To a poor Iranian woman, this was a spectacular achievement. Unfortunately, the correct answer to the question was "the Prophet's daughter."

"Khomeini was furious. He said she should be killed. People were dispatched to hunt her down. But because it was a radio interview with no name, they couldn't find her."

Khomeini wrote a tart letter to the managing director of radio and television two weeks before his famous blast against Rushdie. "I note with great regret and sadness," said the ayatollah, "that the Voice of the Islamic Republic yesterday broadcast a program on a role model for women which makes one ashamed even to speak about it. All those involved with the program will be punished," fumed the eighty-seven-year-old leader of Iran. "If it is proved that there was an intention to insult, the guilty person is without a doubt sentenced to death."

The day of Ayatollah Doi'e's lunch, a huge crowd gathered below the gold minarets of the tomb of the Ayatollah Khomeini. Inside the monument, a cross between the Paris Beaubourg and a Grand Hyatt, a ceiling of shimmering mirrors reflected the glass-cased tomb neatly covered with a cloth and spray of flowers. The floor inside the tomb was heaped with rial notes, Iranian cash, deposited through slits in the glass.

As President Hashemi Rafsanjani, one of Khomeini's closest disciples, spoke on the narrow raised platform at the back of the mausoleum, shots rang out in the crowd. One bullet lodged in the ceiling above Rafsanjani's head. The gunman, in military uniform, was hustled out of the hall. The president looked bewildered. "I thought it was an exploding lightbulb."

The assassination attempt was blamed by the minister of intelligence on a terrorist group, "individuals with notorious records, low beliefs, or no beliefs at all." Cynics in Tehran thought it was staged. Sympathy for the regime was waning dramatically as the economy fell into ruin. "There have been riots recently around the country," said a doctor that night lying on an Isfahan carpet in a frigid outdoor café in Darband, a mountain retreat above Tehran. "The last riot was over bus fares. You don't see it in the papers until maybe two weeks after, there'll be some obscure reference." We were dining by a rushing stream on yogurt with mint and flat bread. "The price of food has gone up a lot. Some things have gone up twenty times."

Corruption was gnawing away at the old revolutionary standards. Drinking and consorting at parties with the opposite sex, punishable by imprisonment, were easily arranged by bribing the Revolutionary Guards. Payment was made in advance, one fee for mixing sexes, the other for alcohol. "Here you can get anything you want," said a louche denizen of North Tehran. "Whiskey, crack, heroin. Just give me two hours. I can get it." The rooftops of Tehran were dotted with odd green boxes, veiled satellite dishes, picking up Star TV from Hong Kong. The Burmese channel was featuring Ginger Rogers movies.

The director of Iranian TV, President Rafsanjani's brother, had just been fired, leading to whispered gossip that the Rafsanjanis might have been doing too well out of the revolution. Control of the National Security Council was wrenched from the president and turned over to a former intelligence chief. The question of who was in control in the Byzantine politics of Tehran was open to speculation. There was no sign that any reshuffling would benefit Salman Rushdie.

In the Majlis, the notion that the *fatwa* could be "fixed," that the dead cleric's judgment against Rushdie could be revoked, was regarded as dangerous political heresy. "Impossible," shouted the dapper Khorosani of the Foreign Affairs Committee whom we visited at the Majlis a few days after our lunch. "To waste time on it is a useless, futile activity. Just forget the man, it's easier." He offered us sweet dried apricots. "You see, what we have to do is let him die, to let the issue just pass away. To keep it alive, I think, is the objective of some of the Western countries who think that by reviving this matter they will be able to find more fault with us."

An aide rushed in to brief him on the budget battle raging on the floor of the Majlis below. Outside the window of the heavily guarded parliament compound, a military helicopter was hovering. "We think that the experience of Rushdie can be viewed as a very educational experience. That after the revival of Islam in our global village, it's good to know the sensitivities of the Muslims so you can be friendly." He laughed heartily. "You have to realize"—he leaned closer—"that inside Iran there are a number of groups who can increase the price for his head. We don't want to say 'stop that' because it is a religious matter. They want to embarrass the government. Cause trouble for us. They are doing pretty well."

Across town on Veliasr Street, there was a particularly festive display of revolutionary zeal. Strings of colored lights and freshly woven garlands draped the entrance of a seven-story building next to one of Tehran's better sock shops. A profusion of posters of Ayatollah Khomeini and his colorless successor as religious leader, Ayatollah Khamenei, were taped to the glass. An Iranian flag lit by neon was stretched over the door. This was the headquarters of the Khordad 15 foundation, named for the date on the Iranian calendar when, in 1963, thousands died in a demonstration instigated by Khomeini against the shah.

Khordad was offering a $3-million bounty for Rushdie's corpse. The offer included martyrdom should the executioner die in the attempt and a stipend for the widow and children. We walked in to find bearded young men milling in and out, punching time cards and discussing real estate deals. Khordad was one of Iran's biggest Bonyads, the religious foundations that seized the multibillion-dollar assets of the shah and the wealthy upper class who fled with him in 1979. Spanking new factories, vast tracts of real estate, fancy hotels, were all parceled out to the Bonyads, run by men the ayatollah trusted. One of them got his start driving the Bronco the day Khomeini came back from Paris. The foundations had considerable portfolios, including holdings abroad. Bonyad Mostasavan—the Foundation of the Oppressed—owned a skyscraper at Rockefeller Plaza in midtown Manhattan.

The young men at Khordad 15 were puzzled by our appearance. There were broad smiles all around at the mention of Salman Rushdie. They seemed to think that we had come in response to the particularly generous reward going for non-Muslims who would do the job. One well-placed mullah, who was a neighbor of Khordad's director in the holy city of Qom, asked us nonchalantly over tea and pistachios, "Do you want to kill Rushdie?"

"Khordad has twenty-five factories," said a well-connected observer of the Tehran political scene. "They make everything from fruit juice to shoes." Ayatollah Hasan Sane'i, the boss of Khordad and the man who originally posted the reward for Rushdie's head, "is a very radical fundamentalist, one of the most important clergy." The observer paused, tracing minute patterns on the paper in front of him. "He is one of the godfathers, so powerful and so big. That's why he doesn't accept any executive positions."

Sane'i was powerful because of his links to the *bazaaris*, the merchants of the bazaar, the pillars of the revolution, who financed Khomeini's crusade against the shah. The *bazaaris* did not approve of "occidentalist" trends, miniskirts, and liberal ideas, which they equated with sexual permissiveness. They believed that business with the West should be allowed. Nothing else.

The Khordad boss agreed to see us. He then abruptly changed his mind.

The central bazaar was a covered market a mile long with vaulted brick ceilings. Every conceivable item was for sale. There were stacks of carpets from Tabriz and Sane'i. You could spot the *bazaaris* around town driving the new Mercedeses with the license plate "Teheran 42." "Downtown has gone uptown," said an observer at the Chola Kebab fast-food restaurant. "The merchants from the bazaar who didn't have obvious connections to the old regime kept their money and now have become very rich." That meant that Khordad 15, who had placed the bounty on Rushdie's head, was well placed behind the scenes.

It was impossible to overestimate the Khomeini legacy. For the fifteen-anniversary celebration, there was an exhibition of paintings at the Museum of the Martyrs. The museum was a confiscated mansion in North Tehran. The roses had been pruned. The swimming pool had been filled. Much of the art was inspired by the war with Iraq, which cost 1 million Iranian lives. In one painting, Khomeini floats in the heavens above a peaceful lake. In the foreground, a field of red poppies melts into a sea of blood. In another work, a mother clutches her son's army jacket. There is a poem attached:

> The blood
> on the martyr's jacket
> smells like heaven.

In one room, there are glass cases full of the personal effects of dead ayatollahs. A pair of cheap glasses, old socks, a half-empty packet of pills. The ayatollahs were all blown up or murdered in terrorist attacks. The blood-soaked turbans are there in the case. There is doleful Persian Muzac playing in the background.

A few days after Ayatollah Doi'e's lunch party, we received a message at the Esteghlal Hotel, the expropriated Hilton. The ayatollah was arranging a special trip for us to the holiest Iranian city, Qom. This was the religious headquarters of the ayatollahs, the very heart of Iranian Shia fundamentalism. Qom was the birthplace of Khomeini.

The ayatollah needed my precise measurements. In Qom, I would need an exceptional veil, long, black, and voluminous, a silky chador that touched the ground as I walked. There were no six-foot veils. The ayatollah was having one specially made. We would be escorted in Qom by his own mullahs. When the seamstress had finished her work, we set out across the painted desert. A great salt lake divided the capital from the holy city. Mount Damavand, a perfect conical volcano, rose out of the salt flats. At the city limits, I struggled into the diabolically slippery chador. The fabric had to be held beneath the chin at all times, which meant that drinking a cup of tea and holding a tape recorder was an impossible feat. A wisp of hair, a glimpse of neck, were sinful sights in Qom.

We were met by the ayatollah's nephew, a remarkably ascetic mullah who looked like he had stepped out of a nineteenth-century painting. Above his robes, his skin looked like the purest white marble. In the center of his forehead, there was a protruding bump, from pounding his head in prayer on the Karbala stones. The sacred stones were made of pressed earth from Karbala in Iraq (which we had last seen in ruins from Saddam's battle with the Shia rebels). He led us to the Mosala Qods central mosque. Under the soaring dome, several thousand of the faithful bowed their heads to touch the Karbala stones on their prayer rugs. I was hustled up rickety wooden stairs to the balcony overflowing with women wearing pale chadors for prayer. In place of "amen," there was a melodic chant of "Death to U.S.A." It rolled over the crowds like a peal of thunder.

There was no sympathy for Rushdie the "apostate" here.

We emerged into the harsh sunlight. Our detachment of mullahs led our procession to the inner sanctum of Qom's religious leaders to hear their views on Rushdie. "I've read the book," said a stern ayatollah in a fine turban and robes. "There's just swearing. There's no logic in it." Sayed Hadi Khosrowshahi held the prestigious job of government adviser in Qom. His last post was ambassador to the Vatican. "It's not just Islam. He's rude to Moses, Jesus. He wrote that Abraham was a bastard. Forty-five Islamic countries, 1.2 billion people, this is not something we can just pass through. It's blasphemy."

The ayatollah sitting in his office crowded with mullahs read the same excerpts from *The Satanic Verses* shipped by diplomatic pouch from the Iranian Embassy in London to the Ministry of Guidance in Tehran and handed to Khomeini. "It took him a day. In the evening he read it and in the morning he issued the *fatwa*," said the ayatollah, one of the very few who knew the chain of events leading to the death sentence. "According to Islam, there's nothing to think about. It's obvious."

"Did you ask at all," said Rushdie, hungry for news of his judges in Tehran, "about this thing of the *fatwa* having not actually been made by Khomeini?" We sadly informed him that this notion, which had generated excitement in the Rushdie camp, had been greeted with derision in the Iranian capital, not to mention Qom. There was a disconnect of galactic proportions between the Iranians who count and Rushdie and his supporters.

"The *fatwa*," said Frances d'Souza, "could be lifted in five minutes." From their modest lodgings in London, her group, Article 19 (named for the universal Declaration of Human Rights section on freedom of expression), has worked tirelessly to mobilize Western governments to support Rushdie. "Five minutes. It was a message delivered to a radio station. No one's seen it. Khomeini could have rescinded the *fatwa* on his deathbed. Future generations," she says, citing Shia law, "are not bound by the words of a dead man."

A *fatwa*, Vice-President Mohajirani had told us, does not have to be written down.

D'Souza believed there may have been serious efforts by the Iranian government to find an escape clause in the *fatwa*. For them, she thought, the *fatwa* was an embarrassment, a bore. There had been so many "in-betweenies," purported emissaries from Tehran. There was the Iranian exile, a multimillionaire industrialist. He threw a dinner that was all Lalique and butlers. D'Souza said she could see Rushdie start to huff and puff but the table was too big so she could not kick him.

Over dinner, the industrialist proposed that someone write four outrageous pages. He would give them to a holy man. It would then be revealed that Khomeini hadn't read the book, but these four pages.

"Completely surreal," says Rushdie, recalling the episode. "You will be asked, 'Did you write this page?' and you will truthfully say, 'No.' Therefore the imam was misled. I said, 'What you're actually proposing is that we introduce into this novel some satanic verses.'" Rushdie laughed. "When we announce that these are in fact interpolations of the devil and remove them, then the text will be purified. If this is how the problem is solved, it's too beautiful. Therefore," he recalled, shaking his head at the memory of the strange scheme, "it's not possible."

A baffled look came across the face of the vice-president at the suggestion that any emissaries had been sanctioned by his government. They had, he said, neglected the imam's judgment. There was a difference between a religious judgment—a *fatwa*—and a governmental order—a *hokm*. Had Khomeini issued the *hokm*, the government would have been obliged to act. If the imam said Rushdie should be killed, the minister of intelligence would be obliged to send a team to kill Rushdie. That was an order. A *fatwa*, he said, is a judgment, a death sentence without a death squad. No "team," he said, was ever dispatched.

Yet one set of emissaries who approached Frances d'Souza in the first year of the *fatwa* seemed to be part of such a team. A diplomat from the Iranian Embassy in London asked her to come to a meeting at the embassy. "He was clearly performing a diplomatic function," said Rushdie, requiring high-level clearance. At the meeting he said, "What do you want?"

The British government expelled the negotiator and two other Iranians on the grounds they were directly, actively involved in the pursuit of Rushdie.

There was a second incident. Just before the Gulf War, the authorities told him, the Iranians paid for a hit team of French contract killers. "It seems," recalled Rushdie, "quite a lot of money was handed over."

"Special Branch's knowledge of Iran is very limited," said d'Souza, "but they say the groups that come over here to do the dirty work are just terribly inept." This begged the question of why a government skilled in the black arts of covert operations would not put their best men on the case. The man who beat and stabbed Rushdie's Italian translator kept demanding Rushdie's address.

A senior administration official in Washington whose job it is to combat terrorism was adamant that the Iranian government, not the occasional religious fanatic or bounty hunter, was stalking Rushdie. "I have good reason to believe even now, *right now*, they are actively seeking to have Rushdie killed. They are very dangerous people. I think the best way to convince people it's real is what happened in Norway. That's real."

William Nygaard, a champion ski jumper and publisher of *The Satanic Verses* in Norway, did not want to talk publicly about what had happened. We had to convince him to speak about the terrible day in October 1993, when he was found in a pool of blood outside his Oslo home, with three large bullet holes in him.

"On the Saturday night," Nygaard told us, "I went to a friend's fiftieth-birthday party, which was also a celebration for the baptism of his child, so it was a good party. The next morning, Sunday, it was raining. Toni Morrison had just gotten the Nobel Prize so I decided to spend the day at home reading her latest novel." On Monday, Nygaard left the house at the leisurely hour of 8:30, heading to a health center for a back massage.

"When I went out to the car, I noticed immediately that the left front tire was flat." It had been slashed. "I'm a clumsy person. I didn't want to fix the tire myself." He decided to call for a mechanic and a taxi. "I opened the front door of the car on the right-hand side to take out the mobile phone and also to stop the car alarm going off. I pushed the button to call the taxi and I heard a small explosion. At the same moment I felt a terrible blow on my lower back."

Nygaard misunderstood the blow. "I thought I had had an electrical shock, because I had a phone in one hand and I was trying to neutralize the alarm with the other. Of course it was really a bullet. It went through my back and stomach. I was still conscious, then the second shot came. I still thought I was getting electrical shocks. I was running. I thought it was important to get out of the electrical zone. There must have been a third shot. It hit me above the knee. I threw myself down the slope. I started screaming. That must have frightened the people who were shooting." Police told Nygaard there had been more than one gunman.

"I was screaming. I was scared. My neighbors might all have left for work. I lay there for ten minutes, I was getting tired. Finally a lady came. A guest from next door."

He was convinced that it was a cleverly organized professional hit. "I would bend down to look at the tire that was cut or get into the driver's seat. They would have had a clear shot."

Nygaard, like the man he published, now lived with around-the-clock police protection. "I am now living in a secret place. Like Salman Rushdie, though not quite as bad. I have police guards. I am transported in a bulletproof car that used to belong to the prime minister of Sweden."

The police have circulated an Identikit portrait of a suspect, described as being of "Middle Eastern appearance." He had a mustache.

The day before Thanksgiving, a month later, a suspicious carload was spotted "staking out" a fashionable northwest Washington address where we were sipping champagne with Rushdie. He had just been received by the president. "Clinton popped out of a room where he was recording a speech about turkeys," Rushdie told us excitedly as he paced. In a corridor, the president engaged in a brave five-minute conversation with the marked man. It was enough for Rushdie that Clinton had made the symbolic gesture, even if his staff shied him away from a photograph. As Rushdie explained to us over more champagne, "They are seriously worried about a major attack on some American installation."

He met Warren Christopher and National Security Adviser Tony Lake, both former Carter officials stung by the disaster of the hostage crisis. They discussed using the Iranian debt as a weapon. "I mean their debt is $44 billion and they're rolling over short-term credits from week to week. The idea would be to squeeze them a little."

After the meeting, the chief justice of Iran called Clinton the most hated man in the Muslim world. The president responded by saying he had met with Rushdie for only two minutes in the corridor, and had meant no offense to Muslims. When we asked the senior terrorism official if Clinton's statement was a retreat, he replied emphatically, "No, no, no. By no means. He was not backing away."

In the holy city of Qom, in a room that was a blur of clerical robes, the Ayatollah Khosrowshahi's disdain for Rushdie and the White House began to flow. "They gave him great status, although he had been rude to 1 billion Muslims. Salman Rushdie is just an excuse. We believe that if we do one-tenth of what the Americans want in Iran, they would get rid of hundreds of Rushdies." The former ambassador to the Vatican was smoldering.

"They killed Kennedy, Martin Luther King. They've planned their terror, their assassinations. The relationship with the Mafia is very obvious. You should know better than us." He fixed his eyes on me. "It's like saying the sun is out."

We excused ourselves, saying we had already taken up too much of his time.

Our ascetic guide, Ayatollah Doi'e's nephew, whisked us out of the room. My slick black veil was slipping off. As we piled into the mullah's car, I stepped on the veil, sat on it, yanking it off my head. The veil and I were at war.

There was something the mullah wanted us to see. His uncle, the aide-de-camp of Khomeini, had given him instructions. The holy city of Qom was built around the Shrine of Fātima the Innocent, sister of Imam Reza, the eighth imam of the Duodecimal Shiites. The Haran of Hazrate Masoumeh was the religious center's holiest site. It was the eye of Iran.

When the great traveler Isabella Bird came by caravan to Qom in 1890, Persians described it as a town that imported corpses and exported mullahs. Bird was shocked by the religious fanaticism. She was determined to enter the sacred Shrine of Fātima, where infidels and Christians were strictly forbidden. She disguised herself. Her scheme was discovered. The explorer never made it through the heavy doors to Iran's inner sanctum.

To my astonishment, the ayatollah's pale nephew led us to the Shrine of Fātima and told us to enter.

Once inside, we were tossed into a seething mass of worshipers. Women and men approached Fātima's solid-silver tomb from different sides of a latticework divide. I was carried in a black wave of veiled bodies through the portico to the women's chambers. They flowed toward the brilliant, intricately carved silver, rubbed by centuries of hands pressing upon it. To touch the tomb meant fulfilling a wish. In an eddy, a mullah sprayed women with rose water. I was heavily doused. Mina, my female companion, heard the comments in Farsi of the crush of women. They whispered about a "foreigner" in their midst. They marveled at my green eyes and tremendous height. I was, they assumed, a convert.

"Thanks be to God," they said. "Her chador is just right."

We were propelled roughly toward the tomb, as though swept toward the rocks by the current of a river. Hundreds of outstretched arms strained to touch the silver, polished like a reflecting pool. Women were sobbing.

As we followed the human current back to the nave, I saw a corpse wrapped in a shroud held aloft on a stretcher over the crowds. The mass of worshipers surged toward it, then fell back. They surged forward again. Some were nearly trampled trying to touch the dead for luck. They tripped on the graves of martyrs and the freshly laid tomb of the last Grand Ayatollah. They wailed. The fervor here was suffocating. Voices rose to a crescendo, echoing in the recesses of the vaulted stone. The stretcher nearly overturned. The faithful gasped, screamed, the pallbearers caught the shroud. This was a crowd that could turn in seconds from the heat of religion to violence. This was like being in a whirlpool, a vortex. In this place, I thought, I have finally reached the ends of the earth.

By the time we drove back across the great salt lake, the dusk light cast the volcano in a purple gloom. The mullahs had loaded us up with tins of Qom's famous pistachio nougat. One of our hosts, soon to be in the top tier of the clergy, had blurted out at the candy counter, "I've never seen an American before." He was sipping Zamzam cola with the daughter of the Great Satan.

I was anxious to go home. I packed away my Qom chador to send it back to the ayatollah. Later I heard he was puzzled that I would return such a magnificent veil. It was, after all, a perfect fit.

FIFTEEN

S.P.E.C.T.R.E.

"**D**ID YOU EVER read Ian Fleming?" a senior administration official whispered to me in his plush Washington office. "These guys are S.P.E.C.T.R.E. All the way back in the fifties, Fleming knew what was going to happen."

Ian Fleming, the creator of James Bond, envisioned a world crime organization staffed from the ranks of the Russian KGB. The administration official was not trying to be funny.

"These guys will kill you," he said urgently. "They're ruthless bastards. They'll kill you in the middle of the night with a vial of something in your room."

By 1995, the Russian Mafia, the phoenix from the ashes of the old Soviet Union, was occupying the thoughts of anyone who was reading classified reports. "It is remarkable," a former White House national security adviser said to me at a candlelit dinner, "Russia is now a criminal enterprise."

I had been exposed to the wild side of the new Russia, just after the elections in the Duma, the Russian parliament, in December 1993. I was there for ABC News. Moscow was unusually warm, Red Square and Kitay-Gorod buried in a sugary snow. The atmosphere was charged after the ultra-nationalist Vladimir Zhirinovsky (he recoiled at the word "fascist") made a strong showing at the voting booths. A quarter of the Russian population earned under thirty-five dollars a month, and discontent with the widespread and ostentatious corruption under Boris Yeltsin had launched a demagogue. Zhirinovsky took fifty-nine seats in the Duma.

There were no snowplows in the Moscow streets. People skated in their boots along the sidewalks. I was there with John Hockenberry of *ABC Day One*, producing a story on the shattered Russian space program. Their launch site was now in a different country, Kazakhstan. The Kazakhs were proposing to share the facilities, now falling apart, with the Iranians. (Khomeini had discoursed at length about religious deportment in space.) At times, problems had been so serious on the ground that astronauts were simply left floating on Mir, the Russian space station, until further notice.

As we were already in Moscow, Roone Arledge, head of ABC News, and his adjutant, Johanna Bistany, wanted us to deliver a story on Zhirinovsky to air on Monday night. It was Wednesday. We had five days to convince Zhirinovsky to do the interview, shoot it, conduct other interviews, plow through file footage, election footage, our own footage, cut the piece, and "bird" it via satellite. It would have to fit a gap left in the show precisely, to the second. This was not a slapped-together news item. It was a long, polished piece, the kind that usually takes two months. It was the television equivalent of a decathlon.

Zhirinovsky's campaign headquarters was on a side street in one of Moscow's old quarters, lined with grand houses that had become tenements. The building was dark. It had not been cleaned, it seemed, since sometime after the battle of Borodino. Water and muck covered the wide, pitted stone steps inside. The cage elevator looked like it had not run since the revolution. On the first-floor landing was the only other tenant in the building. It was the Rock Shop, devoted exclusively to black leather with a few T-shirts printed with tarantulas. I groped my way up the dingy steps, peering at the carpet of cigarette butts, inches deep, on the roof of the dead lift. My destination was the fourth-floor suite of Zhirinovsky and his campaign staff.

Pausing for breath, I walked into a warren lined with beefy men with pink cheeks and weak chins wearing leather jackets. The rest of the claque consisted of an ancient lady reputed to be a philosopher and an aide in a tight bowler hat who spoke twelve languages and believed, firmly, that Zhirinovsky would *restore order to Mother Russia.*

The only artwork on display was a cheap painting of "old Baghdad." Zhirinovsky had sent volunteers from his Youth Brigade to express solidarity with Saddam.

The "law and order" candidate's second-in-command greeted me in the badly decorated outer office. He was a fur salesman. I spent an hour selling him on the concept of American television. During the entire hour, his eyes were glued to my mother's mink coat, taken out of mothballs for this occasion. He suddenly spoke.

"That's Russian."

"I beg your pardon."

"The coat. It's Russian fur. I know. Very nice. Really."

"And the interview?"

"I have a warehouse of furs. The best quality. I would like you to come there."

"Do you think we could bring the cameras tomorrow? Our deadline is very tight and we think Americans should have a chance to see Mr. Zhirinovsky and hear his views as soon as possible."

"The warehouse is not far. My prices are very competitive. Where did you buy that coat?"

"Well, it's an old one."

"I can see, but the mink is, really, the best. Russian. Do you mind if I touch it?"

Later that day, we received a call from the Zhirinovsky campaign headquarters saying that they were optimistic about the interview. Fortunately, we had trudged up those steps before the camera crews from Japanese TV, who secured interviews by simply opening their checkbooks, ruining everyone else's chances. The coat had done a great service. Also, Irena, one of ABC's Russian staff, had been a Zhirinovsky camp follower from the days when the great orator was happy attracting an audience of one table at a luncheonette.

"The Leader," as the faithful called him, received us in a large square room with net curtains and imitation Russian imperial chairs. An impressive map above his desk showed Russia as he would have liked it, stretching across the Bering Strait in a sweeping arc to Alaska. The fifty-first state was nestled under the wing of the falcon, symbol of the "party." The shores of the Arctic above, the shores of the Bering Sea below, the necklace of the Aleutian Islands, Anchorage, the oil fields of the North Slope, all Mother Russia.

Zhirinovsky had blue eyes the color of Sapphire gin. At forty-seven, he had steel-gray hair, a weathered face, and a booming, sonorous voice. Without that voice, he was an ordinary man. When he used the voice to best effect, he could say everything and nothing, leaving the crowd exhilarated, angry, and infected with imperial ambition. He talked with the cadence of a great Shakespearean actor of the "humiliation." The Russian people had been humiliated by perestroika. They were humiliated ever since perestroika. Even now, they were humiliated. He, Vladimir, would protect the people against "anti-Russian sentiments." He and the people, together, would stand up to the Japanese. The Japanese, he bellowed, did nothing but "cry, cry, cry." There were, of course, foreign influences corrupting the motherland. Pepsi-Cola and chewing gum ads were invading the airwaves, like influenza. There were, by the way, not enough Russians on television. Not enough Russian films. All of the programs, he complained loudly, were about Hanukkah.

He knew how to make noise and how to use silence. The room went dead quiet, except for the muffled sounds of the supplicants outside in the waiting room, before he began talking about his youth in Kazakhstan. He went into a kind of trance. He was delivering the soliloquy on the stage of the Bolshoi, the big theater, spilling his anguish in his last rehearsal before the crowds filled in. He threw his booming voice like a net to catch them in the grand tier. He was alone, in the pool of light, unaware that anyone was in the room.

"My father left when I was three months old." He spoke the words slowly, in a kind of howl. "I have no information. He left one note saying, 'Sasha, save yourself. And save the boy.' His name. Wolf. They say it's not a Russian name. His family were all Russian. Perhaps they liked Wolfgang Amadeus Mozart. You cannot say Wolfgang here. You have to say Wolf. I have no information. I was three months old . . ."

He began to hum. He closed his eyes. The song was a Polish

polonaise, his favorite song. "I feel about this song the way I feel about the Russian people."

In Kazakhstan, he said, he was bullied and abused. A Russian, abused by Kazakhs. It was enough to make Russian blood boil. "The people there were living in yurts, in the empty desert. We, Russians, brought civilization, everything, and now they want us out."

On the Alaskan question, he was prepared to give the people of Alaska a choice. When they saw the benefits of returning to Mother Russia, they would beg to call Vladimir Zhirinovsky their leader.

We finished the piece at 4 A.M., Moscow time, an hour before air in New York. The piece slotted in "to time," not a second to spare, and left an unsettling impression of the mental state of the Russian voters.

Russia was unstable. Desperation, lawlessness, confusion, manic-depression, were the symptoms of the dissolution of a superpower. Russians were experiencing sensory deprivation. Everything familiar, everything secure, the jobs, the subsidies, the institutions, the value system, had vanished. It was the equivalent of Americans' being told they should no longer aspire to be rich and famous. They should aspire to translating Serbo-Croatian into ancient Greek.

In Russia, a hefty slice of the elite had been the generals and the scientists. Running the Strategic Rocket Forces or becoming a nuclear physicist, assigned to one of the "secret cities" like Arzamas-16 or Chelyabinsk-70, was what dreams were made of. Now the hustler selling leather jackets was going into currency speculation, commodities exports, and was opening a bank. Moscow was overrun with banks. Teenage girls lined the streets outside the better hotels, clogged the bar of the Metropole to earn the cash to afford a Versace miniskirt. A popular television show in Moscow taught girls the skills they needed to decorate the arm of a Mafia don with a condo in the Côte d'Azur and a bank in Antigua. Moscow was a gritty town of gangsters and molls. Business disputes were settled with a burst of machine-gun fire or a silencer.

The entrepreneurial spirit was sweeping through the government ministries, the intelligence agencies, the military design bureaus, the old mechanisms for the central control of Soviet wealth and production. Special forces officers were reconstituted as private armies. Spies traded intelligence with private firms. Generals sold MIG fighter planes to the highest bidder. The looting of Russia's natural resources, the oil, the minerals, diamonds, timber, by those in the old Nomenklatura who could get their hands on the goods and ship it out was measured in the tens of billions of dollars.

In 1995, Andrew and I were sent by *Vanity Fair* to find out whether the common phrase "everything is for sale in Russia" applied to the Russian nuclear arsenal, including the thousands of tactical nuclear weapons, land mines, depth charges, SADM atomic demolition munitions that fit in a suitcase, Frog artillery that had been withdrawn from Eastern Europe. The Warsaw Pact front line, the old "nuclear battlefield," had been packed up, shipped home, and warehoused. Russia was a nuclear junkyard.

In mid-April we boarded an Aeroflot flight out of springtime Moscow to Murmansk, the hub of Russia's Kola Peninsula, that juts into the Arctic Circle. We flew into a blizzard. At that moment, I thought about the reports that Aeroflot maintenance was the worst in the world. After a bumpy ride, we arrived in a flat landscape of dirty snowdrifts and mile after mile of bare, sick-looking trees. Until a few years before, Murmansk had been closed to foreigners. Murmansk was a military town, surrounded by the bases of the Northern Fleet. Nuclear subs and nuclear icebreakers were based here. There were nuclear intercontinental ballistic missiles and warehouses full of nuclear "confetti," tactical weapons. The whole peninsula around Murmansk was the biggest nuclear repository in Russia. Everyone said the Northern Fleet sailors glowed in the dark.

The city itself was a forest of drab apartment blocks, Soviet concrete slabs, assembled in haste. Statues of Lenin stood proudly in public squares, vacant lots, braced against the frigid wind blowing off the fiords of the Barents Sea. The icons of the revolution, toppled in Moscow and St. Petersburg, here in the north gazed steadfastly over the industrial terrain of the once vital strategic port to Finland and Norway to the west and the radiation-rich tundra, the detritus of the cold war, to the east. Where was the new Russia? Our Khrushchev-era hotel was the Arktika. Lightbulbs were out. Linoleum was cracked. The veneer was peeling. We were just in time for our date with the Russian Navy's chief investigator for the Northern Fleet.

Kulik knocked softly on the door of our grimy room. This was a clandestine meeting. He threw himself into a ragged chair, put his feet on the table, and lit a Russian cigarette, the rough pungent cigarettes with the cardboard filters. "I'm a Russian Tiger," he laughed, the name for investigators of sensitive military cases. He was twenty-five, wearing glasses, jeans, and sneakers. His family had been lawyers in the military for four generations. Kulik had already handled two serious cases of nuclear theft. "There are only two other investigators like me in this country"—Kulik tipped his ash—"and they're both drunkards."

One of the nuclear thefts took place in the Rosta district of Murmansk, ten minutes' drive from the Arktika. Captain Alexei Tikhomirov, scion of a distinguished naval family, walked through a hole in the fence of a nuclear fuel storage depot at 2 A.M. on a November night. He carried a bag and a hacksaw. He approached storage shed 3-30, sawed off the padlock, broke apart three fuel rod assemblies, and stuffed the enriched uranium in his bag. He shoved the bag into the trunk of the car belonging to his accomplice, Captain Oleg Baranov. The two Russian Navy captains sped off down the Murmansk–Severomorsk highway, stopping only to dump a pair of pliers and rubber gloves.

"From start to finish it took forty-three minutes," said Kulik. "Ten to twelve minutes to saw off the lock." There was negligible security in the "guarded zone" of Murmansk. "There were some armed guards, three old women who had no guns. They're afraid of guns. They're afraid of the storage site. There was no light, and one of them told me, 'How can I go there? I'm going to be raped.'" The alarm failed to go off. "Because of the sea, it was wet all the time. It got stuck. For ages the commander was screaming and shouting about a new alarm system. The answer was: no money."

The thief's father was a captain of the "first rank" like the captain in *The Hunt for Red October*. Young Tikhomirov had been in the navy fifteen years. Like everyone else, his salary was arriving "two, three, four months late," said the investigator. His brother Dmitri, a junior lieutenant, had supplied the details of where the fuel was stored and how to get in. The night of the heist, Dmitri stayed on board his ship getting drunk in his cabin with his white rat. "The rat was called Alexander Alexandrovich," the investigator remembered fondly. "He was a favorite of the whole ship. He had a tiny naval uniform and loved vodka. When Dmitri got arrested, the rat was left locked up for three days in the cabin. He was in bad shape when we found him."

They were only arrested months later because a naval officer informed on them. Their asking price was $50,000. "They wanted a new car. They were getting the same salary I am, $210 a month. The main reason they did it is there are no guarantees for your future when you leave the military." When the brothers were arrested, their father, the distinguished retired captain, had a stroke.

Kulik knocked back a couple of carafes of Finnish vodka. He drew a map on a napkin of the Rosta district where the fuel rods had been stolen. We hopped in a taxi and drove down to see if we could break in. It had started to snow again, heavy wet flakes that melted in the mud.

We directed the driver first to the main navy yard gate. Uniformed lady guards with rifles slung over their heavy winter coats scowled at us. "We are not authorized to talk to you," one said. We studied the map and told the driver to take a side road, lined with dirty snow heaps of corroding junk and old barracks. Cement walls had huge slabs broken off. We climbed through the debris of this absurdly porous perimeter while the driver sweated. He was convinced we were spies.

Prowling through the Rosta district, we found a quaint yellow and blue wooden house marked on the napkin. A sign read "Military Unit 31326." It was surrounded by decaying apartment blocks and children's playgrounds. There was an open-air vegetable market. On the other side of a green wooden fence with no barbed wire were the VM-4-AM nuclear reactor cores loaded with uranium 235. Packed snow was wedged against the fence. Children were playing king of the mountain. They, and we, could jump onto piles of snow a mere three feet below. We were yards away from the Quonset huts that contained the fresh nuclear fuel.

Freezing from sloshing around in the snowdrifts, we repaired to the Iceberg Club. The club was the only sign that the Mafia had arrived in Murmansk. We walked into the oasis of soft lights and caviar, where the local mafiosi brought their brassy wives. We wondered whether the group in the next booth was considering the nuclear business.

Kulik believed the stolen uranium was destined for Mafia buyers. "I believe it was for a terrorist act. I've got data on assassinations done with uranium dust. In the analysis after the murder, they can find only the leukemia. You need a very small amount of dust," he confided. "You can put it in a fur hat and they die."

We drove to the Dennis the Menace curiosity shop that sold monster masks at the municipal swimming pool. The younger Tikhomirov brother had a job as a salesman. He was, unfortunately, in jail for assaulting a policeman. "He kicked him in the melon," explained an old military academy schoolmate of Dmitri's from behind the counter. He tried to sell us tapes *(Sax and Sex* and *Gorky Park—Moscow Calling)* and gave every appearance of being stoned out of his mind.

Back in Moscow, we were crammed into the back of a clapped-out Russian compact driving past Red Square, bumper-to-bumper with Mercedes 600s and smoked-glass Lada Samaras full of Russia's new rich. In the front seat was a distinguished nuclear physicist working for the Yeltsin government who was not authorized to have this meeting. The physicist was drawn and deadly serious. "With my own eyes," he told us, "I have seen how they guard the secret of secrets, the pit of a plutonium bomb." He had just been to Tomsk-7, a "secret city" bomb complex where the pits from dismantled bombs were stored. "There are 23,000 containers. Each one contains a few kilos of plutonium" that has been and could be again the core of a nuclear weapon. The storage site in the distant Siberian city had enough plutonium lying around to blow up the planet.

Our very distinguished informant was shocked by what he saw. "The storage place where the containers are, the sheds are built of metal siding. The only thing they could protect you from is the rain." He described two storage sheds inside a barbed-wire perimeter. "One has a code lock on the door, just like the one on my apartment. The other has a padlock. For me this was a very frightening sensation." The containers were two feet high and weighed about a hundred kilos each. "There is no technical control if you want to take one."

We moved the conversation to the bar of the Metropole, filling up with high-priced hookers. No one noticed the handsome older man eating chocolate cake. He drew a diagram for us. Just behind the storage area was a forest. It was outside the closed zone. "You can easily imagine a terrorist," he said, "firing a rocket-propelled grenade from the woods into the storage shed." An inside job, however, required nothing so crude. At the entrance there were no facilities for checking what was inside a truck. There was no radiation detector. It was the traditional system: barbed wire, men with rifles, and a restrictive-pass system. "Circles within circles, like a Russian matroishka doll. So everything depends," he said without confidence, "on the people in the system."

The physicist was very worried about his friends in Tomsk. The plutonium in the shed was in danger of catching fire, which would shower the city of 100,000 with lethal particles. He had already advised his colleagues there to move away. Tomsk-7 is a city already famous for its mutants.

The Russian Ministry of Defense was across the street from Rosy O'Grady's Irish Pub. We had a date with a three-star general from the Twelfth Department. The Twelfth was the elite unit that controlled nuclear weapons. "The green eyeshade guys. If an officer of the Twelfth wanted to move a weapon out," said a Pentagon Defense Intelligence Agency veteran, "he could do it."

The three-star general was Sergei Zelentsov, a soldier-scientist who exploded many bombs at the Soviet test site in Kazakhstan. Zelentsov, who was responsible for the safety systems of all of Russia's nuclear weapons, claimed to us that every weapon had its own passport. The system counted every weapon. It was not off by one. We knew that even the Pentagon miscounted weapons. At one point they lost six Pershing 2 nuclear-tipped missiles. The general said he had full confidence in the care and protection of the plutonium pits at Tomsk-7.

"What is your worst nightmare?" I asked the general.

"The trains," he replied. "I have nightmares about the trains." The trains that moved the weapons across the vast empty spaces of Mother Russia were the most vulnerable targets. Trains could be hijacked or sabotaged. Blow up the track, the train derails, and a nuclear weapon explodes, showering Russia with plutonium.

We found out that the Twelfth Department troops, supposedly immune from the severe trouble in the ranks of the regular Red Army, got very meager perks. Seventy thousand rubles a month (fifteen dollars), a Twelfth Department colonel told us. "Plus two kilos of sausages." His colleagues were due to get a 30 percent raise in May, but inflation was running at 300 percent.

"I see nuclear smuggling," a White House official told us, "as a symptom of a government on the verge of collapse."

The previous December, the police in Prague staked out a late-model Saab parked on Argentina Street in front of a restaurant. A Czech physicist, a Russian, and a Belarussian were sitting inside. When police moved in for the arrest, they found two containers of uranium enriched to 87.5 percent, just short of the quality required to make a bomb. They seized seven pounds. Over the long term, the sellers were offering a ton.

We flew to Prague in April to meet with a Czech spymaster, a slight and soft-spoken man, who had been in the intelligence business only since Václav Havel and his coterie of intellectuals and artists took power. The intelligence man learned his craft as a dissident in the Czech underground. When I was smuggling footage out of Czechoslovakia in 1977 for NBC News, he was leading a double life under the watchful gaze of the Czech secret police. He called our hotel room with instructions out of Le Carré. "Go to Malostranska Square," he murmured. "There is an island in the square where people wait for the tram. There is a kiosk that looks like Uncle Tom's cabin. Meet me there at seven tonight."

It was a half-hour walk to the square in the soft dusk light of late spring. We entered the narrow streets of the baroque old town paved with rough cobblestones and teeming with tourists. The cafés every few yards in Staromestske were jammed. It was a particularly popular place for American students, laden with backpacks. One of the Czech investigators on the case had received a letter. The sender offered him substantial sums in a Swiss bank account to release the Russian smuggler. If he chose not to accept, the sender threatened to explode a small nuclear device in Prague.

The maze of medieval alleyways led to the six-hundred-year-old

Charles Bridge, where a puppet show was drawing a crowd. A musician had laid a table with crystal goblets of varying sizes and shapes. He was playing Mozart in glass. The crowd funneling under the bridge towers joined by a castellated arch was moving in a viscous mass uphill through the artists' quarter of Malo Strana.

Once in the square, we spotted the tram. Uncle Tom's cabin was exactly as described. We ordered coffee in the Kavarna, where Kafka had been a regular customer, and waited. Several tramloads of passengers came and went before our contact arrived, dressed in jeans and a simple jacket. He seemed relaxed but steered us deliberately back into the throng.

We ducked down a side alley, strolled through a leafy park and across the Certovka, the Devil's Stream. We stopped suddenly at an old fisherman's inn by the river Vltava on Kampa Island. "The guys in jail," he said offhandedly, glancing at the board for the catch of the day, "have said very little. They're terrified for their families back in Russia. They say they will talk only if we can get their families out." He paused and lit a cigarette. "That's difficult to do.

"The pattern is first, samples—a couple of grams—to be tested. In all previous cases it was rubbish." The spymaster drew deeply on his cigarette. "This time it was almost weapons grade. It could easily be converted to weapons grade." Material enough for several hundred atomic bombs could have been sold on the Prague pipeline. "For the first time, an expert in the business was involved and weapons grade was involved." The intelligence man spoke quietly. "The fears were justified" about the new Russia. "You can buy anything."

The fish arrived. The spymaster pulled out his mobile phone. "Do you want to go to a party?" he asked.

"Why not?"

He hoped his gloomy predictions were wrong because the Czech Republic was wide open as a transit country. "It's like America at the beginning of the century. It's great for money laundering." He laughed. "We've got a hundred Chinese restaurants in Prague. They're empty. You go in and find the service is terrible. The food is terrible. But they're bringing sacks of money to the bank every day." He lit another cigarette.

We walked through the dark streets to a square we did not recognize. In the middle, there was a Russian tank painted pink. "We will wait here," our friend the spymaster said. Someone whistled. A figure came out of the dark to lead us to a bar down a set of narrow steps in a Prague cellar that smelled like a damp cave. We found a table and ordered a bottle of wine. The spymaster told us he did not know who was clean or dirty in Moscow. What interested him was complicity at the top. "That's what we want to know. That's what the CIA wants to know." The intelligence man smiled. "I'd like to believe that not everything in Russia is corrupt. That not everything is for sale."

The party was picking up. The smoky room was crowded with former dissidents, now running powerful ministries, and chic young Czechs. The band played "Midnight in Moscow, Lunchtime in L.A." The spymaster leaned close.

"I'm thinking of getting out of this line of work."

I smiled and shouted over the din, "So am I."

EPILOGUE

The Trailer

CONVINCING people to tell their secrets is an ordeal. It can take weeks, months, years, to get an interview. Ninety percent of the work is done before you get to the heart of the matter. In the midst of our Russia adventures, Andrew and I had a fantasy. If only we were screenwriters rather than journalists. Even the most hardened criminals long to have the movie made of their lives. We could probe every corner of their past. The Russian Mafia melted at the names Sharon Stone and Al Pacino.

"Why don't you call your friend Walter?" said Andrew. Walter Parkes had just been named head of motion picture development at DreamWorks. "Ask him if we can say we're doing research for Spielberg."

"I can't do that."

"Why not?" Andrew pressed the point.

"Look," I said to end the conversation, "I'll write a treatment for a movie and fax it."

I sat down and stared at my screen. We needed a strong female lead. A White House physicist. And we would open with a nuclear disaster. One of General Zelentsov's Twelfth Department nuclear missile transport trains sabotaged. His worst nightmare. An explosion in the Russian hinterland. We knew from Ambassador Jim Goodby at the State Department that the new Kevlar blankets for the missiles on the trains had not been installed. A theft of nuclear weapons off the train, ending up in?

"Bosnia," Andrew said.

The theft would be the work of an old KGB front company taken over by the Mafia, rather like S.P.E.C.T.R.E. that our Clinton administration friends were so exercised about in their classified cables. But of course, the White House physicist, with her handsome collaborator, saves the day.

I called Parkes in L.A. We had been at Yale together.

"I have a treatment I'd like to send."

"I'm leaving for New York right now. Just fax it to my hotel."

Two hours after he arrived in Manhattan, he called back.

"Steven and I want to make the movie."

"So we can use your name in Moscow?"

"Are you kidding? Of course."

"Make us coproducers?"

"Fine. I love these intellectual action heroes."

When we arrived back from Moscow, there was a call from the coast. It was Joy, assistant to Walter Parkes.

"The limo will pick you up. Now, do you need a greeter?"

"What's a greeter?"

"You know, someone at the airport to make sure you get checked in."

"Are you serious?"

"Listen, I used to work for someone who needed a greeter to get him out of bed."

"I'm sure we can manage."

Andrew and I boarded a flight to Los Angeles. We were going to meet with Steven Spielberg.

The DreamWorks studio had just been born. Headquarters was the old Spielberg company Amblin, a tasteful adobe villa under shade trees in a back lot of Universal Studios. Walter gave us a Southwest nouvelle cuisine lunch in the executive dining room. We toured the conference room, done in Native American art, to see the direct hookup with East Hampton. We then hopped in a jeep and roared off down the freeway to the old L.A. County Jail.

"Steven's shooting a CD-ROM with Quentin Tarantino."

The jail was an abandoned wreck in the slums of L.A. Parked in back was a trailer. This was not the luxury temperature-controlled, bedroom-en-suite model with kitchenette stocked with Evian and finished in faux mahogany. This was a trailer, the kind you find in trailer parks. Spielberg was sitting alone, picking at a fruit salad in a plastic cup. We were at the very epicenter of Hollywood, around which all of the agents driving black BMWs and directors dining at Shutters and writers breakfasting at the Beverly Hills Hotel orbited like lesser planets around the sun.

"Hi," said Spielberg.

He wore an old T-shirt and jeans. He offered to share his banquet. Steven had our *Vanity Fair* Russia piece in his hands. "I love this stuff," he said, putting his feet up. "It reads like a movie. I see the bomb as like the Ark in *Raiders.*" He set the diced cantaloupe aside. "They find it, they lose it, they find it. With this story, it hasn't happened yet. The guy with the bomb in his backpack. So," he said with satisfaction, "I can give you the ending."

He picked up a pen and started to draw. He worked with intense concentration. No one spoke. This was obviously important. There were sweeping lines and small details. At last he was finished. The great director handed me the picture of a small boy and a dinosaur. It was Charlie, face-to-face with a *Tyrannosaurus rex.*

ABOUT THE AUTHOR

Leslie Cockburn grew up in San Francisco and was educated at Yale and the University of London. Her coverage of foreign affairs for print and television has won her numerous awards, including the Emmy, George Polk and Duport–Columbia Awards, the Robert F. Kennedy Award for International Reporting, and the National Press Club Award for Diplomatic Correspondence. She is a Contributing Editor at *Vanity Fair* and a Ferris Professor of Journalism at Princeton University. With her husband, Andrew, she coproduced DreamWorks' *The Peacemaker* and coauthored *One Point Safe*. She lives in Washington, D.C.